W9-AZL-120

BEHIND THE SCENES

Inside Hollywood

A writer's guide to researching the world of movies and TV

John Morgan Wilson

WRITER'S DIGEST BOOKS
CINCINNATI. OHIO

Inside Hollywood. Copyright © 1998 by John Morgan Wilson. Manufactured in the United States of America. All rights reserved. No part of this book may be reproduced in any form or by any electronic or mechanical means including information storage and retrieval systems without permission in writing from the publisher, except by a reviewer, who may quote brief passages in a review. Published by Writer's Digest Books, an imprint of F&W Publications, Inc., 1507 Dana Avenue, Cincinnati, Ohio 45207. (800) 289-0963. First edition.

Other fine Writer's Digest Books are available from your local bookstore or direct from the publisher.

02 01 00 99 98   5 4 3 2 1

Library of Congress Cataloging-in-Publication Data
Wilson, John M.
   Inside Hollywood : a writer's guide to researching the world of movies and TV / by
   John Morgan Wilson.
     p.   cm.
   Includes bibliographical references and index.
   ISBN 0-89879-832-9 (alk. paper)
   1. Motion picture industry—United States. 2. Television—United States. I. Title.
PN1993.5.U6W56   1998   98-4726
384'.8'0973—dc21   CIP

Edited by Jack Heffron
Production edited by Marilyn Daiker
Designed by Sandy Conopeotis Kent
Cover illustration © Tony Stone Images

for Pat H. Broeske
loyal friend, ace reporter and a true Tinseltown dame

About the Author

From his days as a page at CBS nearly thirty years ago to writing and producing television documentaries in the late 1990s, John Morgan Wilson has served his time in the Hollywood trenches. This includes stints as a freelance reader for Showtime, acquisitions coordinator for Viacom Enterprises, frustrated screenwriter whose optioned scripts were never produced, news editor and segment producer for Fox Entertainment News, and writer or writer-producer of more than sixty documentary and reality-based TV episodes, most recently for the Discovery Channel's "Hollywood's Greatest Stunts."

Wilson also knows Hollywood from the outside as a reporter. His freelance articles on the film and television industry have appeared in a dozen major newspapers and many magazines, including the *New York Times*, the *Washington Post*, the *Chicago Tribune Magazine*, *Entertainment Weekly* and *TV Guide*. During much of the 1980s, he worked as a staff editor with the Sunday arts and entertainment section of the *Los Angeles Times*, where he won a Los Angeles Press Club award for excellence in reporting on media issues. He is also a longtime contributor to *Writer's Digest* and author of *The Complete Guide to Magazine Article Writing* (Writer's Digest Books).

On the fiction side, Wilson is the author of *Simple Justice* (Doubleday), which launched the Benjamin Justice mystery series, and won an Edgar Award from the Mystery Writers of America as the best first novel of 1996. *Revision of Justice*, set in the treacherous world of Hollywood screenwriting, was published in 1997, with more Benjamin Justice mysteries planned for the years ahead.

Acknowledgments

Putting this book together was possible only with the advice, support and assistance of many friends and colleagues, including:

Irv Letofsky, the former editor of the *Los Angeles Times*' Sunday arts and entertainment section and managing editor of Fox Entertainment News' daily syndicated show, *Entertainment Daily Journal*. Irv currently serves as a TV critic for the *Hollywood Reporter* and contributes entertainment pieces to such publications as the *New York Times*, the *Washington Post*, the *San Diego Union* and *Entertainment Weekly*.

Pat H. Broeske, former staff writer with the *Los Angeles Times*, and writer-producer for Fox Entertainment News. Her articles have appeared in the *New York Times*, the *Washington Post*, *Rolling Stone*, *Vanity Fair*, *Premiere* and *Entertainment Weekly*, and she serves as the Hollywood markets columnist for *Writer's Digest*. Pat is also the coauthor with Peter Harry Brown of *Howard Hughes: The Untold Story* and *Down at the End of Lonely Street: The Life and Death of Elvis Presley*, both published by Dutton.

Marilyn Beck, a top syndicated Hollywood columnist for more than thirty years. She currently reaches millions of readers five days a week with "Beck/Smith Hollywood Exclusive," cowritten with Stacy Jenel Smith and distributed through Creators Syndicate. Marilyn also writes E! Online's daily "Ask Marilyn" column, has appeared frequently on radio and television, and in 1993 joined E! Entertainment with her regular, on-air Hollywood reports. She is also the author of several books on Hollywood.

Stacy Jenel Smith, coauthor of the aforementioned "Beck/Smith Hollywood Exclusive." Stacy also writes regular features and "Ask Stacy," a popular entertainment column, for Creators Syndicate, serves as an on-air correspondent for the E! Entertainment channel, and reports via the Internet on E! Online. Stacy's freelance pieces have appeared in the *Los Angeles Times*, *Reader's Digest*, *USA Today*, *People* and *Us*.

Gregg Kilday, formerly a senior writer at *Entertainment Weekly*, and staff writer with the *Los Angeles Times* and the *Los Angeles Herald-Examiner*, Gregg has covered the film industry for nearly three decades. His freelance pieces have appeared in *Esquire*, *Vanity Fair*, *American Film*, *Film Comment* and *Out*, among many other top publications. He is currently working on a major Hollywood book.

Darryl D. Pryor, former researcher, story analyst and director of development and production in film and television. Darryl has worked in various production capacities as a crew member on *Colors*, *Heart Condition*, *Beverly Hills Cop III* and other films, and has coproduced and directed electronic press kits for movies as diverse as *House Party* and *Convicts*. He is currently involved in developing and packaging film and TV projects.

Special thanks goes to **Lynn Osborn**, who contributed so much to the organization and research of this book. Lynn worked in the theater for many years as an actor, stage manager, prop master, assistant costume designer, and dresser, and served in the public relations department at San Francisco's American Conservatory Theatre. He currently is program administrator for the Entertainment Management Program at UCLA's Anderson School.

I am also deeply indebted to the following people and organizations for their assistance: Terry Press at DreamWorks/SKG; Nyla Arslanian, president of the Hollywood Arts Council; The Academy of Motion Picture Arts and Sciences and, in particular, the dedicated staff of the Academy's Margaret Herrick Library; The Academy of Television Arts and Sciences, and, especially, Hank Rieger at *Emmy* magazine; the Writer's Guild of America, west; David Horowitz at Warner Bros.; Patricia Polinger and Cathy Tauber at Vidiots in Santa Monica, California; Ana Martinez-Holler at the Hollywood Chamber of Commerce; Jeff Black at Lone Eagle Publishing; Bruce Torrence; and Marie Parker at *People* magazine.

Lastly, I must express my appreciation to everyone at Writer's Digest Books for their patience, skill and support, especially senior editor Jack Heffron and production editor Marilyn Daiker.

— TABLE OF CONTENTS —

Screenwriter; Training Grounds: Where Screenwriters Study; From Submission to Production; The Screenwriter's Union: The Writers Guild of America; Writing for TV; Recommended Books on How Hollywood Works

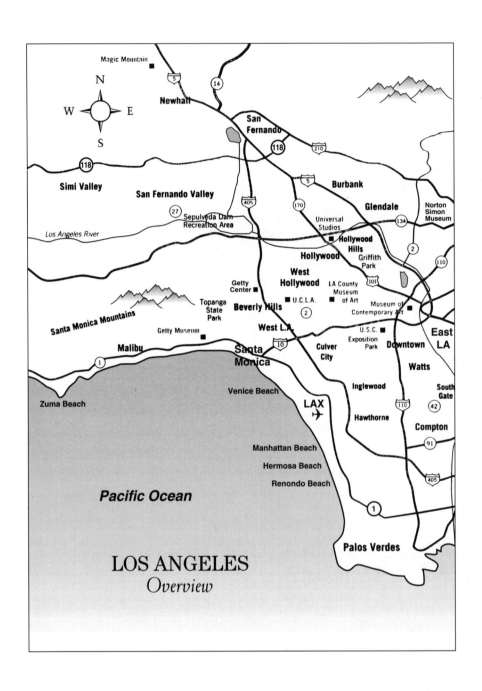

LOS ANGELES
Overview

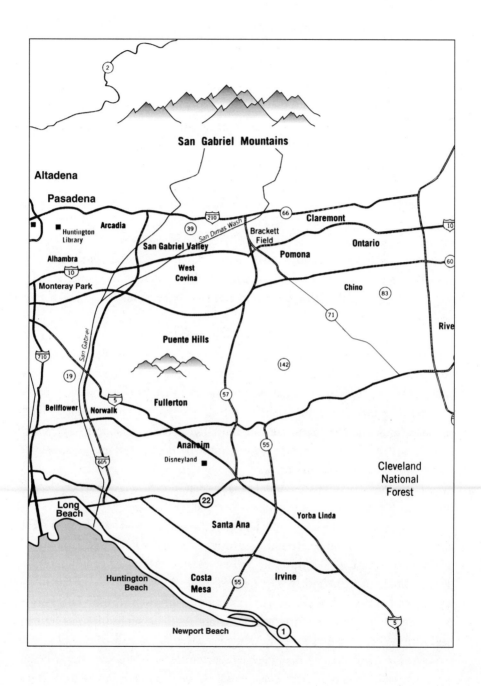

Over the decades, Hollywood has been one of the more popular subjects for writers of all kinds. They've attempted to explore, analyze or simply exploit the Los Angeles-based entertainment industry in countless articles, books, scripts and stage plays. Yet "Tinseltown"—as both a tangible place and a more ephemeral state of mind—is often misunderstood, misrepresented or stereotyped by writers who know it only superficially.

It is very much a company town with specific jobs, roles, terms of vocabulary and professional relationships, which we will cover in concrete detail. Yet creating a writer's resource book about how Hollywood works is no easy task, because Hollywood is so much more than just a workplace. It is the "entertainment capital of the world," a place of enduring myth, a crucible of creativity and a crass marketplace—all within a geographical landscape rich in movie and television lore.

Almost everything about Hollywood—its products, rituals, stars, salaries, market trends, power players—constantly change. It is essentially a cottage industry, without set rules and subject to fast-evolving technology and cycles in audience tastes. Here, ambition, concepts, creative drive and relationships ("who you know") are far more important than college degrees or job resumes. Here, anyone with enough chutzpah can call himself or herself a producer or personal manager. (In California, agents, at least, must be licensed.) Dreamers, artists, businesspeople and hardworking craftspersons created Hollywood and continue to sustain it. Yet scoundrels abound: Lying is a common business practice, deception taken for granted, cheating often rewarded, greed a given.

In the end, screen stories are told and images produced that have a remarkable impact on eyes and minds around the world. It can be argued that Hollywood produces the most popular, prolific and far-reaching forms of communication in the history of mankind. In *The Long Goodbye*, novelist Raymond Chandler wrote, "In Hollywood, anything can happen. Anything at all." John Dos Passos considered it "the most important and the most difficult subject for our time to deal with. Whether we like it or not, it is in that great bargain sale of five- and ten-cent lusts and dreams that the new bottom level of our culture is being created." And in his book *Adventures in the Screen Trade*, screenwriter William Goldman offered this oft-quoted summation: "Nobody in Hollywood knows anything."

Because it's an industry built on dreams and illusions—always in flux, larger-than life, difficult to explain and fully grasp—a "behind-the-scenes" guide to Hollywood must be written in a way that achieves three goals: (1) provides the reader with an understanding of how the industry works in a practical, concrete manner; (2) addresses the less tangible elements that make up Tinseltown, including its lifestyle, social issues, spending habits and mind-set; (3) points readers to other sources for more detailed research and updated information.

I've done my best to achieve these goals in the most comprehensive and accurate manner possible, although it must be noted that sources often vary and conflict in their accounts, particularly in historical matters—something to keep in mind when conducting your own deeper research in specific areas. You'll find that I have organized and formatted this book with many subheads, sidebars, lists, charts, parenthetical references and so on, so that you can skim or jump to different reference points and subject areas to suit your individual needs. Because the subject of Hollywood is so vast, it is impossible to cover it all here—an entire book, for example, could be written on just what the fashions have been in Hollywood through the decades, or how the technology has changed—but you will be pointed to a wide range of additional resources, such as reference books, publications, specialty libraries and archives, films, entertainment databases and Internet Web sites and Hollywood organizations. These will be highlighted along the way, when appropriate, as well as compiled in the appendix. We have also created a comprehensive table of contents and detailed index to further guide you and to make this book as "reader friendly" as possible.

To all the writers and researchers who might find this book useful, may your own projects move forward fruitfully. Or, as they sometimes say in Tinseltown: "Green light it!" "It's a done deal!" "Slam dunk, baby!" (See "Common Hollywood Slang" in Appendix A on page 268.)

John Morgan Wilson
West Hollywood, California

CHAPTER ONE

From Yesterday to Today—An Overview

Hollywood essentially began with the movies, which had their own beginnings in a variety of inventions, techniques and contraptions of the eighteenth and nineteenth centuries in both America and Europe.

But many historians trace the real birth of moviemaking to September 21, 1889, when American inventor Thomas Edison created the first "moving picture," synthesizing and improving upon the work of his predecessors. Two years later, in 1891, Edison patented the first motion picture camera, the Kinetograph, and the next year began exhibiting his short films in penny arcades and peep shows—later known as Kinetoscope parlors—where patrons could view the cheaply made reels. In 1893, in Menlo Park, New Jersey, Edison built the first formal motion picture studio, a small, tar-papered building equipped with a roof that opened to let in the sunlight needed to shoot his Kinetograph films. The motion picture industry was born.

Inspired by Edison's inventions, two French brothers, Louis and Auguste Lumiere, designed the cinematograph, which allowed them to project moving film on a screen large enough to be seen by an entire audience at once. They held the first public movie screening in Paris in 1895 and continued making and showing hundreds of short films over the next few years. The first American movie screening, under Edison's aegis, took place in New York City in 1896. At this point, films were generally documentary in nature, examining topical or real-life subject matter without an attempt to tell a dramatic story.

Around the same time, another Frenchman, magician and theater owner Georges Melies, began to experiment by composing action for the camera (the first "stop-motion" photography), introducing to filmmaking such techniques as dissolves (one scene blending into another) and double exposures. Although his entertainments were essentially filmed stage pieces, Melies took the step of creating fictional stories and elaborate set designs for his movies, and shot roughly four thousand of them between 1896 and 1914, including his 1902, eleven-minute futuristic classic, *A Trip to the Moon*.

Films as popular entertainment were taking shape.

The Age of the Nickelodeon

The turn of the century also saw the proliferation in the United States of the nickelodeon, movie theaters that got their name from their five cent admission price. Silent movie shows gradually edged out vaudeville as the most popular form of entertainment for the masses and by 1907 the gross income from film production exceeded the combined income from burlesque and legitimate theater, and much of Broadway's creative talent was drifting into film work.

Edwin S. Porter's *Life of an American Fireman* (1903) was purportedly the first film with a narrative screen structure—that is, highlighted by crosscutting between space and time, rather than merely shooting actors coming in and out of a scene as with a stage play. Porter's more commercial and entertaining picture, *The Great Train Robbery* (1903), considered by some historians to be the first "real movie," further revolutionized filmmaking and spurred public interest. "With fourteen shots cutting between simultaneous events," according to the editors of *A&E Entertainment Almanac*, "this twelve-minute short establishes the shot as film's basic element and editing as a central narrative device. It is also the first Western."

At this point, the real powers in the film industry were the producers—a small group of businessmen affiliated with Thomas Edison in the Motion Picture Patents Company, also known as the "film trust"—who had a stranglehold on the business through their control of patents, the supply of projection equipment, how many films were produced and of what quality and cost. Through license fees, they were getting rich off the small-time local and regional exhibitors around the country who were trying to free themselves from what they considered an unfair monopoly, an ongoing legal battle led by pioneering exhibitor Carl Laemmle.

Nonetheless, the creative forces of the industry—the directors and photographers—were beginning to gain more clout. None was more prominent than D.W. Griffith, who demonstrated a remarkable ability to express ideas and arouse emotion in his cheap, quickly produced one-reelers for the Biograph Company. A serious, if self-promoting, writer and actor, Griffith rehearsed his casts intensely and boasted of having introduced such innovations as long shots, close-ups and fade-outs that became the foundation of modern filmmaking technique (for an alternative and more international view, see the authoritative *The Story of Cinema*, by David Shipman). By 1911, following the example of the more adventurous European directors, he was making two-reel films, and by 1914, had made a four-reeler, although the eastern financial backers generally felt films should be kept short and simple, and aimed at low-grade tastes.

The year 1914 also marked Europe's full engagement in World War I, which effectively removed the European film industry as any kind of obstacle or competition for the Americans.

Movie Production Moves West

Hollywood became an incorporated city in 1903, but with no intention or desire to become a famous and gaudy film capital. It was developed instead as a scenic residential and resort community, with fine homes on spacious lots, wide streets lined with trees, exclusive private schools and a population that had grown to only 700 by 1905. That small-town serenity and bucolic atmosphere was not to last.

In 1907, while shooting *The Count of Monte Cristo* in Chicago, the Selig Polyscope Company ran into foul weather, and relocated the cast and crew to shoot some scenes in the beachside resort community of Santa Monica, roughly fifteen miles west of Los Angeles. In 1909, realizing that shooting conditions in Southern California were superior to almost anywhere else, the Selig crew returned, setting up headquarters in a converted Chinese laundry in downtown Los Angeles. There, it filmed *The Heart of a Race Tout*, the first movie to be shot in its entirety in California. Not long after, Colonel William Selig relocated his entire company to L.A., triggering an influx of production companies from the East Coast, a number of which settled in or around Hollywood.

In 1910, with a growing population in need of better municipal services, Hollywood became annexed to the city of Los Angeles while remaining a distinct community with its own carefully delineated boundaries. At this point, many of its streets were paved and featured sidewalks, and travel on horses and in horse-

Budgets and Salaries
IN THE EARLY YEARS OF THE FILM BUSINESS

D W. Griffith started out with the Biograph Company as an actor at $5 a day, then as a writer contributing ideas ($15 a day), becoming head of production in 1908 and the company's sole director. In 1908 and 1909, earning $50 a week plus commission, he made 131 one-reel and half-reel films on a budget of roughly $200 per film, with the company clearing $5,000 or more each week. Among his actors was sixteen-year-old Mary Pickford, who was initially paid $10 per day and would go on to become the most important and highly paid woman in the early years of Hollywood and the movie industry. By 1915, when movie production had shifted to Southern California, the bigger studio lots there employed as many as five hundred people or more, who earned salaries from $100 (for the more skilled crafts workers) to $5,000 per week (for top actors), fabulous sums for the time that attracted tens of thousands of men and women to the film business. By 1921, so many aspiring actors were converging on Hollywood that an unemployment crisis developed, and the Chamber of Commerce took out ads to discourage more from coming.

drawn buggies was giving way more and more to automobiles and electric street-cars (known as the Red Car). Still, much of the region remained farm and ranch-land, where acres of oranges and other fruit trees flourished and animals grazed, and the hills that bordered Hollywood on the north were largely undeveloped, though some fine homes were appearing on the lower slopes.

Originally founded by a devout Christian and prohibitionist family, Hollywood continued to enforce strict rules. The drinking of alcohol was forbidden, the riding of bicycles was not allowed on the sidewalks, and gambling was outlawed. Horses, cattle or mules could only be driven through the streets in herds of two hundred or less, with sheep, goats and hogs limited to two thousand, "unless accompanied by competent men in charge," according to the excellent book by Bruce T. Torrence, *Hollywood: The First 100 Years*. To enforce such rules in the city's early years, a two-man police force operated first on horseback, then on bicycles. It was greatly undermanned, however, as more and more film production outfits flooded into the area, tourism increased and Hollywood began to develop into an urban community. By 1913, Cecil B. DeMille, operating out of a small barn at Vine and Selma Streets, produced and directed the first movie to be shot within Hollywood's boundaries—*The Squaw Man*, a Western, filmed

This aerial shot shows the Famous Players-Lasky Studio in 1920, located at Sunset Boulevard and Vine Street, in the heart of Hollywood. The studio was demolished in 1926 as the company relocated to Marathon Street and Van Ness Avenue, eventually evolving into Paramount Pictures. Note the jumble of backlot sets constructed behind the sound stages (middle left) and the surrounding citrus groves, farmland and early residential neighborhoods. (Courtesy of the Bruce Torrence Historical Collection.)

on a $15,000 budget. Hotels, rooming houses and bungalows began sprouting up to accommodate the influx of movie people, along with businesses providing a wide range of services and merchandise. By 1914, with a population approaching eight thousand, barnlike studios popping up all over town, and dozens of crews filming daily in locations throughout the area, tourists flocked to Hollywood by the thousands, hoping to glimpse their favorite star, or at least the star's home. That year, the law enforcement presence in Hollywood had grown to twenty officers, who answered nearly two thousand calls and made 247 arrests.

Of that period, Bruce Torrence writes: "Lemon acreage bought for $700 became $10,000 per acre subdivision property. The name of Hollywood became known throughout the world. Neighboring areas envied Hollywood's publicity and adopted the name. Toluca and Lankershim became North Hollywood. Prospect Park became East Hollywood, Colegrove became South Hollywood, while West Hollywood took in Sherman as far west as Beverly Hills."

One of the arrivals to this Eden-turned-Tinseltown was director D.W. Griffith. Like DeMille and other recent migrants, he was a visionary filmmaker who saw a much greater potential for cinema than Edison or his business associates in the East had ever imagined. Certainly, these independent-minded producers and directors had come west to take advantage of the region's moderate climate, ideal outdoor shooting light, picturesque ocean and mountain backdrops and undeveloped open spaces, which were so suitable for erecting large sets and shooting expansive action scenes. But they also came to put some distance between themselves and the Edison group of autocrats who were attempting to maintain their grip on movie production and distribution, a monopoly that was slowly crumbling under a barrage of antitrust lawsuits.

Another lure was the thriving city of Los Angeles itself. It was being touted as "the promised land" of health and sunshine in unending waves of civic boosterism that was transforming a vast area of desert and farmland into one of the fastest-growing cities in the country, replete with bustling movie theaters.

Griffith was soon making spectacular, full-length epics like *Birth of a Nation* (1915) and *Intolerance* (1916), which further demonstrated his powerful editing and camera techniques and provided such emotive actors as Pickford, Mae Marsh, Lillian Gish and Mabel Normand with more substantial roles. *Birth of a Nation*, which portrayed the South as a victim of post-Civil War Reconstruction (Griffith was southern-born) and blacks as stereotypical heathens, opened to unprecedented public controversy but also widespread acclaim for its cinematic virtuosity. Produced for $60,000 and marketed for $30,000, the film eventually earned a profit of $5 million, all monumental figures for the time. *Intolerance*, filmed at the Fine Arts Studio (formerly the Majestic Reliance Studio) at 4500 Sunset Boulevard in East Hollywood, featured colossal Babylonian sets that continued to stand for years in a vacant lot across the street from the studio, dwarfing the homes in the surrounding neighborhood.

> **"**Millions are to be grabbed out here, and your only competition is idiots. Don't let this get around.**"**
>
> —PRODUCER-DIRECTOR HERMAN J. MANKIEWICZ

Hollywood's First Hotel

The Hollywood Hotel opened in 1903 with forty rooms at the northwest corner of Prospect and Highland Avenues, but did not immediately welcome all visitors. The proprietor reportedly posted a notice that read: *No Dogs or Actors*, to which silent screen star Gloria Swanson responded, "We didn't even get top billing!" After the hotel changed hands a few years later and more than tripled in size, and the film colony continued to grow, the hotel became the social center of Hollywood where the biggest stars of the silent era stayed, dined and danced. Rudolph Valentino and his first bride, Jean Acker, honeymooned there—but were only allowed to register after showing their marriage license. It later gained national fame when Hearst columnist Louella Parsons signed off her radio show with the regular line: "This is Louella Parsons broadcasting from the Hollywood Hotel." The landmark hotel was razed in 1956 when it failed to meet building standards.

Though movies continued to be produced without sound, using title cards to convey dialogue, they were routinely released in color-tinted or toned versions. Other new tools such as tracking shots, car-mounted cameras for chase scenes and wide-screen processes were being developed, along with increasingly sophisticated story lines and subject matter.

As moviemaking burgeoned, the once quiet and puritanical town called Hollywood was destined to become known as the entertainment capital of the world, with the term "Hollywood" coming into wider use in the 1920s to refer not just to a geographical place, but to the film industry as a whole.

The Stars Begin to Shine

According to the *World of Film and Filmmakers*, edited by Don Allen, the word "star" was coined in the early 1900s to describe the most popular silent film actors. Prior to 1909, however, the East Coast film trust refused to reveal the names of its actors, fearing they might become so popular and famous they would begin demanding higher salaries. Thus, the public, which sent the producers thousands of unanswered letters begging for information about their favorite performers, began to refer to them by such nicknames as the "Biograph girl," the "Vitagraph girl" or just "the little girl with the golden curls."

Sensing this public frustration, the independent producers—once again led by Carl Laemmle—began to publicize the names of their own players. Actors

L.A./Hollywood Time Line

(1781-1915)

September 4, 1781: Settlers, half of them of African descent, found Pueblo de Los Angeles.

1839: First official census puts the L.A. population at 2,228.

May 13, 1846: Mexico and the United States go to war.

February 2, 1848: Following the war, the West is ceded to the United States by treaty.

July 4, 1848: The city's first English-language legitimate theater opens.

1850: California admitted to the Union; city of L.A. incorporated under United States law.

December 31, 1881: L.A. is the first American city illuminated by electricity.

1886: Developer Harvey Wilcox purchases a 120-acre tract of ranchland for $150 an acre, which he calls Hollywood and begins subdividing into a residential community.

1900: First known guided tour of Hollywood, which now has five hundred residents, broad, tree-lined avenues and many fine homes.

1902: L.A. entrepreneur Thomas Talley opens the first "electric theater," charging patrons a dime to see motion pictures. It's a huge success; modern movie exhibition is born.

November 14, 1903: Hollywood becomes an independent city.

1907: The first feature footage is shot in L.A. for sequences in *The Count of Monte Cristo.*

1909: *The Heart of a Race Tout*, the first movie to be made completely in California, is filmed (released on July 27, 1909).

February 7, 1910: L.A. annexes Hollywood, which keeps its name.

1910: Hollywood's first theater, the Idyll Hour, opens at 6525 Hollywood Boulevard.

1911: The Vitagraph Company, a pioneering eastern film producer, establishes a studio in Santa Monica to shoot one-reel Westerns, cranking out one a week.

1911: The Nestor Film Company establishes the first Hollywood studio in a former tavern at the northwest corner of Sunset Boulevard and Gower Street.

1911: Carl Laemmle's Universal Film Manufacturing Company acquires the Nestor Film Company.

1913: The Jesse Lasky Feature Plays Company—with Sam Goldwyn and Cecil B. DeMille as partners—sets up West Coast headquarters in a barn at Vine and Selma Streets. DeMille directs *The Squaw Man*, the first feature to be shot in Hollywood.

February 8, 1915: D.W. Griffith's *Birth of a Nation* premieres in Hollywood.

Fans line the sidewalk on Hollywood Boulevard to glimpse celebrities arriving at Grauman's Chinese Theater in 1930 for the premiere of *Morocco*. Today, this section of the boulevard is cluttered with vendors, shops, and multi-plex theaters, but the theater, now known as Mann's Chinese, is much the same. (Courtesy of Bruce Torrence Historical Collection.)

working for the trust, craving recognition and more money, started taking their services to the independents, forcing the trust to finally publicize the names of its players and to increase their wages. It was the beginning of the "star system" that dominates Hollywood moviemaking to this day.

Since many of the first stars had little or no formal dramatic training, their mass appeal seemed to derive from the unique, indefinable quality they projected on camera, a phenomenon that almost overnight transformed fledgling actors into the subjects of widespread fan worship. When star salaries shot up to $10,000 per week in the years just before the twenties—a fantastic wage in the days before the personal income tax—great stage and opera stars suddenly stopped looking down their noses at the film industry and joined the gold rush to Hollywood (where the producers and directors quickly learned that great stage presence didn't always transfer well to the silent screen).

Mary Pickford, known as "America's Sweetheart," the reigning box-office star of the silent era, was earning half a million dollars a year by 1915. So was Charlie Chaplin, the brilliant filmmaker and actor who created the popular "Little Tramp" character. In 1919, Chaplin and Pickford joined with swashbuckling Douglas Fairbanks and director D.W. Griffith to create the United Artists Corporation. This gave them control of the distribution of their own independently produced films, a consolidation of star power that had a profound impact on the business of Hollywood. So powerful was the star mystique during the heyday of the movies in the 1930s and 1940s that novelist Margaret Mitchell developed the leading character of Rhett Butler in her book, *Gone With the Wind*, as a mirror image of Clark Gable's screen personality. When the movie was made, it provided Gable with his most notable and enduring role.

Film historian Gavin Lambert, author of *Nazimova: A Biography*, published in 1997, claims that the great Russian actress Alla Nazimova was the first "real star," because "Nazimova indisputably set the tone for all that is considered both glamorous and decadent in Hollywood, and her residence, the legendary Garden of Allah [at 8080 Sunset Boulevard, now a mini-mall], remains—almost forty years after its destruction—the epitome of movie-star success and excess." Nazimova, a headstrong beauty who lived lavishly and found both men and women desirable, signed a $13,000-a-week contract with Metro Pictures in 1917, making her the highest-paid actress at that time. She would die a virtual has-been in 1945, a victim of her own greed and ego and a sobering example of the fleeting nature of Hollywood fame.

From Silents to Talkies

The use of sound in the motion picture process developed gradually from the early part of the century and into the 1920s, but the public, accustomed to title cards or the accompaniment of live orchestras, was generally lukewarm to the odd notion of hearing actors speak on film.

Nonetheless, in 1927, when Warner Bros. released *The Jazz Singer* with a Vitaphone synchronized sound-on-disc system providing some of the dialogue, the movie was an instant sensation, along with its star, vaudevillian Al Jolson. The first completely talking picture, *Lights of New York*, was released the next year, and the silent era was on its way out. Most of the great silent stars, such as Pola Negri and John Gilbert, were unable to handle dialogue effectively and their careers quickly faded. A few such as Ronald Coleman and Greta Garbo made the transition to even greater popularity, along with many supporting players who rose to stardom in the new age of "talkies."

Another significant change was taking place in the way studios were run and movies were made. In 1923, Irving Thalberg joined Louis B. Mayer Pictures, where he was instrumental in the formation of the future giant, Metro-Goldwyn-Mayer, or MGM. With Mayer overseeing operations as the studio chief, Thalberg served as head of production, keeping directors, productions and budgets under control. For the first time, studio filmmaking was operating in a corporate, businesslike manner, and it signaled a shift in power from the artistic-minded director back to the profit-minded producer. (For reference purposes, both the book and film version of F. Scott Fitzgerald's *The Last Tycoon* offer portraits of a fictionalized Thalberg and the studio system during this period. See lists of Hollywood novels and other research resources on page 34.)

Nonetheless, ultimate power still resided in the corporate boardrooms and head offices in New York City, where the East Coast financial interests controlled distribution, even though the original film trust associated with Thomas Edison had long ago broken up as its members died or sold off their interests.

Censorship and the Production Code

In the wake of several highly publicized Hollywood scandals in the early 1920s (see "Hollywood Scandals Through the Decades" in chapter eight), as well as an increasing amount of racy, sensitive or controversial subject matter finding its way to the silver screen, another kind of power loomed—censorship. It gained strength incrementally through the years along the following time line:

1921: To head off the threat of government restrictions on film content, the film industry establishes the Motion Picture Producers and Distributors Association of America. Headed by former postmaster general Will Hays, the goal of the Hays Office, as it came to be known, is "establishing and maintaining the highest possible moral and artistic standards in motion picture production."

1927: The Hays Office issues specific guidelines for morality on the screen.

1930: The Motion Picture Production Code goes into effect.

1934: Hays issues his Purity Seal of Approval, which is to be withheld from any movie that violates the Code's strict standards.

Some writers and directors found creative ways to work around certain Code restrictions, or boldly challenged it. In 1931, for example, the Hays Office scribbled this warning on the submitted script for the proposed gangster film *Scarface*: "Under no circumstances is this film to be made. The American public . . . find[s] mobsters and hoodlums repugnant. . . . This office will make certain

Scarface is never released." The response of producer Howard Hughes to director Howard Hawks: "Screw the Hays Office. Start the picture and make it as realistic, as exciting, as grisly as possible." *Scarface*, with Paul Muni in the title role, was shot and released to wide popularity, and today is considered a classic.

Throughout the 1930s and 1940s, however, the Hays Office gained increasing influence, backed by conservative politicians, religious groups and other moral watchdog forces. By far the most famous censorship battle involved actress Jane Russell's spectacular cleavage, as displayed in producer-director Howard Hughes' *The Outlaw*, which was involved in a three-year battle with censorship boards—partly engineered by Hughes for publicity purposes—before its release in 1943. While independent producers and distributors often ignored the Code, the major studios largely abided by it until changing public tastes and an anticensorship legal climate led to its dissolution at the end of the 1960s, when movies began to explore controversial subject matter with unprecedented freedom.

General Principles of the Production Code

1. No picture shall be produced that will lower the moral standards of those who see it. Hence the sympathy of the audience shall never be thrown to the side of crime, wrongdoing, evil or sin.

2. Correct standards of life, subject only to the requirements of drama and entertainment, shall be presented.

3. Law, natural or human, shall not be ridiculed, nor shall sympathy be created for its violation.

The following are selected excerpts from the Code:

"**Crimes against the law** . . . shall never be presented in such a way as to throw sympathy with the crime as against law and justice or to inspire others with a desire for imitation. . . . Brutal killings are not to be presented in detail."

"**Methods of crime** shall not be explicitly presented."

"**Illegal drug traffic** must never be presented."

"**The use of liquor** in American life, when not required by the plot for proper characterization, should not be shown."

"**Sex perversion** or any inference to it is forbidden." [This included homosexuality and even the use of the word "pansy."]

"**Miscegenation** [sexual relationship between the white and other races] is forbidden."

"**Sex hygiene and venereal diseases** are not subjects for motion pictures."

From Rural Roads to the Hollywood Freeway

B y the 1940s, Hollywood was a densely developed community of residential neighborhoods clustered around sprawling studio lots, intersected every mile or so in either direction by major thoroughfares bustling with commerce and entertainment, such as Hollywood Boulevard, Santa Monica Boulevard, Melrose Avenue, La Brea Boulevard, Highland Avenue and Vine Street. As the decades passed, cars both dominated and shaped the city. The first freeway to cut through Hollywood was the aptly named Hollywood Freeway (U.S. 101), completed in 1948, which brought even more people into the area, causing it to become one of the most congested communities in Southern California. Today, the Hollywood Freeway carries roughly 300,000 vehicles each day. (For more on L.A.'s car culture, see chapter seven.)

"*Scenes of actual childbirth*, in fact or in silhouette, are never to be presented."

"*Obscenity* in word, gesture, reference, song, joke, or by suggestion . . . is forbidden."

"*Profanity* [this includes the words God, Lord, Jesus, Christ—unless used reverently] or every other profane or vulgar expression however used is forbidden."

"*Complete nudity* is never permitted. . . . *Undressing scenes* should be avoided. . . . *Indecent or undue exposure* is forbidden. . . . *Dancing costumes* intended to permit undue exposure or indecent movements in the dance are forbidden."

"*Religion*. . . . No film or episode may throw ridicule on any religious faith . . . *Ministers of religion* in Their Characters as Ministers of religion should not be used as comic characters or as villains."

For a complete reproduction of the Code, and related anecdotes, see *Hollywood Handbook* (Universe Publishing, 1996), edited by Andre Balazs, pages 82-89.

The Rise and Fall of the Studio System

As the 1930s dawned, talking movies were so popular that much of the film industry remained immune to the Great Depression, with movie attendance ranging from sixty to seventy-five million per week. At this point, five major studios dominated the industry—Twentieth Century Fox, MGM, Paramount Pictures, Warner Bros. and RKO—with Columbia and Universal soon to join

Fans and film extras gather outside the Marathon Street entrance to the Paramount Pictures studio in 1939. These famous gates were emblematic of the major studios in their heyday. Following a redesign of the entrance, the gates are now located inside the lot, preserved for their historic value. (Courtesy of the Bruce Torrence Historical Collection.)

the elite. The devastated economy finally began taking its toll on the smaller film companies in the mid-1930s, and even some of the major studios were seriously damaged, but all survived.

This was the beginning of the so-called Golden Age of Hollywood, with the studio system as its most vibrant and its studio chiefs, or moguls, at their most powerful. During the 1930s and 1940s, according to authors Steve Hanson and Patricia King Hanson in *Lights, Camera, Action: A History of the Movies in the Twentieth Century*, "the mogul was king. So pervasive was the force of his will, legend held, that he could impose his style and taste on every aspect of his studio's product. Individual pictures might bear the name of any one of the company's stable of directors, but there was no doubt in anyone's mind of what was a Louis B. Mayer film or a Samuel Goldwyn film—because it was the studio head who decided what the public should see."

Accordingly, each studio established its own, distinct personality and style, which the Hansons sum up thusly:

- Warner Bros. "developed a new type of film that presented social problems on the screen."
- The Walt Disney Organization "pioneered sophisticated animation."
- Twentieth Century Fox "cheered up moviegoers with stories featuring pint-size Shirley Temple."
- Metro-Goldwyn-Mayer went by a 1930s slogan, "Glorifying the American Screen," that "was manifested in expensively produced pictures featuring 'more stars than there are in the heavens.'"
- Columbia had director Frank Capra, a major director of comedies with a conscience, "that were populist in spirit and also charmingly sentimental."

To see how much of Hollywood looked physically in the 1930s, you might want to view the 1975 film, *The Day of the Locust*, based on the Nathanael West novel, as well as a number of films shot on location in Los Angeles during that period, listed on page 214.

The decade ended with what many still consider the pinnacle year of moviemaking, 1939, and the release of such classics as *Gone With the Wind*, *The Wizard of Oz*, *Stagecoach*, *Wuthering Heights*, *Mr. Smith Goes to Washington* and *Beau Geste*. There would be many more great pictures from Hollywood, but "the business of dreams," as West dubbed the film industry, was forced to face new realities with the impact of World War II and other crises or changes, including:

- A ruling by the Justice Department in 1949 that forced the major studios to divest themselves of their large theater chains, ending their monopoly of both the production and distribution of feature films.
- Also in the late 1940s, the Hollywood talent agencies, led by Dr. Jules Stein and MCA, acquired formidable new power. By the mid-1950s, Stein represented nearly half the stars in Hollywood. By 1962, partly through questionable and exclusive advantages allowed by MCA client Ronald Reagan, then president of the Screen Actors Guild, MCA had taken over Universal Studios and controlled 60 percent of the U.S. entertainment industry. (In turn, certain MCA executives

were allegedly major forces in backing Reagan's political ambitions.)

• During the same period, the rise of anticommunism and "red-baiting," led by Senator Joseph McCarthy, which caused widespread fear in the film industry, derailed or ended hundreds of careers and even led to suicides. To this day, the jailing and blacklisting of members of the so-called "Hollywood Ten"—a group of screenwriters, directors and producers with leftist or Stalinist leanings—for refusing to name names of alleged fellow communists before the House Committee on Un-American Activities, and the "red purge" in Hollywood, led by actor John Wayne, Walt Disney and other political conservatives, remains a bitter issue among historians and many older members of Hollywood's creative community.

• The advent of television in the 1950s, which radically changed American viewing habits, keeping tens of millions of viewers at home and out of movie theaters.

With the coming cultural revolution that would sweep America in the 1960s, the Industry, as the film business had come to be known in Tinseltown, would face its own radical changes.

The Advent of Television

Just as some had predicted that the popularity of movies would destroy radio as a commercial medium, the introduction of television into millions of American homes raised the portent of doom for theatrical films, which proved to be just as shortsighted.

While the concept of transmitting pictures as well as sound dates back to the late 1800s, it took another five decades to develop the technology needed to capture a real life image through a camera's pickup tube, then transmit that image electronically to a television screen. By 1930, RCA engineers were able to create a crude television image, but it would be another eleven years before the National Television Standards Committee, representing fifteen major electronic manufacturers, approved a system it considered worthy for commercial sale.

During those same years, the Hollywood assembly line was cranking out movies. In 1938, the figure was 778, more than at any time since the predepression year of 1928. Producers also generally steered clear of investing in or associating themselves with the developing new medium of television, which was centered in New York City.

Throughout the early 1940s, despite the war, NBC and CBS began offering sporadic programming, primarily boxing and wrestling shows (the first national

L.A./Hollywood Time Line

(1915-1949)

1915: Universal Film Company leaves Sunset-Gower studio and establishes Universal City.

1916: The Lasky company merges with Adolph Zukor's Famous Players Company to form Famous Players-Lasky. Samuel Goldfish leaves the new company to join Edgar Selwyn in forming Goldwyn Pictures Corporation (and later changes his own name to Goldwyn).

1916: The Vitagraph Company moves to a twenty-five-acre lot in Hollywood at Prospect and Talmadge Avenues, later bought out by Harry Warner of Warner Bros.

1918: L.A.'s population now approaches half a million.

1919: Charles Chaplin, D.W. Griffith, Mary Pickford and Douglas Fairbanks create United Artists Corporation, freeing them from studio contracts.

1920: Harry and Jack Cohn and Joe Brandt leave the Universal Company to form a company that would evolve into Columbia Pictures, with Harry Cohn becoming the head of the studio and one of the most feared and disliked moguls in Hollywood.

1920: Roughly two dozen Hollywood studios (total annual payroll: $25 million) now produce most of the nation's five to six hundred movies each year, which are seen weekly by forty million people.

1921: The four founders of United Artists establish the nonprofit Motion Picture and Television Fund, which provides charitable services to film industry employees and retirees.

1923: Irving Thalberg joins Louis B. Mayer Pictures and helps form MGM.

1923: Dedication of the Hollywoodland sign atop Mount Lee, advertising a real estate subdivision. (In 1949, the last four letters would be removed, creating the Hollywood sign.)

1924: Motion picture weekly payroll now exceeds $1.5 million.

January 5, 1926: Ground is broken for Grauman's Chinese Theater on Hollywood Boulevard.

1927: *The Jazz Singer*, the first feature-length talkie, is released to great popularity.

1928: The first television set is sold for $75.

1929: Combined profits of Hollywood studios tops $14 million.

May 19, 1929: First Academy Awards presented at the Hollywood Roosevelt Hotel.

September 3, 1930: *The Hollywood Reporter* begins publication.

September 18, 1932: Failed actress Peg Entwistle leaps to her death from atop the letter "H" in the Hollywoodland sign.

September 6, 1933: *Daily Variety* begins publication.

1935: Technicolor first appears as a three-color system in the film *Becky Sharp*.
1939: Hattie McDaniel becomes the first African-American to win an Oscar for her supporting role in *Gone With the Wind*.
1941: Orson Welles' *Citizen Kane* pushes the creative and technical boundaries of film, redefining the medium for both directors and audiences.
1945: The Federal Communications Commission (created in 1934) establishes the thirteen-channel commercial broadcast spectrum.
October 20, 1947: Senator Joe McCarthy opens "Hollywood Ten" anticommunist hearings in Washington, which end in the 1948 jailing of a group of prominent Hollywood writers, producers and directors.
1949: Cable television introduces better reception in rural areas.

advertisers paid $120 per hour). By 1948, the three major networks, CBS, NBC and ABC, were programming most of the hours between 7 P.M. and 11 P.M., with occasional local programming filling in the rest. The hit shows that would drive the business began to appear about this time: most notably "Texaco Star Theater" with comic Milton Berle and "Your Show of Shows" with Sid Caesar, both on NBC, and "Toast of the Town" (later renamed "The Ed Sullivan Show") on CBS. "By 1950, the pattern was set, and it would not change in any substantive way for the next thirty years," write Howard J. Blumenthal and Oliver R. Goodenough in the well-researched resource guide, *This Business of Television*. "Each of the networks—reduced to three with the demise of DuMont in 1956—worked closely with advertisers and advertising agencies to develop programs that would reach the largest possible audience."

Color TV Hits the Market
In 1954, the first color TV sets were introduced, and the next year, movie attendance dropped to its lowest point since 1923, with Hollywood producing fewer than two hundred pictures. A certain gloom settled over the film industry as more and more men and women on both the business and creative sides either found themselves unemployed or attempted to make the transition to television. Although many of the TV jobs were still in New York, more and more of them were moving to or opening up in L.A. as production gradually moved west. This was where most of the film stars were, the weather was better and the union rules and demands were less stringent.

Even when film people found work in television, however, it could be a demoralizing experience. Most episodes were ground out quickly on a daily or weekly basis, with only a fraction of the time for rehearsal, writing and direction that film allowed.

Although TV's so-called "Golden Era" of the 1950s provided many first-rate dramatic shows, much of what was being done was low-grade fare aimed for the common denominator audience that was glued to "the boob tube." For many making the transition, the pay was not as good. And shows could be cancelled virtually overnight, leaving everyone suddenly unemployed, adding to the general sense of instability.

The studios, which had reigned supreme in Hollywood for so long, were in a grim survival mode. Hurting for revenue, they finally relented and agreed to sell or lease to the networks films made before 1948 for a cumulative price that topped $100 million. By the end of the 1950s, with millions of families gathering each night around TV sets and people buzzing about their favorite TV programs and stars the next day, it was apparent that television was winning the battle for the largest audience. Ultimately, TV would lure away 80 percent of the movie audience, and many studios began converting their sound stages for TV production and selling or leasing their older movies to the networks and local stations. More and more film stars began taking TV work to sustain their careers.

Many filmmakers, on the other hand, while conceding that TV was clearly the new form of mass entertainment, also saw this watershed change as an unexpected advantage that might open new avenues of expression and storytelling techniques on the big screen, as well as the scope of subject matter. Film producers also responded with new ideas, such as:

- Revolutionary technology such as Technicolor, CinemaScope and stereophonic sound.
- Gimmicks such as 3-D, or three-dimensional viewing, with special 3-D glasses.
- The drive-in movie theater, also known as the "passion pit," for the necking and petting that went on in patrons' parked cars, which exploited the growing teenage car culture.
- The low-budget exploitation movie that introduced new genres such as "creature features" and "beach party" movies, which were aimed squarely at teens and their expanding spendable incomes.

Movies were not dead, but merely in evolution.

Location shooting has been commonplace in the Los Angeles area for many years and still occurs on almost any given day, with permit restrictions and fees varying from city to city. In this 1970 photo, a section of Hollywood Boulevard was shut down for the shooting of an action scene in the film *Alex in Wonderland*. Note the use of multiple cameras, including the moving crane (foreground) and the "dolly" (upper right), as well as the well-behaved passersby outside the frame of the shot. Off-duty police officers, paid by the production companies, are required to be present at all location shoots for crowd and traffic control as well as for security. (Courtesy of the Bruce Torrence Historical Collection.)

New Challenges in the 1960s

The year 1966 marked a turning point in the entertainment industry toward "conglomerating"—the clustering through acquisition of many companies under one corporate umbrella. One major development was the takeover of Paramount Pictures by Gulf and Western, whose previous focus had been non-show business fields such as mining and manufacturing (further acquisitions by Gulf and Western would include the TV giant Desilu Productions, theater chains and the Simon and Schuster publishing operations). That same year, Warner Bros. was acquired by the recording company, Seven Arts, a merger that would evolve into the corporate giant, Warner Communications, Inc. By 1976 this company would become perhaps the most powerful company in the record business and a leading player in the growing cable business, with a future that would include book and magazine publishing, its own television network and numerous enterprises outside of show business.

These and other giant mergers resulted in an infusion of executive manpower and corporate wealth that sparked new approaches to doing business geared toward increased profits and more attention to the bottom line. One immediate example was the sale of post-1948 films in blocks to the TV networks. In one week alone in 1966, the three major networks purchased TV rights to a total of 112 films from Paramount, Twentieth Century Fox and MGM, paying more than $9 million for the bunch. After ABC's airing of *Bridge on the River Kwai* attracted sixty-five million viewers that same year, the networks began scheduling feature films five nights a week. The next year, 1967, the studios began producing two-hour "made-for-TV" movies that would become a staple of network programming.

The conglomerate trend would continue unabated in the ensuing decades, with MCA, Inc., originally the Music Corporation of America, achieving gross revenues of more than $800 million by 1976, thanks to such diversified holdings as Decca Records, Universal Pictures and Universal TV. Foreign powers, from the Japanese-owned Sony Corporation to Australian publishing magnate Rupert Murdoch, would join in the merger and buyout frenzy, becoming major forces in the American entertainment industry and continuing to change the way business was conducted in Hollywood.

Television, meanwhile, continued to grow, dictating the direction of other forms of entertainment. By 1970, nearly sixty million American homes had TV sets, nearly half of them in color. Two TV sets in a home was not uncommon, and by 1977, 120 million sets were in use in more than seventy-nine million American homes. The previous year, CBS had become the first advertising medium in history to achieve more than a billion dollars in sales; even ABC, perennially the lowest-rated of the three networks, tallied $954.3 million in advertising revenue that year. Incredibly, the figures would keep soaring.

Other significant post-1960 developments:

The growing power of talent agents. With studios under the command of boards of directors and corporate brass rather than filmmakers, the most established and successful talent agents seized new opportunities. They were able to use their relationships within Hollywood's creative community and their acumen in "packaging" varied elements (stars, director, screenwriter, producer and so on) to move a project forward more profitably and efficiently at the business-minded studios. By 1977, six of the seven production chiefs at the major studios were ex-agents, although one, Columbia's David Begelman, would resign that year in disgrace (see "Hollywood Scandals Through the Decades" in chapter eight). Unlike the all-powerful moguls of the past, they were accountable to the corporate boards and brass, and the resulting friction and executive "revolving door" turnover rate was extremely high.

Rising production costs. In 1977, the average cost of producing a feature film was $4 million, but costs for many projects were rising dramatically. Some of the more expensive films of the period were *New York, New York* ($9 million), *Star Wars* and *The Deep* (each $10 million), *A Bridge Too Far* ($24 million) and *Apocalypse Now* ($26 million).

"As alarming as rising productions costs," wrote Joseph Csida and June Bundy Csida in *American Entertainment: A Unique History of Popular Show Business*, from which many of these figures come, "was the fact that, by the late 1970s, it had often become desirable or necessary to spend as much advertising and promoting a film as to produce it. Faced with sharply rising costs, the moviemakers produced fewer and fewer films, but their track record [at the box office] was quite good." With the huge push for spectacular action and effects in the 1980s and 1990s, a number of films had passed the $150 million production budget limit by 1997, among them *Batman & Robin* ($175 million) and *Titanic* ($200 million plus), which was released in late 1997 to huge box office success.

Ancillary financing. To cope with the inflation in production and promotion costs, many producers began to presell their films, raising financing by selling off rights in ancillary markets before a film's domestic release or even prior to production. In the early 1970s, the top network price paid for feature films before their release was $300,000; after the fevered TV ratings competition of 1975-77, millions were being bid. Even more was offered for films that were proven hits: NBC paid $15 million for TV rights to the two Oscar-winning *Godfather* films, plus a later nine-part miniseries joining the two with previously unseen footage; CBS coughed up $5 million for *Network*; and NBC paid $7 million for *A Bridge Too Far*. Certain independent producers were also beginning to tap foreign distribution territories more heavily, and those with action scripts and top male stars attached could cover most or all of their production costs with foreign money before ever shooting a frame. This led to a plethora of big-budget action pictures featuring all-star casts studded with foreign names, giving films more international appeal and virtually guaranteeing preproduction foreign financing.

The era of the modern blockbuster. When Universal released *Jaws* amid a frenzy of hype and popularity in 1975—achieving a monumental new rental record of $129.5 million in a year that saw studio *grosses* of nearly $2 billion— it ushered in a new era of the box-office blockbuster, which would greatly influence the shape of studio investment and marketing activities in the decades ahead (see "The Age of the Modern Blockbuster" in chapter two).

The X-rated film arrives. In 1967, under pressure because of the frank treatment of sexuality and violence in a growing number of films, the movie industry adopted its own rating system (G—General; PG—Parental Guidance; R— Restricted to persons over seventeen, unless accompanied by a parent; X—no one under eighteen admitted), replacing state censorship boards around the country. By 1976, more than half of all films produced by the studios and major independents were rated R or X, with only 13 percent G-rated. The first outright pornographic film to get major distribution, a Swedish import titled *I Am Curious Yellow*, was a solid box-office hit in 1969. That same year, the X-rated category gained some respectability when director John Schlesinger's *Midnight Cowboy* was released to critical acclaim and went on to win Academy Awards for Best Picture, Best Screenplay and Best Director. Adult-themed films got a similar boost in 1973 when superstar Marlon Brando starred in director Bernardo Bertolucci's X-rated *Last Tango in Paris*.

Throughout the 1970s, "porn palaces" devoted to hard-core fare did a booming business with low-budget sex films like *Deep Throat, The Devil in Miss Jones* and *Behind the Green Door* earning rentals of $1 million or more (at least by some accounts), and porn actresses like Linda Lovelace and Marilyn Chambers finding their particular "star" niche. By the end of the 1980s, the burgeoning home video market had sounded the death knell for porno film exhibition. Today, according to Gil Reavill's *The Best of Los Angeles*, "Of the some 1,400 X-rated tapes released in the U.S. every year, the huge majority— perhaps 95 percent—are produced in Los Angeles. The San Fernando Valley is the home turf for these tapes, which are sometimes churned out at the rate

> **❝** If you suck a woman's breast, it's rated *X*. If you cut it off, it gets an *R*. **❞**
> —JACK NICHOLSON

of two a day." (The 1997 feature film *Boogie Nights* chronicles the porn indus-try in the 1970s.)

Superstar salaries. Film stars have always been well paid, but Elizabeth Taylor was probably the first million-dollar player when she was paid $125,000 per week for sixteen weeks of work, plus substantial bonuses, to star in *Cleopatra* (1963). Marlon Brando, Steve McQueen and a few other top stars had earned salaries in the million dollar range by 1970. But it was in the late 1970s, with the sudden escalation of film production costs and the expansion of the interna-tional film market, that star salaries skyrocketed into the multimillions, creating the climate for the modern superstar salary. Robert Redford reportedly got $2 to $3 million for four weeks of work on *A Bridge Too Far* (1977), Gene Hackman was paid $4 million for *March or Die* (1977), Marlon Brando received $2.25 million for a cameo in *Superman* (1978), Burt Reynolds earned $5 million for *Cannonball Run* (1981) and Sean Connery got $4 million for *Never Say Never Again* (1982).

Fees like these laid the groundwork for Sylvester Stallone, who stunned the film industry in 1983 when he negotiated a payment of $15 million to star in *Rocky IV.* Some actors—notably Jack Nicholson, playing a supporting role in *Batman* (1989)—earned even bigger paychecks by signing for a guaranteed per-centage of the picture's gross. Stallone upped the ante again in 1995 when he signed a three-picture deal with Universal for a reported $60 million. By 1997, after relative newcomer Jim Carrey was paid $20 million to star in *The Cable Guy*, more established male stars like Tom Cruise and Bruce Willis were de-manding even larger figures. Several leading ladies, Demi Moore, Sandra Bullock, Whitney Houston and Julia Roberts among them, had climbed into the $10 to $15 million range, and press reports claimed that Mel Gibson would be paid an astronomical $50 million to star in *Lethal Weapon IV.*

The growth of cable and pay TV. The first cable TV services went on the air in 1949, and by 1971 more than five million families across the country had subscribed to CATV systems. "The spur to the expansion of cable in the cities was the conversion of Home Box Office (HBO) into an instant national network when it began distributing its programming by satellite in 1975," according to *Les Brown's Encyclopedia of Television.* "Its wide acceptance was a signal to entrepreneurs of a monumental cultural change: the willingness of people to pay for television." In 1977, the FCC approved the first over-the-air pay TV system, launched in Los Angeles by National Television Subscription. That same year, HBO was transmitting movies, sports shows and other specialty programming to roughly 350 distribution systems, reaching more than half a million subscribers. By 1982, depending on the source one consults, from twenty-three to twenty-nine million American households were cable subscribers, a figure that rose to roughly sixty million over the next decade. Cable channels like HBO, Showtime and Nickelodeon not only were operating successfully, but were producing original programming of their own (in addition to broadcasting feature films), and CNN, the first twenty-four-hour all-news channel, was a huge success. Meanwhile, the developing satellite TV market was opening up the viewing universe even wider for millions of Americans.

The introduction of the videocassette and VCR. 1977 was also the year videocassette player-recorders hit the American market full force. They were designed for hookup with most TV sets with the capability to record TV programs while the viewer was away from home or to screen home or prerecorded videos. The message to the public was clear: Viewers could tape their favorite shows and watch them when they chose; they were no longer slaves to the networks' schedules. In addition to a wide range of educational and documentary material already on the market, the Video Club of America began offering hit feature films on cassette for as little as $39.95. Advertisements also began to appear offering porn titles for sale. By the end of 1977, the sale of VCRs was showing sharp growth. Simultaneously, for the first time in the history of television, viewership was declining. Millions of viewers were tuning out the networks and turning to other venues for entertainment. By 1990, sixty-five million VCRs were in operation in American homes, and video sales and rentals accounted for a significant part of a feature film's revenue, a trend that grew throughout the decade as thousands of video rental stores opened across the country.

The merchandising explosion. With the release of *Star Wars* in 1977 and a bonanza of product tie-ins that would eventually be worth billions, the studios finally recognized the incredible merchandising potential in their movies, something only Disney had realized until that time. The result was not only a glut of movie-related merchandise, but feature films that were conceived and produced to exploit their merchandising potential and sequels that kept the licensing money rolling in. (See "The Merchandising Phenomenon" in chapter two.)

The rise of the independent distributor. In the 1980s, a number of "minimajors" challenged the major studios by both producing and releasing their films. Most failed to survive, but those who did—notably New Line Cinema and Miramax Films—had a profound impact on the kind of movies being produced and how they were marketed. A new wave of independent production continued through the 1990s, significantly changing the Hollywood business landscape. (See "The Independents" in chapter two.)

The "fourth network" is born. In 1987, the Fox Broadcasting Company challenged ABC, CBS and NBC by becoming the fourth network, taking direct aim at younger and ethnic viewers by programming irreverent, youth-oriented or racially-distinct shows like "The Simpsons," "Married With Children," "Beverly Hills 90210" and "In Living Color." The strategy succeeded, and Fox, despite its lower overall ratings, sliced off a disproportionate amount of the advertising pie because of the high demographics of its youthful audience. By creating a "brand name" and distinct programming identity, it forced the other networks into attempting the same and changed the face of commercial television. By 1991, the three major networks, once the only source of TV programming in America, drew only 65 percent of the total viewership and continued to lose roughly 2 to 3 percent of their audience each year. The addition of the Warner Bros. and Paramount networks to the chain in the 1990s, though less successful, added to viewer choices and further eroded the dominance of the Big Three.

Just as television had given the movie industry its greatest crisis at midcentury, the TV business was now going through a crisis of its own as it faced the coming millennium. The impact this had on those who worked in Hollywood was to send many scurrying to new media and new markets, looking for new avenues of expression and a paycheck.

The Hollywood Memorabilia Market

The booming market for Hollywood memorabilia offers writers and researchers a rich source of insight into the minds and behavior of starstruck fans in general and a fascinating Hollywood subculture in particular. It is also a valuable study for countless colorful and revealing details from the history, lore and changing visual styles of Tinseltown, as well as visual examples of evolving marketing and merchandising techniques.

How the memorabilia boom got started is difficult to pinpoint, but freelance reporter and television producer Rhys Thomas, who exhaustively researched the phenomenon for a two-part series in the *Los Angeles Times*, credits its explosion, at least in Hollywood, as much to Kent Warner as any other individual. Warner, a Hollywood costumer who had access to movie warehouses and TV wardrobe departments all over town, was an avid collector of old cars, 78 recordings, and vintage radios and television sets, particularly those from the 1930s. When he

L.A./Hollywood Time Line

1950-1997

1950: First nationwide TV program airs ("See It Now" with Edward R. Murrow).

1952: Resolving a lengthy antitrust lawsuit, the Justice Department orders the major studios to divest themselves of their theater chains, ending their production-distribution monopoly.

1953: *The Robe* is released in CinemaScope, ushering in a new era of wide-screen processes.

1954: Disney and Warner Bros. are the first movie studios to produce TV shows.

1954: Gross revenue for TV hits $593 million, surpassing radio for the first time.

July 17, 1955: Disneyland opens in nearby Anaheim, which is in burgeoning Orange County.

September 30, 1955: James Dean dies in a desert car crash at age twenty-four in the same year his first two films, *East of Eden* and *Rebel Without a Cause*, are released and just after completing his third and final film, *Giant*.

1955: 70mm film is introduced commercially with *Oklahoma!*

1956: When *Gone With the Wind* airs on TV, 52 percent of all TV households tune in.

1959. Cheating on popular, prime-time TV quiz shows erupts into national scandal.

1959: L.A.'s population now exceeds 2.4 million.

1960: Millions of women stop bathing in the shower after seeing a horrific murder scene set in a shower in director Alfred Hitchcock's *Psycho*.

1960: Seventy million TV viewers watch the Kennedy-Nixon presidential debate.

1962: Federal antimonopoly regulation forces the studios to leave the talent agency business.

1962: First transatlantic TV transmission occurs via satellite.

1964: Color TV introduced widely into American homes.

1964: Sidney Poitier becomes the first African-American to win an Academy Award for a starring performance for his role in *Lilies of the Field*.

1968: The MPAA introduces the film rating system with G, PG, R and X.

1969: *Midnight Cowboy* becomes the first (and only) X-rated movie to win the Best Picture Oscar.

August 9, 1969: Actress Sharon Tate and four others are murdered by Manson Family members in the Benedict Canyon home rented by Tate's husband, director Roman Polanski.

1969: The low-budget *Easy Rider* is a major critical and box-office hit, making Jack Nicholson a star and generating a wave of largely unsuccessful studio imitations.

1970: FCC mandates the separation of TV networks and studios.

1971: Stanley Kubrick's critically acclaimed *A Clockwork Orange*, replete with disturbing images and explorations of violence, ushers in a new era of permissiveness on screen.

1971: Producer Norman Lear's "All in the Family" shatters the "happy family" sitcom stereotype and starts a trend in more frank, socially conscious TV programming.

1972: HBO, owned by Time, Inc., is established as the first pay cable network.

1976: *Rocky* unveils the first feature film use of the steadicam camera.

1977: ABC airs *Roots*, a twelve-hour eight-part miniseries based on Alex Haley's history of African-Americanism, which is seen in a record 36.38 million American homes.

November 11, 1978: Ceremonies are held to unveil the renovated Hollywood sign.

1979: Director Michael Cimino's film, *Heaven's Gate*, goes so far over budget and is such a box-office bomb in its 1980 release that it contributes to the collapse of United Artists and becomes an enduring symbol of Hollywood egomania run amok.

1980: Robert Redford founds the nonprofit Sundance Institute and Sundance Film Festival in Park City, Utah, to support independent, alternative and regional filmmakers.

November 4, 1980: Ronald Reagan, a former B-actor married to former B-actress Nancy Davis and ex-husband of Oscar-winning actress Jane Wyman, is elected U.S. President.

1981: A Supreme Court decision allows TV cameras in the courtroom.

1983: Sylvester Stallone stuns the film industry and triggers an industrywide escalation of star salaries when he is paid $15 million to star in *Rocky IV*.

1986: Barry Diller, president of Rupert Murdoch's News Corporation, founds the "fourth network," the Fox Broadcasting Company.

1987: Dawn Steel is named president of Columbia Pictures, becoming the first woman to head a major studio.

1988: Only 2 percent of all U.S. households lack a TV set.

1990: NC-17 rating (no children under seventeen) replaces the MPAA's X rating.

1990: The public "outing" of closeted gay celebrities and Hollywood executives by certain militant gay journalists becomes a heated issue in L.A.

1991: The brutal police beating of Rodney King is taped by a citizen and aired on TV, triggering a wave of "video-driven" television news events.

1991: A record high nineteen African-Americans are signed to direct feature films, signaling a potential new wave of black filmmaking led by the success of director Spike Lee.

1992: Syndicated columnist Art Buchwald wins a lawsuit against actor Eddie Murphy and Paramount Pictures for plagiarism over the literary origins of *Coming to America*.

1992: Johnny Carson, perhaps the single most successful performer in TV history, retires after thirty years as host of the "Tonight Show."

1992: Actor-producer-director Edward James Olmos is allegedly targeted for death after offending leaders of the so-called Mexican Mafia with his barrio-themed film, *American Me*. Two other persons associated with the movie later die violent and unexplained deaths.

1992: Director Steven Spielberg's *Jurassic Park* grosses more than a billion dollars worldwide, eclipsing his *E.T.* as the most successful movie of all time in pure dollars.

1993: The Avid Media Composer system, used to cut the film *Lost in Yonkers*, revolutionizes the editing process by allowing the digitizing and computer intercutting of film.

1993: Actor Brandon Lee, son of the late martial arts movie legend, Bruce Lee, dies during the filming of *The Crow* when he is accidentally struck by a bullet from a prop gun.

1994: Steven Spielberg founds a new studio, DreamWorks/SKG, with wealthy music mogul David Geffen and Jeffrey Katzenberg, former Disney production chief.

1995: Actor Christopher Reeve (*Superman*) is paralyzed from the neck down in a horse-jumping accident. (In 1997, working in his wheelchair, he makes his directing debut with HBO's AIDS-themed film, *The Gloaming*.)

1996: Federal legislation greatly deregulates telecommunications, vastly opening up production and marketing opportunities for broadcast and cable companies.

1996: Comic actor Jim Carrey, a newcomer to movie stardom, is paid $20 million to star in *The Cable Guy*, triggering another escalation in star salaries.

1997: TV star Ellen DeGeneres comes out publicly as a lesbian, prior to the same, precedent-setting transformation of her title character on the ABC sitcom, "Ellen."

1997: Steven Spielberg's new studio, DreamWorks/SKG, releases its first movie, *The Peacemaker*.

1997: At close to $200 million, *Titanic* becomes the most expensive movie ever released, and also one of the most commercially successful.

discovered in the early 1970s that the studios were throwing out some of the most famous clothes worn by Hollywood's biggest stars in their classic roles, he began smuggling as many pieces as he could off studio lots to spare them from the dumpster. (In fact, he found many already *in* the dumpster.) Among his finds was the original pair of Ruby Slippers worn by Judy Garland in the 1939 MGM musical, *The Wizard of Oz*. The slippers, one of several pairs, had acquired legendary status in the world of movie buffs and were probably worth $15,000 to $25,000 at the time on the underground collecting market. By 1988, when sold at a widely publicized event at Sotheby's, the legendary New York auction house, the shoes brought a price of $165,000. Today, their value to wealthy collectors is estimated by some experts to exceed $1 million.

Thomas, who pieced together the mysterious story of the famous shoes in his book, *The Ruby Slippers of Oz* (Tale Weaver Publishing, 1989), credits Warner with almost single-handedly triggering the memorabilia boom by amassing hundreds of items valued for their historical and nostalgic value. At first intending to keep them for himself, Warner, who died of AIDS in 1984, before Thomas was able to interview him, eventually began feeding them into the underground memorabilia marketplace, where the legal ownership of many of the items was a matter of question; greed, intrigue, deception and outright fraud abounded.

Today, the collecting and trading of entertainment-related memorabilia is a legitimate, worldwide, multimillion dollar market. Its participants range from serious (some would say fanatical) collectors such as James Comisar, whose Beverly Hills apartment is crammed with more than five thousand TV treasures, including Johnny Carson's desk and "Carnac the Magnificent" turban; to a Las Vegas dentist who has tried to sell the plaque he claims to have scraped off Elvis Presley's teeth; to British writer Brian Mills, author of *Movie Star Memorabilia: A Collector's Guide*, which categorizes and catalogs such collectibles as vintage "annuals" (fan magazines of earlier decades), cigarette cards, postcards, posters, signed photographs, and movie props and souvenirs.

As recently as 1997, prices set at auction for such items include $4,000 to $7,000 for Dorothy Lamour's sarong worn in *Typhoon*; $30,000 to $50,000 for Clark Gable's personal script for *Gone With the Wind* and his Oscar for *It Happened One Night*; $12,000-$16,000 for a tricorder used on TV's "Star Trek" series; and $1,000 to $1,500 for the bed used by Michael Douglas and Sharon Stone in *Basic Instinct*. Although private collecting drives the market, it's not uncommon to find show business items donated to benefit charity, with the proceeds tax deductible. Among the most prized movie items on the market, besides the Ruby Slippers, according to the experts are: Charlie Chaplin's hat, cane and floppy shoes from his film roles as the Little Tramp; Vivien Leigh's coach gown from *Gone With the Wind*; Dooley Wilson's piano from *Casablanca*; Marilyn Monroe's "subway dress" from *Seven Year Itch*; Rudolph Valentino's "suit of lights" from *Blood and Sand*; the hat worn by the Wicked Witch in *The*

Wizard of Oz; the Rosebud sled from *Citizen Kane*; Adam West's TV "Batman" outfit; and Rita Hayworth's *Gilda* dress.

Original movie posters lead the market in sheer volume, with prices influenced by the poster's rarity, its quality and size, the popularity of the film or stars and the prestige of the illustrator. Driving up prices more than anything, though, is the heat of bidding fever generated and sometimes secretly manipulated by savvy professional auctioneers. The size of posters can range from the popular "one-sheet" (27″×41″) and "quad" (30″×40″), both of which can be easily framed and hung, and the smaller "lobby card" (11″×14″), up to the gargantuan, billboard-sized "forty sheet," and nearly a dozen sizes in between. Original horror film posters, particularly from Universal Pictures of the 1920s and 1930s, generally bring the highest prices, frequently over $100,000. Among the highest recent prices reportedly paid at auction are $450,000 for *The Mummy* (a Boris Karloff feature), $180,000 for *Frankenstein* and $100,000 for *King Kong*.

Hollywood memorabilia trading reached a new pinnacle in the spring of 1997 when the legendary New York auction house Christie's opened its first West Coast office in Beverly Hills, competing directly in L.A. with its major rival, Sotheby's.

Further Resources for Studying Hollywood

Over the decades, dozens of feature films and documentaries have been made and hundreds of novels and nonfiction books written that depict and explore Hollywood and its entertainment industry. Selected lists in all three categories follow.

Nonfiction Books

What follows is a very select list. Many other nonfiction and reference titles on Hollywood are noted throughout the book where appropriate or compiled in the appendix.

> *American Entertainment: A Unique History of Popular Show Business*, Joseph Csida and June Bundy Csida
> *Backstory: Interviews With Screenwriters of Hollywood's Golden Age*, Pat McGilligan
> *Censored Hollywood: Sex, Sin and Violence on Screen*, Frank Miller
> *City of Nets: Hollywood in the 1940s*, Otto Friedrich
> *City of Quartz*, Mike Davis
> *David O. Selznick's Hollywood*, Ronald Haver
> *Disney That Never Was, The*, Charles Solomon

Sources for Buying or Studying Hollywood Memorabilia

Among the more helpful movie book/poster/memorabilia shops in Los Angeles are the venerable Larry Edmunds Cinema Bookshop, 6644 Hollywood Blvd., (213) 463-3273; Hollywood Poster Exchange, La Cienega Blvd.; the Last Moving Picture Company, Hollywood Blvd.; the Hollywood Book and Poster Company, 6349 Hollywood Blvd., Hollywood, CA 90028, (213) 465-8764; Backlot Books, 7278-A Sunset Blvd., Hollywood, CA 90046; (213) 876-6070; Book City Collectibles, 6631 Hollywood Blvd., Hollywood, CA 90028, (213) 466-0120; The Collectors Bookstore, 1708 N. Vine St., Hollywood, CA 90028, (213) 467-3296; and Eddie Brandt Saturday Matinee, 6310 Colfax Ave., North Hollywood, CA 91606, (818) 506-4242.

Other memorabilia sources include the Universal Autograph Collectors Club (P.O. Box 6181, Washington, DC 20504-6181), founded in 1965, and Jay-Bee Magazines (134 West St., New York, NY 10001, 212/675-1600), among many other memorabilia shops and organizations nationwide. As they say, consult your local directory.

Due to Circumstances Beyond Our Control, Fred W. Friendly

Empire of Their Own: How the Jews Invented Hollywood, An, Neal Gabler

Enchanted Drawings: The History of Animation, Charles Solomon

Film Before Griffith, edited by John L. Fell

From Sambo to Superspade: The Black Experience in Motion Pictures, Daniel J. Leab

Genius of the System: Hollywood Filmmaking in the Studio Era, The, Thomas Schatz

Goldwyn, A. Scott Berg

Great Movie Stars: The Golden Years, The, David Shipman

Hollywood Be Thy Name: The Warner Brothers Story, Cass Warner-Sperline and
  Cork Millner with Jack Warner, Jr.

Hollywood: The Dream Factory, Hortense Powdermaker

Hollywood: The First Hundred Years, Bruce T. Torrence

*Hollywood: Stars and Starlets, Tycoons and Flesh-Peddlers, Moviemakers and
  Moneymakers, Frauds and Geniuses, Hopefuls and Has-Beens, Great Lovers and Sex
  Symbols*, Garson Kanin

*Inside Warner Bros. (1935-1951): The Battles, the Brainstorms, and the Bickering—
  From the Files of Hollywood's Greatest Studio*, Rudy Behlmer

Lights, Camera, Action!: A History of the Movies in the Twentieth Century, Steve
  Hanson and Patricia King Hanson

Making of Citizen Kane, The, Robert Carringer
Mary Pickford: America's Sweetheart, Scott Eyman
MGM: When the Lion Roars, Peter Hay
Monster, John Gregory Dunne
Movies, The, Richard Griffith and Arthur Mayer
Naming Names, Victor S. Navasky
Out of Thin Air, Reuven Frank
Parade's Gone By, The, Kevin Brownlow
Pickford: The Woman Who Made Hollywood, Eileen Whitfield
Raising Kane: The Citizen Kane Book, Pauline Kael
Reel Power: The Struggle for Influence and Success in the New Hollywood, Mark Litvak
RKO Story, The, Richard Jewell and Vernon Harbin
Story of Cinema, The, David Shipman
Studio, The, John Gregory Dunne
Tender Comrades: A Backstory of the Hollywood Blacklist, Patrick McGilligan and
    Paul Buhle
Twentieth Century's Fox: Darryl F. Zanuck and the Culture of Hollywood, George F.
    Custen
Without Lying Down: Frances Marion and the Powerful Women of Hollywood, Cari
    Beauchamp
Working in Hollywood: 64 Film Professionals Talk About Moviemaking, Alexandra
    Brouwer and Thomas Lee Wright

A select list of Hollywood biographies and autobiographies, including a few that appear here, can
be found at the end of chapter four.

Fiction

Especially recommended are *The Last Tycoon*, by F. Scott Fitzgerald; *Day of the
Locust*, by Nathanael West; *Hollywood*, by Gore Vidal; *Get Shorty*, by Elmore
Leonard; *Movieola*, by Garson Kanin; *Tinsel*, by William Goldman; and *What
Makes Sammy Run?* by Budd Schulberg.

Other titles include:
Barbarous Coast, The, Ross Macdonald
Bondage, Patti Davis
Celebrity, Thomas Thompson
Dead Celebs, The, Lindsay Maracotta
Dead Hollywood Mom's Society, The, Lindsay Maracotta

Fedora, Thomas Tryon

Force Majeure, Bruce Wagner

Glamourpuss, Christian McLaughlin

Graveyard for Lunatics, A, Ray Bradbury

Hollywood, Charles Bukowski

Hollywood Education, A, David Freeman

Hollywood Gothic, Thomas Gifford

Hollywood Husbands, Jackie Collins

Hollywood Wives, Jackie Collins

Inconvenient Woman, An, Dominick Dunne

Laurel Canyon, Steve Krantz

Myra Breckenridge, Gore Vidal

Only Make Believe, Marilyn Beck with Stacy Jenel Smith

Pay or Play, Jon Boorstin

Play It as It Lays, Joan Didion

PlayLand, John Gregory Dunne

Popcorn, Ben Elton

Pretenders, The, Gwen Davis

Revision of Justice, John Morgan Wilson (yes, yours truly)

Feature Films

You will find most of the following films listed alphabetically by title and described in some detail in *Leonard Maltin's Movie and Video Guide*. Especially recommended are *Sunset Boulevard* (1950), *The Bad and the Beautiful* (1952), *The Day of the Locust* (1975), *The Last Tycoon* (1976), *Nickelodeon* (1976), *The Stunt Man* (1979), *Barton Fink* (1991) and *Chaplin* (1992). Other titles include:

Abbot and Costello in Hollywood (1945)

Alex in Wonderland (1970)

The Barefoot Contessa (1954)

Beloved Infidel (1959)

The Big Knife (1955)

Boogie Nights (1997)

California Suite (1978)

A Face in the Crowd (1957)

Fedora (1978)

The Front (1976) (New York setting)

The Goddess (1958)

Guilty by Suspicion (1991)

Harlow (1965)

Hearts of the West (1975)

Hollywood Boulevard (1936)

Hollywood Boulevard (1976)

Hollywood Canteen (1944)

Hollywood Cavalcade (1939)

Hollywood Hotel (1937)

Hollywood or Bust (1956)

Hollywood Revue of 1929 (1929)

Hollywood Shuffle (1987)

Inside Daisy Clover (1965)

The Last Command (1928)

Merton of the Movies (1924, 1932, 1947)

Mommie Dearest (1981)

Movie Crazy (1932)

Myra Breckenridge (1970)

The Oscar (1966)

The Party (1968)

The Player (1992)

Play It as It Lays (1972)

Postcards From the Edge (1990)

Show People (1928)

Silent Movie (1976)

Singin' in the Rain (1952)

Soapdish (1991)

S.O.B. (1981)

Stand-In (1937)

The Star (1952)

Star Dust (1940)

Star 80 (1983)

A Star Is Born (1937, 1954)

Stranded (1927)

Sullivan's Travels (1941)

Swimming With Sharks (1994)

Tootsie (1982) (New York setting)

Two Weeks in Another Town (1962)

Valley of the Dolls (1967)

The Way We Were (1973)

W.C. Fields and Me (1976)

Whatever Happened to Baby Jane? (1962)

What Price Hollywood? (1932)

The Wild Party (1975)

The World's Greatest Lover (1977)

Documentaries

These titles may be considerably more difficult to find. Most were researched for their availability by Patricia Pollinger and Cathy Tauber, who stock many of the titles at their video store, Vidiots, which is often praised by film buffs as one of the best in the Los Angeles area (302 Pico Blvd., Santa Monica, CA 90405; 310/392-8508).

American Cinema (five volumes) (1995)

Art of Illusion: One Hundred Years of Hollywood (1990)

The Celluloid Closet (1995)

Here's Looking at You: The History of Warner Bros. Studio (1991)

Hollywood Chronicles (thirteen volumes) (1991)

Hollywood on Trial (1976)

Hollywood: When the Lion Roars (three volumes) (1992)

Just Shuffling Along: The Black Stereotype in Motion Pictures (1988)

Legacy of the Hollywood Blacklist (1987)

Library of Congress: Origins of Cinema (six volumes) (1995)
Power and Fear: The Hollywood Graylist (date unknown)
Rhinoskin: The Making of a Movie Star (1987)
Sex and Buttered Popcorn (1991)
That's Dancing (1985)
That's Entertainment! (1974)
That's Entertainment! II (1976)
That's Entertainment! III (1994)

Research Suggestion

To get a clear idea of what Hollywood and life there looked like through the decades, make special use of the many oversized pictures books that are heavily illustrated with period photographs and can be found in public and specialty libraries, general and specialty bookstores, archives and historic organizations, and the like. Many of these are listed in Appendix B. Also, see chapter seven for listings of guide and reference books on Hollywood and of movies shot on Los Angeles locations from the 1920s on.

CHAPTER TWO

The Movie Industry

Two core groups dominate the Hollywood feature film system: the major studios and the independents. This division, however, is not as simple as it sounds.

In the modern age of mergers and consolidation, the major studios have changed ownership, size, shape, name and sometimes even location—something to keep in mind as you write about Hollywood in the present, since the present is tomorrow's history. The term "independents" can refer either to an independent distributor or an independent production company (more on that later). The record of the independents through the years has been anything but stable and predictable, and many have operated with ongoing financing and distribution deals with the major studios, or been absorbed outright by the majors. It's also common for a "production company" to be formed—for legal and financial reasons—for the sole purpose of producing only one film, after which it no longer exists, except on paper.

In this chapter, we'll sort all of this out so you will have a clearer understanding of how the movie industry is structured and functions.

What the Major Studios Do

The chief function of a film studio is the production, acquisition, distribution and marketing of motion pictures, with distribution and marketing its most essential activities.

The movie theater marketplace, first domestic (North American), then foreign, is generally where the biggest sums are made or lost and where a picture's popularity and/or critical stature is established. (Some American pictures, particularly action-thrillers, now make more money overseas than at home.) Domestic theatrical release is followed by the exploitation of such crucial ancillary markets as video, pay-per-view, cable, network TV, syndication and merchandising (not necessarily in that order), which continue to generate revenue from a movie many years after its initial run in theaters. (This formula may be altered, of course, for movies that go straight to video, or play in theaters very briefly.)

As a general rule, a major studio in the 1990s releases between fifteen and thirty features yearly. This figure is far below the high production levels seen during the studios' heyday of the 1930s and 1940s when they produced fifty to one hundred films a year. Each major studio will usually produce many, if not most, of the pictures it releases, but it may also acquire films for distribution from foreign or American independent production companies.

Rising Costs

According to figures compiled by the Motion Picture Association of America, by 1997, the average negative cost for a studio picture was $39.8 million, with another $19.8 million spent on average to distribute or market each film—with the costs rising all the time. Total budgets of $100 million or more had become almost common, and a number of productions were approaching or passing the $200 million mark.

One reason for these enormous costs is studio overhead: keeping a company running with a full-time staff, production and corporate facilities, and all that that entails. Universal Studios, for example, employs nine thousand persons worldwide, with more than half of those people working in Los Angeles. (Overall, in 1998, more than a quarter million people were directly employed in the movie and television industry, according to the Los Angeles Economic Development Council, with many more economically dependent in some way on production.)

The nature of the creative process, market trends and studio decision-making also add to the overhead. The traditional studio movie deal is structured, according to Gail Resnik and Scott Trost in *All You Need to Know About the Movie and TV Business* (Fireside, 1996), as follows: "Up until a project is approved, or *green lighted*, the studio *absorbs* (pays for) all costs of buying the book, script, or life story and hiring the writers, along with possible fees for the producer who brought in the project. As soon as the project comes in the door (meaning the studio has either purchased or optioned the story), it's considered to be in development. A studio will have a number of projects in different stages of development at one time. It's not unusual for a major studio to have more than one hundred projects in some stage of readiness at one time, and perhaps 10 percent of those will actually make it to production." Of those that go into production, only a small percentage will show a profit, at least initially; in many cases, a film must earn its money back over an eight- to ten-year period as it plays off in ancillary markets at home and around the world.

Another cost factor is the existence of labor unions, which add, by some estimates, 30 percent or more to film budgets at the studio level in terms of higher wages, overtime and fringe benefits. This is something independent producers can avoid if they are not signatories to guild contracts (see "Hollywood Labor Unions" in chapter four), or if they take their productions to other states where unions have less control over craft and technical job hiring.

Superstar salaries are also soaring, along with the payments to other top creative talent, with some stars earning paychecks for a single performance that a few years before would have covered the entire shooting budget of a major motion picture. (See "Superstar Salaries," in chapter one.)

A less calculable factor is the traditionally lavish Hollywood lifestyle, particularly at the studio level. One notoriously extravagant executive team, which jointly ran a major studio until they drove it nearly to financial ruin, reportedly spent $5,000 a week just to have fresh floral arrangements placed about their corporate offices. Recently, when a studio cashier lost her $30,000-a-year job during industrywide downsizing, she said bitterly: "They spend more than that just catering one of their parties."

When major stars are filming on location, it is customary to accord them expenses for their personal hairstylists, physical trainers, masseurs and masseuses, even friends and family members, who are often flown in, housed, fed and paid for by the studio. Top executives and above-the-line talent rarely travel,

---

Home Viewing, Studio Style

Seagram Co. has spent $276,544 to date to build a movie screening room at the Los Angeles home of Frank Biondi, Jr., chief executive of the company's Universal Studios Inc. entertainment unit [who was also paid a salary of] $7.3 million in the fiscal year ended in June, including a $5.85 million bonus.

—ITEM IN THE *LOS ANGELES TIMES BUSINESS* SECTION
SEPTEMBER 27, 1997

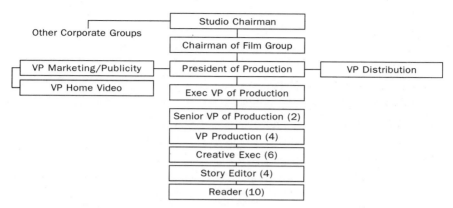

Chart of organization for a generic studio production department. (Copyright Hugh Taylor, courtesy of Lone Eagle Publishing.)

dine or shop in any manner except first class, and sign it off at studio expense whenever possible. All this helps drive studio overhead sky high. (For more on Tinseltown's luxurious lifestyle and spending habits, see chapter eight.)

Internal Studio Structure

With two exceptions, noted further on, the major studios are huge, multilayered companies with a complex executive hierarchy built around several key departments (see chart above), which work out of offices on busy studio lots. Those key departments are:

Production. This department is responsible for the creation of studio product or "releases," overseen by dozens of production executives who come under the jurisdiction of the president of production, or the "head of production." This is where the deals are made: the purchasing of screenplays or other literary material, the negotiating with producers, the signing of major stars or directors and so on. This is also the top of the Hollywood heap, the place so many of Hollywood's most ambitious and talented men and women want to be, including many of those already successful in television, which yields many creative talents who go on to work in feature films. The pressure in these office suites can be enormous since the fortunes of the studio, and corporate shareholders, rise and fall with the quality and success of the film projects that are chosen, developed and green lighted into production.

Physical production. Budgeting, cost overruns, scheduling, union matters and other practical aspects of a film's production come within the jurisdiction of this department. Although each movie has its own producer, who is responsible for day-to-day production matters, the studio maintains its own, expert production executives to monitor projects in production, whether they are being shot on location or the studio lot. Here, the concerns are less creative and political and more practical and budgetary, although dealing with the egos and personality quirks of the creative talent comes with the job.

Acquisition. This less prestigious but essential department consists of executives and their assistants whose job is to scout or "chase" films for release. As long as distribution rights to a film project are still available, that project is a "freeball," in acquisition parlance. These projects may be at various stages—in development, preproduction, production or completed—and the studio might become involved to varying degrees as a financing partner in exchange for various distribution rights. (For a more detailed breakdown, see *The Movie Business Book*, edited by Jason E. Squire, and *The Hollywood Job-Hunter's Survival Guide*, by Hugh Taylor.) When a film is acquired in this manner, it is called a "pickup." The acquisition department works closely with, or even as part of, the production department, and production executives are frequently actively involved in scouting potential pickups.

Distribution. Distribution covers a wide range of responsibilities, but its most important task is picking the release dates for the studio's movies, a highly strategic decision that affects virtually everyone else in the other studio departments and can mean the difference between a film "finding its audience," or being overlooked or destroyed by competing titles. In 1996, for example, Paramount Pictures waited until early fall to release *The First Wives Club*, a comedy starring three middle-aged actresses about women dealing with aging. It proved a surprise hit, in part, the studio believed, because it had been released *after* the summer glut of more lightweight or action-oriented pictures aimed at a younger audience, and when adult audiences were hungry for something a bit more sophisticated. The following September, the studio repeated exactly the same strategy in releasing the gay-themed adult comedy, *In & Out*, again to surprising success. This juggling act demands a keen knowledge of the competition and the marketplace, elaborate planning and scheduling, and a gambler's instinct and daring—with stakes that run into the hundreds of millions of dollars.

Other distribution responsibilities include the release of "trailers" (coming attractions) months before the release of the film itself; reserving screens for exhibition in both individual theaters and chains (known as "booking"); deciding how "wide" to open a film (how many theaters to book for opening day), which might range from "platforming" a smaller film (booking it at first into only a few or a few dozen theaters in major cities) to "going wide" with a bigger picture in roughly 1,500 to 3,000 theaters at once; deciding whether to go wider in the weeks thereafter, or pull back the number of theaters; delivering a flawless print of the film to each booked theater around the country by opening day; and so on.

Working closely with distribution is the marketing department and its subdivisions, publicity and advertising.

Marketing. Along with production and distribution, this is the other prestige and power department within the hierarchy. Marketing is where decisions are made on how to "position" a film with the public, that is, how to mount a "campaign" to create a public perception of the picture. For example, will a film be "sold" as an erotic thriller or a more arty *film noir*? Will it be aimed at the teenage crowd or a somewhat older audience? Advertised more heavily in the major cities or the suburbs, on TV or in print, on MTV or the networks, FM radio or AM? Should an ending or other scenes in the completed movie be reshot, the running time trimmed for a faster pace, the film recut to amplify a particular performer's role—and how big of a part should audience testing play in these decisions? When and where will sneak previews be scheduled, and with what other films? And so on.

Marketing works closely with advertising to carry out this crucial phase of promotion, and must be concerned each step of the way with not offending or alienating the top creative personnel associated with the film, who may or may not agree with how the picture is being handled. Ultimately, however—except in cases involving the most powerful, above-the-line talent—the studio has the final say in marketing decisions.

Advertising. This department creates the visual and audio tools needed to promote the product: the logo, posters, trailers, billboards and print and electronic spots that will help sell the film to the public.

Publicity. Publicists are responsible for generating free exposure for a film in a wide range of media outlets, which might include entertainment columns, magazine or newspaper articles and profiles, talk shows, news and magazine shows, and, more recently, outlets on the Internet. Publicity also coordinates press "junkets" (group gatherings of reporters) and publicity tours to various cities, and oversees the creation and distribution of electronic press kits (EPKs) for use by visual media. The studio publicists customarily work in close contact with personal publicists at top Hollywood public relations firms handling stars and other talent. (It is customary for all of these promotional departments to work with outside individuals and firms in the creation of copywriting, press kits, graphic design and other specialized services.)

Although executives within these departments work closely with each other on the movies they are assigned, they also frequently clash as they attempt to impress their vision or viewpoint about how a film should be cut, distributed and marketed. Final decisions often rest in the hands of the executive with the most political clout within the studio, including the studio chairman when necessary.

Ancillary or "aftermarket" departments. Each studio has vice presidents in charge of the primary post-theatrical markets: home video, cable, domestic television (movie) sales, foreign distribution and institutional distribution. Reporting to the president of the studio, their job is to work in an orchestrated way with the other departments to avoid conflicting efforts, while maximizing the sale of the studio's product in their particular market. This involves a series of "release windows"—exclusive periods of release in each market—scheduled to maximize potential revenue from one market before the product moves to a less profitable market (e.g., theatrical before video, cable before syndication).

The Current Major Studios

At this writing, the major studios are comprised of seven long-time survivors of the studio system, plus a notable newcomer, for a total of eight (although one, MGM/UA, has downsized to an almost marginal level). Together, they belong to and comprise the Motion Picture Association of America, Inc. (MPAA). The eight current majors, with a sampling of their modern era film titles, currently include the following:

Walt Disney Studios. Known also just as "Disney." It has two in-house divisions, Touchstone Pictures and Walt Disney Pictures, which specialize in more adult and lower-budget features and family fare, respectively. (Disney shut down its less successful Hollywood Pictures division in 1997.) Disney has also acquired independent distributor Miramax Films, which has been extremely successful with offbeat and less expensive "specialty" films. Disney is one of the most successful studios of the 1990s, under the leadership of top executive Michael Eisner. Films: *Good Morning, Vietnam*; *Three Men and a Baby*; *Who Framed Roger Rabbit?*; *The Lion King*.

Warner Bros. (owned by Time Warner). Uneven track record in recent years, but with a long history of classic films. Films: *All the President's Men, The Exorcist, Batman, Contact*.

46

How Many People Work There?

With one or two exceptions, each major studio employs at least several thousand people in Hollywood and many more who work around the country and throughout the world. Most of the studio lots are like little cities—parking is always at a premium—bustling with employees who work in a complex of areas, including legal and business affairs, accounting, operations and maintenance, postproduction, home video, music, research and various departments within production, such as costume, wardrobe and makeup.

As for the three key executive divisions mentioned above—production, distribution and marketing—they break down something like this (Hollywood only):

PRODUCTION The smallest of the three because so much work is done by outside production companies or nonstaff personnel (such as script readers), the production divisions generally maintain staffs of forty to sixty, with a newer and more streamlined company like DreamWorks/SKG at the lower end.

DISTRIBUTION The range here is quite broad, from about thirty at DreamWorks/SKG up to 150 for the larger, more established companies.

MARKETING Because marketing encompasses the busy advertising and publicity departments, it generally fields staffs of about 150 to 200.

Note: The same top three departments at the "mini-majors" or independent distributors, such as Miramax or Fine Line Features, work with considerably smaller staffs.

Sony Pictures Entertainment. What started out as Columbia Pictures (*Funny Girl, Lawrence of Arabia, Kramer vs. Kramer*), and later merged with Tri-Star (*Rambo*), was then swallowed up by the giant Sony Corporation, and renamed Sony Pictures Entertainment. Often referred to as "Columbia Tri-Star" since Sony produces films individually in both divisions. Films: *Men in Black, The Cable Guy, Air Force One, My Best Friend's Wedding, Hook.*

Paramount Pictures. Now owned by Viacom, Inc., and still going strong after all of these decades. Films: *The Godfather, Raiders of the Lost Ark, Trading Places, Face/Off.*

Twentieth Century Fox. Known widely as "Fox." Revitalized in the 1990s under production president Joe Roth, who then moved to Disney. Films: *Alien, 9 to 5, Star Wars, Home Alone, Grumpy Old Men, Titanic.*

Universal Pictures. Formerly known as MCA/Universal, and now jointly owned by Seagram Co. (the majority partner) and Japan's Matsushita Electric Industrial. After being a consistently leading power at the box office in the

Visitors tour the lot of the Warner Brothers Studio. (Copyright Warner Brothers, used by permission.)

1970s and 1980s, it has a checkered success record in the 1990s with intermittent blockbusters. Films: *American Graffiti, On Golden Pond, E.T., Jurassic Park*.

MGM/UA (Metro-Goldwyn-Mayer/United Artists). Once the mighty MGM (*Gone With the Wind, The Wizard of Oz, 2001: A Space Odyssey*), which later merged with another older studio, UA (*West Side Story, Rocky*, many James Bond films), this company is now attempting to rebuild as a full-fledged major after a financial takeover and breakup of assets reduced it to little more than a film library. Films: *Rain Man, Wargames, The Goodbye Girl, Manhattan, Stargate, Goldeneye*.

DreamWorks/SKG. The new multimedia company was founded in 1994 by three major Hollywood players—producer-director Steven Spielberg, music mogul David Geffen and former Disney production president Jeffrey Katzenberg—who plan to create a less hierarchical studio (for example, no formal titles for anyone). DreamWorks/SKG brings enormous money, talent and energy into the arena, and will be the studio everyone in Hollywood is watching as the millennium approaches. Its first production, *The Peacemaker*, was released in the fall of 1997. Other early titles: *Amistad, Mouse Hunt, Deep Impact*.

The three major Hollywood players who created and control the DreamWorks/SKG studio: David Geffen, Jeffrey Katzenberg and Steven Spielberg. (Photo by George Lange. Courtesy of DreamWorks/SKG.)

The Independents

Traditionally, an "independent" has been any film production and distribution company that works outside of the studio system. They are much smaller and more compact and streamlined than the huge studios, typically employing from a few dozen to a couple of hundred people, and operating with considerably less overhead, bureaucracy and executive layers.

The essential difference between the major studios and the independents comes down to one thing: money reserves. Studios, in a sense, are big banks or lending institutions, which finance individual film projects (or "multipic" deals), then release the finished product nationwide through their complex, highly sophisticated distribution systems. Their financial resources are so great—constantly fed by revenues from their vast libraries of old films and other company ventures, such as television and merchandising—that they are able not only to bankroll expensive productions and marketing campaigns, but to survive

The MPAA and the Movie Ratings System

The Motion Picture Association of America (MPAA) was founded in 1922 to represent the combined interests of the American film production and distribution industry in the United States. Since 1966, it has been headed by president Jack Valenti, a former top aide to President Lyndon Johnson, who is the recognized spokesman for the industry in the United States and around the world. As president of the Motion Picture Export Association, Valenti also represents the member companies in negotiating film treaties and settling marketing issues, notably film piracy problems, with foreign governments. Although the MPAA may seem a rather esoteric organization to Hollywood outsiders and to some readers of this book, Valenti has for three decades been an extremely vocal, visible and influential presence in the film industry.

Valenti was also responsible for forging the modern movie ratings system for parental guidance in the late 1960s to help ease out the restrictive Hays Code (see "Censorship and the Production Code" in chapter one). Today, all movies distributed by MPAA members are rated according to content by the MPAA ratings board to provide parents with "advance information" regarding a movie's content. Producers and directors frequently clash with the MPAA over ratings and many feel its ratings board is an unfairly restrictive censorship body. A producer who is displeased with the rating his or her movie has received can appeal to the MPAA ratings appeal board, which is the final arbiter.

The current ratings:

G: General Audience—All ages admitted. **PG:** Parental Guidance Suggested; some material may not be suitable for children. **PG-13:** Parents strongly cautioned. Some material may be inappropriate for children under 13. **R:** Restricted, under seventeen requires accompanying parent or adult guardian. **NC-17:** No children under seventeen admitted.

financially if these risky ventures fail at the box office. Independents, on the other hand, can be wiped out by only one such costly failure.

Nonetheless, over the decades, independent distributors have attempted to carve out a share of the feature film marketplace, with varying degrees of success.

"The independent moviemaking sensibility can be traced in the modern movie era to John Cassavetes' distribution company in the 1960s," Jason E. Squires, an adjunct professor at the USC School of Cinema-Television and editor of *The Movie Business Book*, wrote recently in the *Los Angeles Times*, "and back further to the original 'United Artists'—Chaplin, Fairbanks, Pickford and

Exhibition: The All Important Box-Office

The way studios make money, at least at the initial theatrical release level, is fairly simple: Each studio negotiates terms with theaters for the right to show (exhibit) a given motion picture. The theaters (exhibitors) sell the tickets at the box office and turn over a percentage to the studios, less certain operating costs. Generally, at least with bigger pictures, theaters take a smaller percentage in the first weeks of release—sometimes as low as 10 percent—and more as the weeks go by, increasing up to 50 percent. In many cases, most of the profits theaters see come not from ticket sales but from the concessions they sell (e.g., popcorn and candy).

The total amount of ticket sales for a movie is the film's box-office "gross." The "rentals" represent the amount the distributor (studio) gets, which on average is 50 percent of the box-office gross and is sometimes referred to as the "distributor's gross." "Film rental is the crucial figure," veteran film reporter A.D. Murphy has written in *Variety*, "because film rentals pay for the production, promotion and prints of the film as well as for participations in gross when the creative talent is in the superstar echelon" (as opposed to "net profit" participation for others, which often amounts to nothing when all of the studio accounting is done).

At one time, the major studios monopolized both production and exhibition—essentially taking *all* of the money—by owning and running their own theater chains. In 1952, after a three-year legal battle, the studios were forced by federal antitrust decree to choose between the two, and opted for production. In the deregulation climate of the late 1980s, however, studios began buying up individual theaters and theater chains, once again controlling how and where many movies will be shown, and making it more difficult than ever for the independent to survive. (For a detailed breakdown of the complex movie exhibition business, see chapters seven through nine in *The Movie Business Book*.)

A primary source for tracking movie grosses is Exhibitor Relations (116 N. Robertson Blvd., #606, Los Angeles, CA 90048; 310/657-2005). Operated by president John Krier, it disseminates a wide range of information to the media, including film release schedules, opening weekend grosses, cumulative grosses and so on.

Krier estimates that by 1998, with the rise of the multiplex theater, including many smaller-capacity screening rooms, there were roughly 30,000 theater screens across the country, up from about 14,000 in 1970.

The current top ten markets for feature film revenue in the U.S. and Canada are: (1) New York Metropolitan Area, (2) Los Angeles, (3) Washington, DC, (4) Philadelphia, (5) San Francisco Bay Area, (6) Chicago, (7) Toronto, (8) San Diego, (9) Orange County, California, (10) Detroit.

Griffith in 1919—with stops along the way for other pioneers including Joseph E. Levine, Samuel Goldwyn and Walt Disney."

Excluding low-budget exploitation movies and foreign imports, the vast majority of feature films were made and distributed by the major studios well into the 1960s. Then, in 1969, the box-office success of *Easy Rider* led to an explosion of independent production and the emergence of impressive new filmmakers such as Bob Rafelson (*Five Easy Pieces*), Terrence Malick (*Badlands*), Martin Scorscese (*Mean Streets*) and numerous others who did their early work outside the studio system. Independent filmmaking took on a new prestige, bolstered by growing media attention and box-office success. Along with it came the growth of upstart, independent distribution companies that either produced their own films, acquired completed films for distribution or both, and put them into limited distribution.

By the 1980s, a number of high-profile independents were attempting to duplicate the strategies of the majors by producing big, expensive films, then releasing them nationwide (at that time, roughly 1,000 to 1,500 theaters). By the end of the decade, lacking the cash to keep producing new pictures to feed their distribution pipeline, most of the independent distributors had folded, filed for bankruptcy or radically reorganized and scaled back their ambitions.

A few independents, however, managed not only to survive but to thrive by concentrating on low-budget films for niche audiences, using shrewd marketing campaigns and focused distribution and thereby maximizing their return on their minimal investment. One of the most successful was New Line Cinema. Ira Deutchman, former senior vice president of New Line Cinema and president of one of its two production divisions, Fine Line Features (the other is New Line Pictures), writing in *The Movie Business Book*, compared studio and independent distributors this way: "The primary difference is in marketing styles. Studios, by needing to feed an enormous overhead machine, are forced by their very nature to swing for the fences every time out. This requires a marketing style that works on the macro—reaching out for large numbers. We [the independents], however, are practitioners of micromarketing—sticking our fingers into little pockets of business and scaling down the economics accordingly. . . . Compared with the majors, the profit margin is smaller, but the risk is smaller as well."

In the early 1990s, however, some of those "small" films turned into bona fide blockbusters. Gramercy's modestly budgeted *Four Weddings and a Funeral* has reportedly grossed $250 million worldwide. Miramax, while spending an average of $12.5 million to produce its films, racked up a string of impressive worldwide grosses with such pictures as *The Piano* ($40 million), *The Crying Game* ($62 million) and *Pulp Fiction* ($200 million). In 1990, New Line Cinema grossed more than $100 million in the U.S. alone with its *Teenage Mutant Ninja Turtles*, and $25 million for its black teen comedy, *House Party*, which it produced for about $3 million.

These figures were not lost on the major studios, which began acquiring the more active independent distribution companies—Miramax to Disney, New Line Cinema to Time Warner—or developing in-house units that served the same purpose, such as Sony's Classics Division and Searchlight Films at Twentieth Century Fox. (It's worth noting that this duplicates a similar studio trend that came and went in the 1970s and 1980s). Even as the studios forged these new alliances with independents, however, most studio brass seemed to regard the smaller, independent film as a marginal business venture. The studios' focus would continue to be the manufacturing and marketing of big-budget productions in an attempt to create blockbuster movies that could reach the biggest worldwide audience possible.

The studios, however, cannot make all of those movies alone. That's where the independent producers come in.

The Independent Producers

Independent producers and production companies are another animal completely from the independents that handle their own distribution and, in essence, attempt to operate as ministudios. There are hundreds of these production-only outfits scattered throughout Southern California, ranging in size from lofty, well-financed companies with studio financing deals, such as Imagine Films and Castle Rock Entertainment (see "Major Studios and Independent Producers" later in this chapter), to budding entrepreneurs and even scam artists who call themselves "producers" and operate out of one-person offices or dingy apartments.

Most independent producers ("indies") fall somewhere in the middle and they constitute a vital, thriving, energetic portion of working Hollywood, responsible for employing thousands of people; optioning and developing hundreds, if not thousands, of screenplays; generating countless motion pictures; and growing in size and stature as they develop solid track records over time or score the surprise hit that suddenly puts them on the map. It's important to understand that *moviemaking in Hollywood is as much about the less-visible independent producers as it is about the mighty and more glamorous studios*, a point often

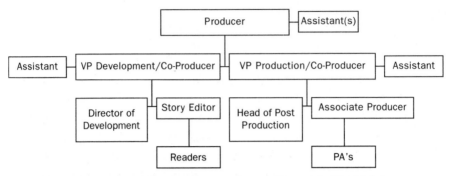

Chart of organization for a large production company. (Copyright Hugh Taylor, courtesy of Lone Eagle Publishing.)

overlooked or misunderstood by outsiders. They are the worker bees in the production game, the ones who are scouting, reading and developing material with just as much hope and hunger as those at the studios, if not more.

While a few dozen independent producers have the kind of financial backing that allows them to develop and shoot big budget pictures, the majority of independent producers are always scrambling for money with $3 to $7 million being a fairly common shooting budget. This endless quest for working capital is referred to as "trying to put the deal together": would-be producers searching anywhere they can for investors willing to put up part of the financing based on a script and attached "elements" (stars and a director who have committed to the project), in exchange for a piece of the potential profits. (For a more detailed breakdown of this process, see *The Beginning Filmmaker's Business Guide* by Renee Harmon.) The ones who stick with it to get their movies made are those who seem to possess patience and determination bordering on obsession.

Case in point: Robert Townsend, a young actor who shot to fame during the indie boom of the 1980s. As an African-American facing typecasting and limited roles, Townsend decided to write, produce and direct a comedy based on his Tinseltown experiences, which he called *Hollywood Shuffle*. His financing strategy was simple: He applied for every credit card offered him after he graduated from college—some three dozen cards with generous credit limits—then used them to run up his production expenses. When a major studio picked up his low-budget movie and released it successfully in 1987, he covered all of his costs and much more.

Similar success stories fueled the dreams of aspiring filmmakers, and more and more "small" independent films hit the market, which had grown to include cable TV outlets and home video sales and rentals. The trend reached a new plateau in 1995 with the success of youthful director Quentin Tarentino's gritty, offbeat Miramax production, *Pulp Fiction*. The film was such a huge box-office and critical hit that it made Tarentino an instant "hot" director and generated a new wave of independent production and indie-studio deal-making.

With the gradual rise of the independent producer over three decades and a wider range of choices for a film audience that continues to grow more diverse and discriminating, the marketplace now supports more independent filmmakers and nonmainstream subject matter than ever before. That means that Hollywood is abuzz with would-be filmmakers knocking on studio or production company doors or trying to "put the deal together" on their own.

For every Robert Townsend and Quentin Tarentino, however, there are countless producers who never produce anything, or go broke trying.

The "True" Independent

There is yet another level of independent production, what some call the "truly" independent producer: filmmakers so passionate about their art that they manage to make their films with or without the backing of established, traditional sources, even when their budgets seem impossibly small. Making a profit, let alone an enormous profit, which drives most of Hollywood, is not their primary goal. They operate on the fringes of Hollywood, with their chief purpose being *to get their movie made, the way they want to make it, without outside interference.*

Among the more prominent independent filmmakers of the last two decades: Robert Altman, John Sayles, Robert Young, Alan Rudolph, Henry Jaglom, Jim Jarmusch, Susan Seidelman, Charles Burnett, Gregory Nava, Abel Ferrara, Spike Lee, Julie Dash, Wayne Wang, Joel and Ethan Coen, Steven Soderbergh, Gus van Sant, Alison Anders, John Waters, Nancy Savoca, Gregg Araki. (A few went on to make studio deals, giving up varying degrees of autonomy.)

Henry Jaglom (*Sitting Ducks, Eating*), who financed his early films in the 1970s with investments from dentists who benefited from lucrative tax shelter deals (no longer legal), insists that the truly committed filmmaker will do whatever it takes to make his or her films: "To make a movie, you need as much money as you've got, not a penny more," he writes in *The Movie Business Book*. "If it's just $20,000 you can raise, take a video camera and go make a movie. Someone will see it and you'll be on your way. Don't talk about it; do it. This is a great time for independent filmmakers because of all the new formats that need to be fed."

Many have followed Jaglom's path, helping to create a worldwide audience for the small or intensely personal picture that now includes a circuit of film festivals numbering in the hundreds (see "Film Festivals" in Appendix B). There is also a growing number of independent filmmaker organizations and support groups, such as The Independent Features Project/West (1625 West Olympic Blvd., Santa Monica, CA 90404; 310/475-4379; www.ifpwest.org), which sponsors the annual Spirit Awards and other events (see "Professional Organizations and Associations" in the appendix). By far the most prominent—combining support and mentoring programs, a film festival, and a production company—is the Sundance Film Institute, which was founded by Robert Redford. The annual Sundance Film Festival, held in the mountain community of Park City, Utah, was originally attended largely by young, aspiring filmmakers and film buffs; today, it is very much a Hollywood affair, as agents, producers and studio executives flock into town each year in search of new talent or films for acquisition.

Lured by big budgets and paychecks, power and worldwide audiences, many independent filmmakers are inevitably swallowed up by the studio system. Some go on to great success, while others fail to survive the ruthlessness of studio politics, the vagaries of the marketplace, the fierce competition and the pressure to keep churning out commercial hits.

Ironically, even some of those who make careers in Hollywood will later admit that they made their most personally satisfying films on shoestring budgets, back when they were the captains of their own ships and "truly independent."

Major Studios and Independent Producers

What follows is a list of the major studios and selected independent production companies that operate with a high profile in Los Angeles at this writing. Representative film titles are listed for each independent. In some cases, independents have studio deals and locations as noted. Be aware that phone numbers and other details are subject to change. (*Denotes a major studio.)

Studio tours are offered by Paramount, Warner Bros. and Universal. For details, see the sidebar "Studio and Network Tours and Tickets" on page 208. A writer who is planning to include a studio lot as subject matter or background material in his or her work may be able to get research assistance or even arrange a personal tour through the studio's public relations department, especially if the writer is working under contract to a bona fide publisher. Also, numerous illustrated books on studio history exist (see the Nonfiction/Reference Books

Section of Appendix B, as well as the sidebar on the Margaret Herrick Library, page 69).

Amblin Entertainment (100 Universal City Plaza, Bungalow 477, Universal City, CA 91608; 818/777-4600). This is Steven Spielberg's personal company, housed in homey, Santa Fe-style offices built especially for him on the Universal lot as an expression of the studio's gratitude for his many hit films. It is in the process of being absorbed into his new studio, DreamWorks/SKG (see below). Films: *E.T., Jurassic Park, Schindler's List.*

Avenue Pictures (11111 Santa Monica Blvd., Suite 2110, Los Angeles, CA 90025; 310/996-6800). Films: *Short Cuts, The Player, Restoration.*

Baltimore Pictures (818/954-2666; otherwise, see Warner Bros.). This is the company of writer-director-producer Barry Levinson. Films: *Bugsy, Tin Men, Quiz Show.*

Bruckheimer Films, Jerry (1631 Tenth St., Santa Monica, CA 90404; 310/664-6260). With the late Don Simpson, Bruckheimer produced such blockbuster hits as *Beverly Hills Cop* and *Top Gun.* Now he's on his own. Titles: *Con Air, The Rock.*

Carolco Pictures (4665 Lankershim Blvd., Suite 420, North Hollywood, CA 91602; 818/754-0744). Once a major force among independents, Carolco has been financially shaken in recent years, and now operates only marginally. Films: *Rambo, Terminator 2, Cliffhanger.*

Castle Rock Entertainment (335 N. Maple Dr., #135, Beverly Hills, CA 90210; 310/285-2300). Castle Rock, owned in part by actor-producer-director Rob Reiner, is located in a plush high-rise on a quiet, tree-lined street in the "flats" of Beverly Hills. Once a powerhouse among independents and now a subsidiary of Time Warner, Castle Rock has suffered financially in recent years. Films: *A Few Good Men, City Slickers, In the Line of Fire.*

Cherry Alley Productions (225 Arizona Ave., Suite 350, Santa Monica, CA 90401; 310/458-8886). This is actress Goldie Hawn's new company after the breakup of the Hawn-Sylbert Movie Co., which produced films including *Deceived, Overboard* and *Protocol.*

***Columbia Pictures** (see Sony Pictures Entertainment).

Davis Entertainment Co. (2121 Avenue of the Stars, Suite 2900, Los Angeles, CA 90067; 310/556-3550). Films: *Predator, The Firm, Grumpy Old Men.*

***DreamWorks/SKG** (See Amblin Entertainment; 818/733-7000). This studio is the new kid on the block among the majors, with offices spread out in roughly half a dozen locations across the city, from Glendale to Marina del Rey, and another office in New York.

Goldwyn Co., Samuel (10203 Santa Monica Blvd., Los Angeles, CA 90067; 310/552-2255). After serious financial problems, the future of this venerable company that championed the unusual or more artistic independent film is uncertain under its new owner, MGM/UA. Films: *Longtime Companions*; *The Wedding Banquet*; *Eat Drink, Man Woman*.

Gramercy (see Polygram).

Imagine Entertainment (1925 Century Park East, 23rd Floor, Los Angeles, CA 90067; 310/277-1663). Owned partly by actor-director Ron Howard, Imagine occupies spacious high-rise offices in Century City. Films: *Apollo 13*; *Backdraft*; *Liar, Liar*; *Far and Away*.

Interscope Communications, Inc. (10900 Wilshire Blvd., Suite 1400, Los Angeles, CA 90024; 310/208-8525). Films: *Terminal Velocity*, *The Hand That Rocks the Cradle*.

Kopelson Entertainment, Arnold (2121 Avenue of the Stars, Suite 1400, Los Angeles, CA 90067; 310/369-7500). Films: *Platoon*, *The Fugitive*, *Falling Down*.

Ladd Company, The (see Paramount Pictures). Presiding over this company is Alan Ladd, Jr., a former studio executive and son of the late Alan Ladd, the tough-guy star of the 1940s and 1950s. Films: *Braveheart*, *The Brady Bunch*.

Live Entertainment, Inc. (15400 Sherman Way, Suite 500, Van Nuys, CA 91406; 818/908-0303). Films: *Dirty Dancing*, *Reservoir Dogs*.

Miramax Films (7966 Beverly Blvd., Los Angeles, CA 90048; 213/951-4200). Although now part of the Disney family, this successful independent has offices away from the Disney lot on the city's west side. Films: *The Crying Game*, *The Piano*, *Pulp Fiction*.

*MGM/UA (2500 Broadway, Santa Monica, CA 90404; 310/449-3000). MGM was once one of the great Hollywood studios, and occupied a legendary lot in Culver City whose streets are named after its most famous stars, which is now the home of Sony Pictures Entertainment. MGM, in a rebuilding phase, is now housed in an attractive, newer office building about three miles from the ocean in the seaside city of Santa Monica.

Morgan Creek Productions (see Warner Bros.). A very successful company. Films: *Major League*, *Ace Ventura*, *Wild America*.

New Line Cinema, Fine Line Features (116 N. Robertson #200, Los Angeles, CA 90048; 310/854-5811). New Line is considered a mini-major because of its volume of product and success in both production and independent distribution and, more recently, its infusion of capital after being acquired by Time Warner. Films: *Teenage Mutant Ninja Turtles, Dumb and Dumber, House Party, Menace II Society.*

New World Entertainment (headquartered in New York with animation in L.A.).

Northern Lights Entertainment (see Walt Disney Pictures). This is the company that produces the films of director Ivan Reitman. Films: *Ghostbusters, Stripes, Kindergarten Cop.*

Obst Productions, Lynda (310/369-2993; otherwise see Twentieth Century Fox). Films: *Sleepless in Seattle, The Fisher King, Contact.*

Orion Pictures (1888 Century Park East, Los Angeles, CA 90067; 310/282-0550). Once a thriving mini-major with a healthy release schedule, Orion went bankrupt in 1991 and is now operating as part of Metromedia Entertainment Group, which has been acquired by MGM/UA. Films: *Dominick and Eugene, The Lady in Red, Ulee's Gold.*

*Paramount Studios (5555 Melrose Ave., Los Angeles, CA 90038; 213/956-5000). Paramount is still housed in its original home behind its famous gates, which have been seen in countless photographs and even some movies, and through which hundreds of Hollywood's biggest stars have passed. Although modern touches can be found in certain areas of the lot, particularly in the executive offices and dining facilities, many of the old backlot streets, sets and vintage production offices remain.

Peters Entertainment (see Warner Bros.). Chairman Jon Peters is the former partner of Peter Guber, who as a team were responsible for such hits as *Batman, Rain Man, Flashdance.*

Polygram Filmed Entertainment (9348 Civic Center Dr., Suite 300, Beverly Hills, CA 90210; 310/777-7700). Includes Gramercy. Films: *Four Weddings and a Funeral, Posse, Jason's Lyric.*

Propaganda Films (940 N. Mansfield Ave., Los Angeles, CA 90038; 213/462-6400). Known for offbeat fare. Films: *Wild at Heart, Kalifornia, Red Rock West.*

RKO Pictures, Inc. (1801 Avenue of the Stars, Suite 448, Los Angeles, CA 90067; 310/277-0707). RKO was a major studio in earlier decades, but is now a relatively small production company (with a sizable library of vintage RKO movies) with offices in L.A. and New York. Films: *Hamburger Hill, Narrow Margin.*

Rastar Productions (see Sony Pictures Studios). Veteran producer Ray Stark is the chairman of this company, which has a long deal/relationship

BEHIND THE SCENES: INSIDE HOLLYWOOD

with Columbia Pictures. Films: *Lost in Yonkers, Steel Magnolias, Barbarians at the Gate* and many earlier hits.

Robinson, Phil Alden (see Universal Pictures). Robinson is a writer-director who produces his own projects. Films: *Sneakers, All of Me, Field of Dreams.*

Rudin Productions, Scott (see Paramount Pictures). Films: *In and Out, Sister Act, The Addams Family.*

Silver Pictures (see Warner Bros.). Chairman Joel Silver is a colorful producer known for his successful action pictures. Films: *Lethal Weapon, Die Hard, Demolition Man.*

*Sony Pictures Entertainment (Columbia Tri-Star) (10202 W. Washington Blvd., Culver City, CA 90232; 310/244-4000). See MGM/UA above.

Sundance Institute (225 Santa Monica Blvd., 8th Floor, Santa Monica, CA 90401; 310/394-4662). This is the L.A. office of the organization founded in Park City, Utah, by Robert Redford to support independent filmmakers. Titles: *Desert Bloom, A Dry White Season, Reservoir Dogs.*

Tisch Co., The Steve (3815 Hughes Ave., Culver City, CA 90232; 310/838-2500). Titles: *Risky Business; Forrest Gump; Corrina, Corrina.*

Touchstone Pictures (a division of Walt Disney Pictures, listed below).

Tri-Star Pictures (see Sony Pictures Entertainment).

*Twentieth Century Fox (10201 W. Pico Blvd., Los Angeles, CA 90064; 310/369-1000). Much of the former, sprawling Fox lot was sold off decades ago in a real estate bonanza that resulted in Century City. What remains is a cramped, busy lot for both TV and film production, including its legendary New York street sets, original commissary and bungalow screening rooms.

United Artists Pictures (see MGM/UA). Films: *Rob Roy, Tank Girl.*

*Universal Studios (MCA/Universal) (100 Universal City Plaza, Universal City, CA 91608; 818/777-1000). This is very much a working lot, anchored near its entrance by the famous "Black Tower" executive high-rise building, although much of its land has been converted for its world-famous theme park, Universal City Walk, theaters and other attractions.

Viacom. A major, international multimedia company, New York-based.

*Walt Disney Pictures (500 S. Buena Vista St., Burbank, CA 91521; 818/560-1000). Housed on a crowded valley lot with its streets and lanes named for its most popular cartoon characters, i.e. Mickey and Goofy.

*Warner Bros. Studios (4000 Warner Blvd., Burbank, CA 91522; 818/954-6000). Warners occupies the sprawling complex known as The Burbank Studios, where many of the old bungalows and backlot sets are still intact, along with warehouses filled with props, clothes and other memorabilia from classic Warners pictures.

Zanuck Co., The (202 N. Cannon Dr., Beverly Hills, CA 90210; 310/274-0261). With former partner David Brown, Richard Zanuck made such classics as *Jaws*, *The Sting* and *The Verdict*. He is now partnered with wife Lili. Titles: *Rush*, *Wild Bill*, *Mulholland Falls*.

(For a more complete and current listing, consult recent editions of the *Hollywood Creative Directory* or the *Pacific Coast Studio Directory*. See Appendix B for additional resources).

The Age of the Modern Blockbuster

For more than three decades after its release by MGM in 1939, *Gone With the Wind* was the undisputed box-office champ, with domestic rentals of $77.6 million (rentals being that portion taken by the distributor after theaters take their slice of the ticket grosses, as explained on page 51). It was an astounding figure for the time considering that most tickets back then cost a quarter; by comparison, MGM's *The Wizard of Oz*, the second biggest film of 1939, reaped rentals of $4.5 million.

Then in 1972, Paramount released *The Godfather*, which netted $86.2 million, almost double the amount reached by the studio's previous top success, *Love Story* (1970). Although *The Godfather* followed the publication of Mario Puzo's best-selling Mafia saga novel, Paramount had actually nurtured it as a screen project from the beginning. Before his book was written, the studio purchased a twenty-page outline from Puzo for $7,500, then paid him an additional $80,000 and installed him on the Paramount lot, where he finished the novel under the studio's aegis (this according to Susan Sackett in *The Hollywood Reporter Book of Box Office Hits*). This creation of an "event" movie through shrewd planning and careful promotion—and the astounding box-office returns it brought in—signaled the coming of the modern studio blockbuster.

Perhaps more than any single picture, *Jaws* (1975) was the quintessential studio event movie and first true modern blockbuster. It was released amid an unprecedented frenzy of hype and popularity, and set a new rental record of

> **““***Jaws* was not a novel, it was a story written by a committee, a piece of shit.**””**
> —ACTOR ROBERT SHAW, WHO COSTARRED IN THE FILM *JAWS*

The Top Ten Domestic Grossing Films of All Time
(THROUGH 1997)

1. *Star Wars* (Twentieth Century Fox, 1977): $460.9 million
2. *E.T.* (Universal, 1982): $399.8 million
3. *Jurassic Park* (Universal, 1993): $356.7 million
4. *Titanic* (Paramount, 1997): $337 million (at this writing)
5. *Forrest Gump* (Paramount, 1994): $329.6 million
6. *The Lion King* (Disney/Buena Vista, 1994): $312.8 million
7. *Return of the Jedi* (Twentieth Century Fox, 1983): $309.1 million
8. *Independence Day* (Twentieth Century Fox, 1996): $306.1 million
9. *The Empire Strikes Back* (Twentieth Century Fox, 1980): $290.1 million
10. *Home Alone* (Twentieth Century Fox, 1990): $285.7 million

Although the reporting of international grosses is somewhat less reliable than domestic grosses, these films generally made at least as much if not more money in foreign release. *Jurassic Park*, generally regarded as the top world grosser, reached $914 million in worldwide ticket sales. In 1997 the *Los Angeles Times* estimated that *Jurassic Park* had returned profits of $700 million to Universal and director-producer Steven Spielberg, derived from ticket sales, merchandising, video sales and sales to television, but not counting theme park revenues. *Titanic*, only recently released, may become the first film ever to gross $1 billion worldwide.

$129.5 million, part of a record year in which gross box-office receipts in the U.S. totaled $1.9 billion. In *Variety*, reporter Leonard Klady wrote: "Basically there are two types of blockbusters—Before *Jaws* and After *Jaws*."

Two years later, *Star Wars* netted $193.5 million in rentals for Twentieth Century Fox, a figure topped by Universal's *E.T.* in 1982, with rentals of $228.7 million. The make-or-break blockbuster, with tens of millions invested in marketing and promotion, had become part of every studio's agenda, along with a trend toward film sequels that continues unabated.

The Merchandising Phenomenon

Although Disney was successful for decades in exploiting its popular animation movies for merchandising revenue, it wasn't until 1977, with the release of *Star Wars*, that the other studios woke up to the merchandising potential in their own feature films.

Explaining "Net Profits" and "Points"

Motion picture profits come in two varieties: "net" and "gross." Top creative talent, customarily stars, directors, producers and writers, participate in a film's revenue according to the stipulations in their individual contracts, that is to say, whether they have a percentage of the net or the gross (or, in some cases, no profit participation at all).

Some key terms to understand:

NET The net is what's left *after* the studio takes its distribution fee, expenses and negative cost (see "Professional Hollywood Terms" in Appendix A).

GROSS This is the revenue taken in by a studio (roughly half the ticket sales) *before* it deducts the aforementioned costs.

FIRST DOLLAR GROSS This is the revenue calculated "off the top" as the very first money comes in from distribution (a.k.a. "distributor's gross").

POINTS "Net points" or "gross points" refer to a stipulated percentage of a picture's profits. Five net points, then, equals five percent of the net profits.

BREAKEVEN This is the point when a film has paid off its costs and goes into profits, which is determined by studio accounting procedures.

ROLLING BREAKEVEN A studio accounting practice by which a studio deducts *all* costs of a film, including payments to *gross participants* as those payments are made, which sometimes keeps even very successful movies from ever showing a net profit.

BACKEND A deal whereby a talent defers all or most of his or her salary in exchange for a gross participation at the back end (when the money comes in). Some deals like this have earned actors paychecks in the tens of millions of dollars, while greatly diminishing the paychecks of those with less favorable net point deals.

BOOTSTRAPPING Using profit points on one film as leverage or barter to get more favorable deals on future projects.

The most important consideration in making a deal for gross or net points is where along the accounting timetable the points kick in—that is, from first dollar (the best deal), and other levels down the scale to breakeven (the worst deal).

What kind of deal a creative talent is able to make depends on a variety of circumstances, including the size of the film's budget, how the movie is being financed, the savvy and power of the negotiating agent and, most importantly, the stature and popularity of the talent and how badly the producers and director want that person for a particular role (writing assignment, directing job and so on).

Newcomers who lack negotiating leverage generally get a net point deal—two-and-a-half net points for a first-time screenwriter is quite common, for example—and it is just as common that they never see any money beyond their initial, up-front payment.

CONTINUED ON NEXT PAGE

In recent years, a number of stars and other top creative talent have taken to auditing the accounts on films they've worked on, and frequently the studios have been forced to pay up. In some cases, just the *threat* of an audit has been enough to shake loose profit payments that are overdue, but easily hidden by a studio's complicated, sometimes mysterious, bookkeeping practices (a.k.a. *creative accounting*).

Use of the *Star Wars* logo and characters on posters, T-shirts, toys, lunch boxes and other merchandise proved to be a bonanza more profitable than the film itself. To date, it is estimated that *Star Wars* and its sequels have sold between $3 and $4 billion in merchandise around the globe. Because of an unusually shrewd deal that producer-director George Lucas cut for himself with Fox prior to making the sequels, he has reaped the lion's share of the profits; at the time, studios did not even have merchandising departments.

Taking his cue from Lucas and *Star Wars*, Steven Spielberg struck merchandising gold with *E.T.*, which achieved a worldwide gross of $619 million in its initial release in 1982-83, to become the most popular movie of all time to that date. So popular was the space alien character E.T. that Spielberg was able to license more than two hundred E.T. products, ranging from cereal and toys to women's undergarments with E.T.'s face stitched on the leg.

Since the heady discovery of movie merchandising revenue in the 1970s, every studio has established a special division to handle such tie-ins, and it is thought that some movies are now conceived primarily as wellsprings for lucrative merchandising spin-offs or to boost merchandising lines already being manufactured. When *Superman* was released in 1978, the title character was already a comic book icon, but the success of the movie and its sequels gave a boost to its merchandising potential and by the end of the decade, *Superman* licensing deals totaled more than a thousand. Likewise, even before *Teenage Mutant Ninja Turtles* was released as a movie in 1990, toys based on the comic book and TV characters had grossed over $1 billion, but sales shot up dramatically with the worldwide promotion and success of the movie. Similarly, the 1989 release of *Batman* resulted in reported retail tie-in sales of $1.5 billion worldwide, more than twice the film's ticket sales.

Licensing deals don't always work out, of course, and it is the licensee who takes the biggest risk by making a multimillion investment in merchandise and advertising while gambling that a movie will be a hit. When movies such as *Flash*

Gordon, *Dick Tracy*, *The Rocketeer* and *The Hunchback of Notre Dame* failed to fulfill box-office expectations, more than a few retailers were left with unsold tie-in products on their shelves, and some merchandisers were reportedly left with sizable losses. When *Batman & Robin* and the animated *Hercules* fell short of anticipated blockbuster figures in the summer of 1997, some industry analysts felt the glut and greed of commercial tie-ins was beginning to cheapen the image of certain movies and turn off audiences. "When a movie is made for McDonald's and the retailers, it loses sight of the story and audience," said Arthur Rockwell of the brokerage firm Yaeger Capital Markets. "Like *Batman & Robin*, *Hercules* is seen less as a movie than as a giant marketing venture."

The merchandising phenomenon has also become a problem for actors and actresses who object to their likenesses being used to sell products, fearing commercialization, overexposure, an implied endorsement of the product or the mishandling of their image. A number of legal and contractual disagreements reportedly arose over the use of stars' likenesses connected to merchandising deals on such films as *Hook*, *The Doors* and *Robin Hood: Prince of Thieves*. According to the *Hollywood Reporter*, for example, a Taco Bell fast-food promotion tied to *Robin Hood* fell through because the star, Kevin Costner, did not want his image associated with the merchandising campaign. There were still numerous other tie-ins for the film, however, including a *Robin Hood: Prince of Thieves* cereal from Ralston Purina featuring arrow-shaped cereal pieces and a generic Robin Hood image on the box rather than a likeness of Costner.

Problems can also arise over who created and controls or shares in a merchandising bonanza generated from a particular character or film, as happened with Disney's *The Mighty Ducks*. The 1992 comedy revolving around a peewee hockey team spawned two sequels and a profitable line of Mighty Ducks merchandise, much of it generated by a Disney-owned pro hockey team, which was expressly named the Mighty Ducks because of the films. The writer of the original screenplay, who had come up with the Mighty Ducks name, subsequently filed a lawsuit seeking 5 percent of Disney's take from all Mighty Ducks merchandise. The writer cited language in the basic Writer's Guild of America agreement that says a writer is entitled to that percentage of the moneys from merchandisers to a studio, when that studio exploits an object or other entity "first described in literary material written by the writer."

Today, with merchandising a multibillion dollar business, participation in movie-related merchandising revenue is a vital point in virtually every contract negotiation involving high-level talent.

Named by Academy librarian Margaret Herrick, who thought the figure resembled her uncle, the Oscar statuette has long been a symbol of quality and success in the film industry. (Copyrighted property of the Academy of Motion Picture Arts and Sciences. Used by permission.)

Oscar's Special Role in Hollywood

The Academy of Motion Pictures Arts and Sciences—the organization that each year hands out the Academy Awards or Oscars—became a legal corporation on May 4, 1927.

The driving force behind the Academy was studio mogul Louis B. Mayer, the head of Metro-Goldwyn-Mayer, who opened membership to those who "had contributed in a distinguished way to the arts and sciences of motion picture production." Its chief goals in the beginning were to mediate labor disputes, promote technical advances and help improve the image of the Hollywood film industry by working with the Hays Office. The first Academy members—231 of Hollywood's more distinguished actors, writers, producers, directors and technicians—paid $100 each to join.

It was soon decided to bestow "awards of merit" for each of those five creative branches at the Academy's annual banquet. By July 1928, a voting system was in place, with members voting for nominees in their respective branches. The winners were chosen by a central board of five judges comprised of one representative from each branch. On February 18, without much fanfare, the names of the winners were printed on the back page of the *Academy Bulletin*, with honorable mention given to the other nominees. The banquet itself was held three months later at the Hollywood Roosevelt Hotel, and small golden statuettes were handed out in twelve categories.

When Academy librarian Margaret Herrick saw one of the trophies for the first time, she reportedly exclaimed, "Oh, it looks just like Uncle Oscar!" The name stuck, and the award came to be known informally as the Oscar, and the annual awards show as "The Oscars."

In the early years, the Oscars was a rather clubby affair, with little tangible professional or promotional value for individuals or individual films that won. Some stars failed to show up at the banquet to pick up their trophies, and even after the awards show became nationally televised in 1953 (the first TV rights were sold for $100,000), nominees sometimes spurned their invitations. The reasons included disinterest, disrespect for the self-promotional aspects of the show, a dislike of the competitive process that pitted creative people against each other, or more personal political reasons.

Yet as more and more top Hollywood stars attended, gaining increasing media coverage, the unique situation of seeing so many well-dressed celebrities together in one place at one time—live and on camera—appealed to a public hungry for Hollywood's larger-than-life glamour. Throughout the 1960s and 1970s,

---

❝The Oscar is the most valuable, but least expensive, item of worldwide public relations ever invented by any industry.❞

—DIRECTOR FRANK CAPRA

❝The Academy Awards are obscene, dirty and no better than a beauty contest.❞

—ACTOR DUSTIN HOFFMAN

the annual Academy Awards show, which was usually held on a Monday night in March (never during the movie-going weekend), grew in terms of both its stature and popularity, becoming a much-anticipated, nationwide event.

Today, the annual Oscar broadcast is seen by an estimated one billion people around the world. Television rights are sold for several million dollars yearly. An Oscar can catapult an actor or director to A-list status virtually overnight, and can add tens of millions of dollars to box-office and video revenues. Each year, the studios, and sometimes personal publicists representing star clients, engineer expensive Oscar campaigns at both the nomination and selection stage, attempting to gain consideration or sway Academy voters. Charges of greed and manipulation by critics of the Oscar voting process and the event itself have plagued the Academy for decades, yet it remains the single most widely watched, talked about and written about entertainment awards show in the world. (For a selected list of other award shows, see Appendix B.)

The Oscar statuette is the copyrighted property of the Academy of Motion Pictures Arts and Sciences and the phrases "Academy Awards" and "Oscar" are registered trademarks. Inquiries on these issues should be addressed to: Scott Miller, Legal Rights Coordinator, Academy of Motion Pictures Arts and Sciences, 8949 Wilshire Blvd., Beverly Hills, CA 90211.

Excellent resources on Oscar history include the scholarly *Sixty-Five Years of the Oscar: The Official History of the Academy Awards*, by Robert Osborne (soon to be updated), and *Academy Awards: An Ungar Reference Index*, by Richard Shale. For less reverent but quite useful accounts, see *Inside Oscar: The Unofficial History of the Academy Awards*, a year-by-year chronicle rich with anecdotes, by Mason Wiley and Damien Bona; the well-researched and deliciously dishy *Oscar Dearest: Six Decades of Scandal, Politics and Greed Behind Hollywood's Academy Awards, 1927-1986*, by Peter H. Brown and Jim Pinkston; and *The Real Oscar: The Story Behind the Academy Awards*, an opinionated but informative book by Peter H. Brown.

> **❝**Awards are nice, but I'd much rather have a job.**❞**
> —OSCAR-WINNING ACTRESS JANE DARWELL

Hollywood's Research Treasure: The Margaret Herrick Library

Founded in 1931 as the Library of the Academy of Motion Pictures Arts and Sciences, and later renamed for a former Academy librarian and long-time executive director, the Margaret Herrick Library in Beverly Hills is world-renowned for its noncirculating reference and research collection, which is devoted to the history and development of the motion picture as an art form and industry.

The Margaret Herrick library is located at the Academy of Motion Picture Arts and Sciences' Center for Motion Picture Study in Beverly Hills, shown here. (Photo by Nick Springett Photography for AMPAS.)

Housed in a 40,000 square foot renovated historic building, the library's vast holdings include books, periodicals and pamphlets, files of clippings, still photographs, screenplays and special collections that relate to the motion picture industry and its history. Open to the public (for serious research purposes only), the library is widely regarded by film journalists, scholars and other researchers in Southern California as the premiere research center of its type.

Each year, some 14,000 visitors are carefully screened by security personnel before admittance. The Academy's National Film Information Service handles hundreds of information and photograph requests by mail, and its telephone reference service answers nearly 30,000 questions each year.

Donations to the library of film production records and memoranda, correspondence, still photographs, scripts, posters, books, periodicals and related material of historical value are tax deductible.

Schedule: Open weekdays except Wednesday; library hours: 10 A.M. to 6 P.M.; phone reference: 9 A.M. to 5 P.M.
Address: 333 South La Cienega Blvd., Beverly Hills, CA 90211
Phone: (310) 247-3020.

For a list of other specialty libraries related to Hollywood, see Appendix B.

CHAPTER THREE

The Television Business

At one time, "television" essentially meant the three major networks: CBS (the Columbia Broadcasting System), NBC (the National Broadcasting Co.), and ABC (the American Broadcasting Co.). These three broadcast giants dominated the production and distribution of TV programming, to the virtual exclusion of any competition.

Today, the universe of television is vastly more expansive, and continues to change with the rapid evolution of technology and marketing. According to figures compiled by Nielsen Media Research, a leading television monitoring organization, the average American home in 1997 could choose among forty-five separate channels, double the number available in the average home in 1990; 12 percent of all homes had access to seventy channels. Three out of four homes were equipped with two or more TV sets, and more than 80 percent had at least one VCR.

There are now three predominate means of distributing TV programming: the aforementioned network (broadcast), syndication and cable. The majority of programming for these outlets is produced by four sources: the studios, the networks, independent producers and local broadcast and cable stations. This includes one-shot programs—specials, made-for-TV movies, miniseries—or on-going series. While the corporate headquarters of the largest broadcast and cable companies are in New York, close to its large financial center, much of the production is done in Los Angeles, frequently divided among various production studios in different parts of the city.

In this chapter, we will take a closer look at these three basic areas of television that are such a vital part of Hollywood's creative and business activity, as well as the fast-emerging new media, such as direct broadcast satellite, the Internet and interactive TV. Anyone who intends to write about Hollywood in this new "digital era" should understand that as the twenty-first century approaches, we are on the brink of radical changes in the way entertainment programming is made available, received, used and enjoyed, particularly by home audiences. This is an area to watch closely because the changes are likely to come very fast, especially in the area of computerization and the world of Internet entertainment. They will undoubtedly have significant impact on the creative and business practices of Hollywood, where many industry leaders are already scurrying to adapt to and catch up with technological innovation.

For now, however, broadcast, syndication, and cable are still the predominate forces, with broadcast being the venerable giant, which is where we will begin.

Network Television

The three major networks continue to be CBS, NBC and ABC. They broadcast their programming over two types of TV stations: owned-and-operated stations ("O&Os") and affiliates. Each network owns seven O&Os in major cities ("major markets"), which serve as the flagship stations for the networks around the country. The affiliates, roughly two hundred allied with each network blanketing the rest of the country, are independently owned but carry network programming. In certain circumstances, an affiliate will carry limited programming from a competing network or networks.

The networks generate the bulk of their revenue by selling national advertising time ("commercials"), roughly eight minutes out of every half hour of broadcast time. The key selling period, when the audience is greatest and the commercial rates are highest, is 8 P.M. to 11 P.M., or "prime time." Several national ratings services monitor the size of the viewing audience for particular programs in specific time slots. (See "The All-Important Ratings" on page 76).

With some exceptions determined by demographics (especially age), the higher these audience ratings, the higher the advertising rates the networks are able to charge. That is why "the ratings race" among the networks and among different shows in particular time slots is so fierce. Millions of dollars in revenue can ride on a single ratings point representing a few hundred thousand viewing households. The networks pay the affiliates a nominal sum to carry their programming and much of their national advertising, but leave the affiliates some open time slots in which to sell local advertising of their own. These negotiated

---

The Broadcast TV Networks

American Broadcasting Companies, Inc. (ABC)
East Coast: 1330 Avenue of the Americas, New York, NY 10019. (212) 887-7777
West Coast: 4151 Prospect Ave., Los Angeles, CA 90027. (213) 557-7777

Columbia Broadcasting System, Inc. (CBS)
East Coast: 51 West 52nd St., New York, N.Y. (212) 975-4321
West Coast: CBS Television City, 7800 Beverly Blvd., Los Angeles, CA 90036.
  (213) 852-2345

National Broadcasting Co. (NBC)
East Coast: 30 Rockefeller Plaza, New York, N.Y. 10020. (212) 664-4444
West Coast: 3000 West Alameda Ave., Burbank, CA 91505. (818) 840-4444

Fox, Broadcasting, Corp.
East Coast: 40 West 57th St., New York, N.Y. 10019. (212) 977-5500
West Coast: 10201 West Pico Blvd., Los Angeles, CA 90035. (213) 277-2211

For similar data on WBN and UPN, see Warner Bros. Studios and Paramount Pictures, respectively, in the list of major studios and independents in chapter two.

---

arrangements, known as "barter" may vary from station to station, depending on the size of the market and other factors.

The Fox Broadcasting Corp. (FBC) is known as the fourth network because of its late entry into the major network competition and its smaller audience share. Fox broadcasts over a collection of stations formerly belonging to the Metromedia Group, which serve as the Fox O&Os, and more than a hundred affiliate stations around the country that broadcast on the UHF (ultra-high frequency) band. It also broadcasts on a handful of former CBS affiliates that Fox acquired in "affiliate raids" that increased Fox's market reach to more than 90 percent of the country. Fox is now considered one of the four major national networks with a number of long-running hit shows to its credit ("The Simpsons," "The X-Files," "Married With Children," "Cops," "Beverly Hills 90210") and its bold entry in the 1990s into the programming of professional sports, notably with NFL football.

Two more recent entries in the network pack are Warner Bros.' WB Network and the United Paramount Network (UPN), both affiliated with major studios, which have less market penetration than Fox and have been struggling as fledgling networks as Fox did in its infancy.

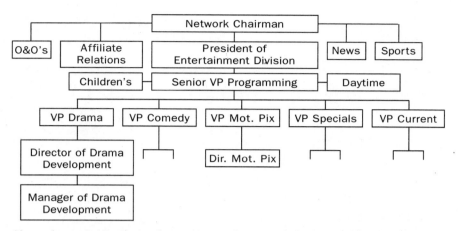

Chart of organization for a television network. (Copyright Hugh Taylor, courtesy of Lone Eagle Publishing.)

The Internal Network Structure

The networks are comprised of several key departments and executives (see the network organization chart, above).

Entertainment Division

This division is the heart of each network, responsible for the all-important prime-time programming. "While the network as a corporation has interests in news, sports and radio," writes Hugh Taylor, in *The Hollywood Job-Hunter's Survival Guide*, "only the Entertainment Division is really considered part of the Hollywood establishment." Likewise, the president of the entertainment division, also known as the head of programming, "is the most important person at the network. He or she makes every important programming decision. It is a position of tremendous power and influence." (Ultimate power, however, resides with the network chairman in New York.)

In Hollywood, heads of the entertainment division are given the same kind of attention and scrutiny from the media as the studio production chiefs, because they hold so much power over what America sees, what shows get renewed or cancelled, the careers and employment situations of so many people and how well a network does financially year in and year out. Some, such as the late Brandon Tartikoff, who was the youthful (and quite successful) president of production at NBC, become celebrities in their own right. However, they rarely attain quite the sense of glamour and prestige as their counterparts at the movie studios, where some of the TV chiefs are destined to one day work (it happens much less often the other way around).

Under the head of programming sit several senior vice presidents in charge of various departments, who work in relative obscurity, at least to those outside the business.

Vice President of Current Programming

This executive oversees all ongoing series, from the writing through the production and final editing of an episode before it airs. The most successful and powerful producers such as Aaron Spelling ("Charlie's Angels," "Dynasty," "Beverly Hills 90210," "Melrose Place") and Steven Bochco ("Hill Street Blues," "L.A. Law," "NYPD Blue") are able to work with relatively little network interference, but the final word on program content always resides with the network.

Vice Presidents of Drama and Comedy

This position requires maintaining relationships in the Hollywood creative community to bring new shows in their respective areas to the network, and overseeing the development and production of "pilots," prototype shows that serve as test runs for possible new series. Knowing hundreds of creative people, having a keen script and casting sense, working well with producers and writers, and being able to handle the pressure of network politics and the grind of production are all requisites of the job.

Vice President of Motion Pictures

This person supervises the development and production of made-for-television movies (also known as movies of the week or MOWs), as well as miniseries. There is sometimes a separate Vice President for Miniseries.

Under these vice presidents are the directors, managers, assistants and others who hope to work their way up the figurative network ladder. They are generally willing to work long, exhausting hours to do it, knowing that there are hundreds, perhaps thousands of others aspiring to fill those relatively few slots.

The Network-Producer Relationship

The networks get most of their programming by paying a "license fee" to a producer or production company that owns a show, which gives the network the right to air each episode a certain number of times before those broadcast rights revert to the show's owner.

This license fee covers only part of the show's production costs. This is known as "deficit financing" on the producer's end. In deficit financing, the producers are gambling that the show will run long enough on the network to build a supply of episodes big enough to be syndicated in reruns on the hundreds of local stations around the country, where most successful series recoup their losses and earn enormous profits. A four- to five-year network run is generally needed to establish a show's popularity and create enough episodes to fill the most lucrative syndication packages, although shows with shorter runs and fewer episodes are frequently sold for repeat viewing on cable channels. (See "Syndication," on page 80.)

Because of the high costs, extreme production demands, network politics and other factors, breaking into television as a producer is considerably more difficult than in the more freewheeling and creative atmosphere of feature films, where holding the rights to a great script and getting it to the right people can transform a producer's status almost instantly. TV production is a more methodical and detail-oriented process. Relationships, including those with agents and star talent, are extremely important and usually built over time. And a producer's dependability in the face of grinding writing and production schedules is a valued asset, along with a track record of delivering hit shows.

Most successful TV producers began their careers as writers or worked their way up the network ladder as executives before becoming independent producers. They learned the intricacies of the network system, along with the technical and financial aspects of production. Several hundred producers or writer-producers work in the medium, yet the list of those who consistently have shows on the air, season in and season out, is relatively small. "Star producers," such as the aforementioned Spelling and Bochco, might have several shows on the air at one time, yet even the success tracks of these mighty producers become derailed with changing audience tastes and viewing habits. Spelling, perhaps the single most successful producer now working in terms of the number of hit shows he has had on the air, hit a dormant stretch during the 1980s before making a comeback with a number of popular shows on Fox. Norman Lear, one of the most honored and successful producers in the 1970s with such highly-rated shows as "All in the Family," "Maude," "Good Times," and "The Jeffersons," became less of a TV presence as situation comedies faded in popularity before "The Cosby Show" revived the genre in the mid-1980s.

Because of the enormous investment a network makes in a series, particularly if the producer or a major star is able to negotiate a guaranteed thirteen-episode commitment, the networks are willing to work only with producers who have proven over time that they can deliver slick, entertaining shows, meeting meticulous technical standards on time, week after week.

Even then, the skill of a producer means nothing, unless he or she can "deliver the numbers," meaning good ratings.

The All-Important Ratings

There's a common saying in the Hollywood television community: *The ratings are everything*. If that's an overstatement, it's not by much.

A rating, as defined in *Les Brown's Encyclopedia of Television*, is the "established unit of audience measurement in TV, carried over from radio, which represents the percentage of households tuned to a given program in a time period from the universe of households equipped to receive television."

Over the decades, the primary research service used to measure national ratings has been the A.C. Nielsen Media Research, which shares most of the monitoring of local markets (local stations) with its chief competitor, the Arbitron Ratings Company. In the past, Nielsen has used a variety of information-gathering techniques, including an electronic black box monitoring device attached to TV sets in the homes of so-called "Nielsen families," and diaries filled out by family members noting their viewing patterns. Currently, Nielsen relies on electronic "PeopleMeters," which collect minute-by-minute viewing information in several thousand households, with plans to have more advanced research technology in place by the end of the century.

The data from these several thousand viewing sites, which are selected through standard research techniques to provide a representative sample of American homes, are then projected to represent about ninety million households with TV sets. Television ratings appear in the press on a "ratings chart" that usually shows a split figure for each show (or network), such as 23.6/40. The first number (in this case, 23.6) is the "rating"; the second number (40) is the "share." The rating is the percentage of *total number of homes with television sets* that were tuned to a given program or network during its time period; the share represents the percentage of the *sets in use* that were tuned in to that show. Thus, a rating/share of 23.6/40, based on a total of ninety million TV households in the U.S., would mean that about *21.2 million homes* were tuned in to that particular show, while *40 percent of all the sets in use* were tuned in.

Three times a year, covering more than four hundred local markets between them, Arbitron and Nielsen conduct surveys that sweep the entire country to measure viewing patterns that local stations (network affiliates and independents) then use as criteria for establishing advertising rates. These have become known as "sweep periods" or "sweep weeks," during which the networks try to schedule special programming and many local stations engage in a frenzy of promotion and sometimes sensational news programming to boost viewership.

Through the years, as commercial rates along with production costs have soared, ratings have become the crucial bottom line standard used to measure a show's success and determine whether it is renewed or canceled.

The Impact of Ratings on Jobs and People

Until the late 1970s, it was common for the networks to give new shows a period of many months, even a year or more, to catch on with the public and develop a loyal audience. "All in the Family," for example, languished for months in the ratings after it was introduced by CBS as a "second season entry" in January 1971. A landmark situation comedy noted for its mature themes and frank dialogue, it developed a massive following during summer reruns and subsequently rode atop the ratings chart for most of the decade, spawning a number of successful "spin-off" shows—programs built around characters first introduced on the original show. "All in the Family," for example, spawned "Maude," "The Jeffersons," and "Good Times."

Today, with some notable exceptions, new shows are rarely given more than a few weeks to find an audience before being pulled from the lineup either permanently, or for revamping. Now and then, a network will even cancel a show after only *one* airing if the ratings are disastrously low and the "network brass" senses that the show will never "click" with a large enough audience.

Because of this constant threat of cancellation, the ratings hover like a dark shadow over television production in Hollywood, particularly when a show is first going on the air or suffering a serious ratings decline. During these times, one finds the production staff, cast, agents and even some crew members waiting with great anticipation for the "overnights"—the initial ratings that come in from the major cities the day after a show airs. These are generally faxed or telephoned from the network, where the executives have gotten them from the ratings services the moment they are available. (Complete ratings for the entire country come in a day or two after the overnights.) It is difficult to overestimate the value placed on the overnights and the tension the anticipation generates, since so many jobs, possibly even careers, ride on whether the ratings are favorable or weak. Producers, writers, actors and others associated with new shows admit they sometimes toss and turn during the night following the broadcast of their first show, feverish with dreams about the ratings.

Back in 1977, while on assignment for the *New York Times*, I happened to be on the set of "Lou Grant," a show spun off "The Mary Tyler Moore Show" and starring Ed Asner in the title role of a tough-talking but tenderhearted newspaper editor. The show was produced by Moore's then-husband, Grant Tinker, an enormously successful producer who would later serve as the production chief at NBC. Initial ratings on the show were low, and the network was ordering only one episode at a time, waiting to see if the show developed a larger audience. The mood on the set was tense and gloomy; even the large tray of donuts and fruit set out for the cast and crew was largely untouched. As I came in, the slim, silver-haired Tinker was on the phone to a network executive, negotiating, in his gracious and gentlemanly way, for more patience and support. The gruff and burly Asner paced nearby, silently fuming. Finally, he grabbed the phone from Tinker's hands and bellowed into the phone, "Either give us a decent order or cancel us! But don't keep stringing us along one show at a time! I don't care about myself, but, dammit, there are people here who don't know if they will still have a job next week!" (The show eventually caught on and became quite popular. CBS cancelled it in the fall of 1982, citing declining ratings, though many felt the cancellation was due to Asner's outspoken political views against U.S. military involvement in Central America.)

So crucial are the ratings that producers and others associated with the show look for any silver lining they can find when the overnights appear cloudy. Only recently, I spoke to the executive producer of a high-profile, one-hour drama that had initially aired two nights earlier on one of the big three networks. I asked him how the overnights were, and he replied enthusiastically, "Quite good. We're very pleased." When I saw the ratings listed in the *Los Angeles Times* a day or two after that, I found his show ranked fifty-fifth among all programs, right about in the middle of the rankings, with ratings that seemed mediocre at best. Nonetheless, the show had performed better than any previous show for the network on that evening in that time slot in several years, giving my friend, the executive producer, the silver lining he needed to interpret the ratings as positive.

The meaning and impact of ratings, as this incident illustrates, cannot be interpreted simply by the numbers. When a show airs, on what network and to what kind of audience, as well as the cost of the show and other factors, are all taken into account when network executives decide to renew or cancel. A friend

The Decline in the Network Audience

Overall, the audience for network broadcast shows has been gradually eroding for more than two decades, although a continuingly expanding population keeps each network's nightly viewership in the tens of millions, with forty to fifty million viewers tuning in for the most popular programs.

During one survey period in early 1997, researchers calculated that ABC, CBS and NBC accounted for only 40 percent of the viewing audience on an average night, and just short of half the audience if the Fox ratings were factored in. During a similar period five years earlier, the Big Three had accounted for 54 percent of that audience (when Fox was only broadcasting four nights a week, instead of its current full schedule). As recently as three decades ago, the three networks had accounted for more than 90 percent of all viewers on any given night.

Clearly, the addition of new networks, wide-ranging cable programming, the popularity of the Internet and other new technologies including the remote control, which encourages "channel surfing," are having a serious impact on viewing patterns. One former network executive, who now runs a cable network, likened the networks' audience erosion to "getting pecked to death by ducks."

Yet, at least for now, the networks appear to be in a holding pattern, programming much as they always have and hoping they can keep a large enough audience to survive.

of mine, for example, once starred in a situation comedy that aired in the half-hour time slot on a prime weekday viewing night following a sitcom from the same producer. At the time, the other show was the number one rated series on the air, and "delivered" an enormous potential audience as a "lead-in." Even though my friend's show was consistently ranked in the top twenty among all programs, it was cancelled after fourteen weeks because it failed to "hold" much of its huge lead-in audience, losing too many valuable viewers and with them, too many advertising dollars.

Fox TV's "Cops," on the other hand, which has enjoyed a steady run since 1989, is generally ranked among the sixties and seventies among all shows, which is quite low by most standards, but not necessarily for the fourth network. More importantly, "Cops" is a cinema verite-style show with extremely low production costs and overhead; airs on Saturday night, the night of the week with the lowest TV viewership; and appeals to a youthful male audience that is especially attractive to advertisers. Consequently, its "low" ratings are actually quite solid as well as consistent, and it has remained as the Fox "anchor" show each Saturday evening.

Syndication

A syndicator is a company that licenses distribution rights to the programming it controls to local stations, a process known as syndication.

There are two types of syndicated programming: (1) first-run syndication—programs such as "Entertainment Tonight" or "American Gladiators" that are produced expressly for sale and transmission through syndication; and (2) off-network—shows produced for initial viewing on network prime time, such as "Cheers" or "Cops," which are later sold as reruns.

During the early decades of commercial television, the networks produced and owned all of their shows and syndicated these programs themselves. In the 1970s, however, the Federal Communications Commission (FCC) found this practice to be monopolistic, and restricted the networks from owning the same prime-time programming they broadcast—financial-syndication rules known in the business as "fin-syn." This had a huge impact on the balance of economic power, giving the producers of hit shows access to the off-network syndication gold mine.

The more popular a show, the more valuable an asset it becomes as a rerun commodity, particularly if it fits the half-hour format for easy local scheduling. "The Cosby Show," a situation comedy that aired on NBC and dominated the Nielsen ratings for much of the 1980s and early 1990s, generated millions of dollars in profits for the network during its long run. The show itself, however, was created and owned by an independent producer, Carsey-Werner, in partnership with its star, Bill Cosby. Carsey-Werner's distribution partner, Viacom, engineered a bidding war among local stations for rerun rights to "The Cosby Show" that broke all records at the time, reportedly driving the total past $500 million. NBC did not share in this enormous syndication revenue.

In the wake of the broadcast networks' declining audience shares and the increase of competition from cable in the 1990s, however, the FCC has lifted the fin-syn restrictions and the networks are back in the production-syndication business.

Cable Television

Cable refers to programming delivered through underground and overground cables hooked up to individual homes. The overall cable programming system, according to *All You Need to Know About the Movie and TV Business*, breaks down this way:

- Local cable operators, which are separate from the national cable services that supply the programming, make their money by providing the cable equipment that carries the signal to each home and by charging subscribers a monthly service fee.
- If the cable service is national, it delivers the programming to a satellite, which in turn sends the signal to dishes owned by local cable operators.
- The local operators then transmit the programs via cable to subscriber homes (unless the home is equipped with its own satellite dish, newer technology that is part of a much smaller but growing market).

How does the supplier make its money? Just as a producer licenses the right to a network to show its programs for a limited number of runs, a cable supplier typically does the same with a local or regional cable service. (This can include the sale of movies in bunches, or "packages," for a particular number of airings.) National advertising rates are based on the size of the audience a national cable service is able to deliver; in some cases, local cable services pay a fee for the right to receive national programming. As a public service to the communities they serve, local cable services are also required by the FCC to provide "public access programming"—uncensored programming time for use by citizens at their discretion and at nominal cost.

Most, if not all, of the major cable companies—Home Box Office (HBO), Showtime, the USA Network, the Disney Channel, Lifetime Television, Turner Network Television (TNT)—produce original programming to supplement the programming they acquire from other production or distribution entities. Like the studios, the cable networks build their own film and programming "libraries," which they exploit in other markets, from domestic TV syndication to foreign theatrical release (theater exhibition in foreign markets).

The cable production divisions are structured much like those at the networks and movie studios, though generally on a smaller scale in terms of the number of employees and bureaucratic and administrative layers. While many are located in New York, the rest are widely scattered between the two coasts. They tend to be corporate, rather than creative, in look and atmosphere since they do not operate like production studios as the broadcast networks traditionally have done. With the exception of sports and news programming, the bulk of their production is created by producers and production companies working

Cable Networks (Selected List)

Arts and Entertainment Network (A&E)
555 Fifth Ave., New York, NY 10017 (212) 661-4500

Bravo Cable Network
150 Crossways Park West, Woodbury, NY 11797 (516) 364-2222

Cable News Network (CNN)
One CNN Plaza, Atlanta, GA 30348-5366 (404) 827-1500

Cable Satellite Public Affairs Network (C-SPAN)
444 North Capitol St. NW, Washington, DC 20001 (202) 737-3220

Cinemax Cable Pay Television
1100 Avenue of the Americas, New York, NY 10036 (212) 512-1000

The Comedy Channel
120A East 23rd St., New York, NY 10010 (212) 512-8900

The Discovery Channel
8201 Corporate Drive, Suite 1200, Landover, MA 20785 (301) 577-1999

The Disney Channel
3800 West Alameda Ave., Burbank, CA 91505 (818) 569-7711

ESPN, Inc.
605 Third Ave., New York, NY. 10158 (212) 916-9200

The Family Channel
1000 Centerville Turnpike, Virginia Beach, VA 23463 (804) 523-7151

Home Box Office (HBO)
1100 Avenue of the Americas, New York, NY 10036 (212) 512-1000
West Coast: 2049 Century Park East, Los Angeles, CA 90067 (213) 201-9200

Lifetime Television
Kaufman Astoria Studios, 36-12 35th Ave., Astoria, NY 11106 (718) 706-3503
West Coast: 10880 Wilshire Blvd., Suite 201, Los Angeles, CA 90024 (213)
    850-0373

MTV Networks
1515 Broadway, New York, NY 10036 (212) 258-8000

The Nashville Network (TNN)
1451 Elm Hill Pike, Nashville, TN 37210 (615) 361-0366

Nickelodeon
1515 Broadway, New York, NY 10036 (212) 258-7500

Prime Network International
250 Steele Street, Suite 300, Denver, CO 80206 (303) 355-7777

Showtime Entertainment Corp./The Movie Channel
1633 Broadway, New York, NY 10019 (212) 708-1600
West Coast: 10900 Wilshire Blvd., Los Angeles, CA 90024 (213) 208-2340

Sportschannel
150 Media Crossways, Woodbury, NY 11797 (516) 364-3650

Turner Broadcasting System, Inc.
(TNT, TBS). See **CNN** (404) 827-1700

USA Network
1230 Avenue of the Americas, New York, NY 10020 (212) 408-9100

---

elsewhere, in production facilities throughout the country, with heavy concentrations in Los Angeles and New York.

Much of cable's success can be attributed to: (1) its higher-quality reception capability, even when transmitting network broadcasting; (2) its ability to avoid network-style "mass appeal" shows with programming that targets niche audiences—movie channels (e.g., Cinemax, The Movie Channel), sports channels (ESPN), news channels (CNN), documentary channels (Discovery Channel, History Channel), educational channels (Learning Channel), music/youth culture channels (MTV), ethnic channels (the Black Entertainment Network), and so on; and (3) original programming, particularly on HBO, that tends to be bolder and more sophisticated than just about anything found on broadcast network TV. (HBO's slogan in the late 1990s: *It's not TV. It's HBO.*

Most analysts believe that by the end of the century, the aggregate viewing of the basic cable channels will equal or surpass the collective audience of ABC, CBS and NBC, a milestone that some feel has already been reached.

Rating TV Content for Sex, Language and Violence

In 1997, the television industry, under mounting public and political pressure, agreed to a new ratings system under which it would label programs that contain sex, violence and coarse language, in an effort to fend off the possibility of government intervention and censorship.

The new parental guideline ratings were: **V** (violence), **S** (sexual situations), **L** (coarse language), **D** (suggestive dialogue) and **FV** (fantasy violence).

These code letters were added to a system already in place that used **TV-Y7** (directed to older children), **TV-PG** (parental guidance suggested) and **TV-14** (parents strongly cautioned) for parental guidelines, which many parents' groups found too weak or vague. Under the new system, then, a show could conceivably be rated **TV-14-V-L-S-D**, presumably giving a parent more "information" about program content.

Television industry executives negotiated the new ratings system with a number of national organizations, including the National PTA, the National Education Association, the American Medical Association, and Children Now. Parties on both sides of the negotiating table saw the ratings as a compromise, particularly the activist groups that wanted more specific ratings that indicated the *level* of violence or sexuality in a given program. NBC refused to endorse the agreement, concerned about the possible threat to First Amendment free speech rights. Several labor guilds—the Writers Guild of America, the Directors Guild of America and the Screen Actors Guild—publicly voiced similar concerns about creative and artistic freedoms. Meanwhile, a major study sponsored by the National Cable Television Association found that such ratings were actually likely to have a "forbidden fruit" effect and *entice* younger viewers to watch the shows labeled for violence and sex.

With the new ratings system, the television industry continued laying the groundwork for the so-called V-chip, a device still in development that will be built into televisions and allow parents to program their sets to block out programming they deem objectionable.

Network "Standards and Practices": The Internal Censors

Each broadcast network has a department of internal censors or watchdogs traditionally known as "standards and practices" that is responsible for reviewing each script prior to shooting to look for material the network might find objectionable. This typically includes profanity, nudity, extreme violence, controversial references to race or religion, smoking, drinking and the like. Standards and practices is also concerned with trademark infringement or brand name references. As one TV writer told me, "They might tell you that you can show a Coke can once, but not twice. Or you can show the name once, but the next time, you have to turn the can around."

In earlier decades, standards and practices wielded considerable clout, able to dictate what a producer could or could not put in a show, and sanitizing scripts to ridiculous extremes. The word "pregnant," for example, was forbidden from TV until the 1960s ("with child" was allowed) and couples, even married ones, could not be shown sharing the same bed.

That began to sharply change in the 1970s as powerful producers like Norman Lear began to boldly challenge the boundaries and restrictions. In the 1980s, producer Steven Bochco, known in the TV world as "standards and practices' worst nightmare," stretched the limits in virtually all areas, including male and female nudity, which he scripted into shows ranging from "Bay City Blues" to "NYPD Blue" in the 1990s. As Bochco led the way, other producers followed, and today, standards and practices people wield far less influence over producers and programming. More often than not, insiders say, they come timidly asking for changes, rather than demanding them.

They are the most careful, and retain some clout, when it comes to scripts for the so-called "family hour" of viewing (6 to 8 P.M.), which remains television's most sensitive time slot. As in the old days, writers and producers still play the game of deliberately inserting objectionable material to be used as bargaining chips. "You put in two hells," a writer for "Step by Step" told me recently, "so you can keep one damn."

Two Decades of Pressure

Since the late 1970s, a number of TV "watchdog" groups claiming to represent Christian, profamily or antiviolence points of view have agitated, lobbied and spearheaded boycotts against entertainment companies and advertisers that sponsor programming these groups deem offensive, with varied results.

A 1989 campaign against an episode of ABC's "thirtysomething" that showed two gay men in bed reportedly cost the network $1.5 million in lost advertising revenue when sponsors pulled out, and additional revenues when the episode was subsequently pulled from the rerun schedule. That same year, another campaign against Fox TV's racy and irreverent family sitcom, "Married With Children," backfired by generating unexpected publicity for the show, giving it a big boost in the ratings and helping to turn it into a long-running hit.

Among the more high-profile groups attempting to "clean up" television during the past two decades: Viewers for Quality Television, Center for Media Education, American Family Association (Rev. Donald Wildmon), Media Research Center, Focus on the Family, Americans for Responsible Television and Christian Leaders for Responsible Television.

Sizable religious organizations, not necessarily media-oriented, such as the Christian Coalition, sometimes actively protest against Hollywood. In 1995, for example, the Catholic League, claiming 350,000 members, called on all Catholics to boycott the Walt Disney Company because it was releasing the controversial movie, *Priest*, through a subsidiary, Miramax Films. Two years later, a conference of Southern Baptists voted to boycott Disney and its ABC sitcom, "Ellen," whose title character "came out" as a lesbian during the 1996-97 season, along with the series star, Ellen DeGeneres. (See "The Gay Factor" in chapter eight.)

Despite the boycotts, *Priest* was released into theaters and on video as scheduled, and the "coming out" episode of "Ellen" drew one of the largest national viewing audiences of the season, although it was pulled from the schedules of a few Bible Belt stations.

The Emmy Awards: TV's Oscar

What the Academy Awards are to the movie industry, the Emmy Awards are to the television business, although the Emmys come with less prominence, glamour and worldwide promotional value.

The first Emmys were conferred on January 25, 1949, at the Hollywood Athletic Club by the newly formed Academy of Television Arts and Sciences, in recognition of outstanding professional achievement. The name Emmy was suggested by Harry Lubcke, a pioneer television engineer and Academy president at the time, as a variation on "Immy," a nickname for the recently developed image orthicon tube.

In its early years, the awards show was largely a local affair, but began a coast-to-coast telecast in 1955. Like the Oscar telecast, it quickly became a national television event, peaking in popularity in 1957, when 73.4 percent of the nation's viewing audience tuned in. That same year, the National Academy of Television Arts and Sciences was formed, and administered the awards from that point through 1976.

"In 1977," writes Alex McNeil in *Total Television*, "tension between the Hollywood and New York chapters of the National Academy led to the secession of the Hollywood group, which was reborn as the Academy of Television Arts and Sciences." Following a series of lawsuits over rights to the Emmy statuette and ceremonies, a compromise was struck that permitted the Hollywood branch to confer the Emmys for prime-time entertainment programs and the New York-based National Academy to award Emmys for daytime, sports, local shows and news programs. "Despite a troubled history of internecine warfare, boycotts and frequently boring telecasts," McNeil writes, the Emmys remained popular for many years.

Angela Lansbury holds an Emmy statuette that she won for her long-running dramatic series "Murder, She Wrote." The television industry's equivalent of the Oscar, the Emmy endures as a symbol of professional achievement. (Photo courtesy of Academy of Television Arts and Sciences.)

Until the mid-1980s, the Academy of Television Arts and Sciences rotated the popular Emmy Awards Show between the then three established networks. At that point, the Academy signed a lucrative exclusive contract with Fox, which was in the early stages of building a fourth network. This resulted in a dramatic decline in viewership for the Emmy show, and by 1990 the ratings had slipped to a low of 8.2 and a 14 share. Since then, with the advent of a four-way rotation of the show, ratings have improved but remain well below the earlier peak numbers.

One factor in the public's diminished interest may be the sheer volume of Emmys handed out through the years—thousands in dozens of categories—and the repetitiveness of winning shows and individuals. Some long-running series, notably "The Mary Tyler Moore Show," "Hill Street Blues," and "Cheers" have won more than two dozen Emmys each. ("Cheers" holds the record for number of nominations with 117.) In some cases, stars have voiced concern about the self-promotional aspects of the telecast, and a few, after winning several personal Emmys, have asked that their names no longer be considered for nomination. Often, though, the most honored individuals through the years may be less familiar to the public, such as producer-director Dwight Hemion, who has received forty-six Emmy nominations and seventeen wins, more than any other individual. (All of these figures dated through 1997.) For many viewers, no doubt, the number of Emmys handed out can be numbing.

Nonetheless, many within the industry still consider the Emmy a notable honor and benchmark of success. The awards process now includes cable television programming; in 1997, for the first time, a cable channel, HBO, received more nominations (ninety) than any of the major networks (NBC had eighty-nine).

For many years, the Academy of Television Arts and Sciences (5220 Lankershim Blvd., North Hollywood, CA 91601; 818/754-2800) maintained archives with reference books on television, directories of distributors of television shows, biographies of television figures, still photos, a clipping file and information on the Emmy Awards. The bulk of that collection has been donated to the University of Southern California Cinema-Television Library (213/740-7610), which contains over three hundred donor collections, the complete Warner Bros. archives and half a dozen partial collections from other studios, covering both film and TV. It is open to the public for serious research purposes.

The Academy continues to publish its official magazine, *Emmy*, a respected journal that covers the history, personalities and issues of television.

Note: The term "Emmy," and its statuette image, are trademarks registered by the Academy of Motion Pictures Arts and Sciences. For an unofficial but well-researched history of the Emmy awards, see *The Emmys: Star Wars, Showdowns and the Supreme Test of TV's Best*, by Thomas O'Neil.

New Technology and Emerging Media

Today, most of us take for granted two seemingly simple pieces of electronic equipment: the remote control and the VCR. Yet each has had a profound impact on the way we watch television. What lies ahead?

Here are some new technologies that are already shaping and will continue reshaping the television business in the new millennium.

Pay-Per-View. Specialty programming such as movies, concerts and sports events, paid for on a selected, show-by-show basis, implemented by telephone orders and addressable converters hooked up to television sets in cable-equipped households. After orders are placed, the signal for the selected event is unscrambled for the duration of the viewing time. According to *Les Brown's Encyclopedia of Television*, "Pay-per-view is expected by the cable industry to evolve ultimately into programming-on-demand, envisioned as the ideal pay system, allowing viewers to decide what they want to see from thousands of options and ordering it up." So far, after more than a decade in the marketplace, the results of pay-per-view have been mixed, with feature films generally doing poorly and heavyweight championship fights performing the best.

Direct Broadcast Satellite. This is technology that facilitates the transmission of broadcast-quality signals from a space satellite to home antennas without the need for a TV station or cable company. Although there are fewer than three million satellite antennas currently in use in the U.S., the market is growing. Media mogul Rupert Murdoch plans to launch a satellite service capable of beaming up to five hundred channels into homes, an ambitious venture that threatens the cable industry and faces a complicated legal and marketing battle.

Fiber Optics. Fiber-optic cable, a finger-thin cable comprised of slender, flexible fibers of glass or plastic, is being developed as a replacement for the much thicker and more cumbersome copper coaxial cable, which is currently used to transmit signals from local cable suppliers into homes. Already in wide use in both cable TV and telephone installations, fiber optics, along with satellite transmission, could be the two chief means of television transmission in the new century.

Digital and High-Definition TV (HDTV). "A technology that provides a TV picture and sound vastly superior to present broadcast standards," according to *Les Brown's Encyclopedia of Television*, "with an image resolution resembling 35mm motion pictures. HDTV is without question the television of the future." Introduced in Japan in the 1970s, two other systems have since been developed in Europe and the U.S., where the first digital sets are planned for marketing to the public in late 1998. Meanwhile, a legal battle has been raging in the broadcast industry as station and network executives worry about how they are going to work out a reasonable timetable and cover the multibillion dollar costs of converting from standard analog broadcasting equipment to digital high-definition.

Digital Video Disc (DVD). Also known as the Digital Versatile Disc, this is the new technological breakthrough that its manufacturers hope will replace videocassettes, laserdiscs, CDs and CD-ROMs by virtue of its extremely high-quality picture and sound and its remarkable versatility. (It also promises up to twenty-five times the storage capacity of current CDs or CD-ROMs at about the same price). *Premiere* calls it a "dream format in an age when entertainment companies have their fingers in almost all media. This one disc can be a movie medium, a music medium, a computer-software medium, a video-game medium." Some technical kinks are still being worked out, including the technology's copy-protection system, but a number of DVD titles have already hit the market.

Internet and Interactive TV. A merging of computer and television technology that invites the viewer to become directly involved with the programming rather than watching passively in the traditional manner of TV consumption. Spurred by the video game craze that changed the viewing habits of the Nintendo generation, interactive TV is already commonplace in tens of millions of homes in such primitive forms as pay-per-view programs, home shopping channels and shows that invite viewer participation through 1-900 call-in numbers.

However, these rather simplistic uses are quickly being eclipsed in sophistication and popularity by interactive systems that allow viewers to choose how much or what kind of news reports they wish to see, direct the plots of dramatic programs and control the camera angles as they watch sporting events, among countless other functions. A few examples of the coming revolution in Internet/interactive programming:

- In the spring of 1997, ABC aired a one-hour docudrama, "Cold Case," with its own Internet web site, and invited viewers on-line to try to solve the mystery as the show progressed. It was purportedly the first time a major U.S. television network made the Internet an integral part of its programming.

- WebTV Networks is selling technology that turns traditional TV sets into Web-surfing devices. Intel Corporation and Compaq Computer are also marketing technology designed to deliver digital-quality television with all of the interactive and Net-surfing capabilities of personal computers. Said an Intel executive: "The PC is the future of broadcasting."

- By the late 1990s, every major studio had an Internet division, and outside the studios, a new "cyber-infrastructure," replete with Hollywood-style company names like CyberStudio and American Cybercast, had developed. A 1997 study by the Bay Area Economic Forum concluded that Los Angeles multimedia firms—Internet-based entertainment industries such as CD-ROM, virtual-imaging and Web page design—employed roughly 133,000 people, more than the combined total of those in the field in the New York and San Francisco areas.

- Microsoft founder Bill Gates has created the Microsoft Network (MSN), an attempt to develop the methodology needed for a cyberspace entertainment and information empire by melding the Internet and television, what one MSN executive calls "the studio of the twenty-first century." Gates and Microsoft are already in the television production business, working with the United Paramount Network on a new show that Gates is reportedly enhancing with $25,000 to $50,000 of his own money per episode. The show will air on UPN as a regular series, but it will also allow viewers with the proper equipment to watch the program in one corner of the screen, with interactive features occupying the rest of the screen—windows that allow the viewer to write electronic fan mail, for instance, or pull up star photos and biographies.

The "proper equipment," of course, will be Microsoft equipment, specifically Windows 98. "Having already obliterated its major competitors in PC operating system software with Windows," reports the *Los Angeles Times*, "and largely obliterated rivals in such PC applications as word processing and spreadsheets, Microsoft, they fear, may now be preparing to ensnare the TV world." Some predict that if Gates is able to force the broadcast industry to accept his technological standards, his reach into and control of entertainment could be enormous, even monopolistic, and he has been embroiled in a number of related lawsuits.

Some of these technologies, of course, are still in the early stages or have yet to live up to early expectations. Yet with personal computers now such a pervasive part of American culture and life, particularly for the young, revolutionary change in the way entertainment is distributed and received seems inevitable in the new century. Television, in particular, will become more interactive, more involving, more viewer controllable and a much greater sensory experience than that to which the passive couch potato has grown accustomed.

For now, Hollywood continues to work much as it has for decades, with the bulk of work being done at the networks, studios and individual production companies. But as the Internet attracts more and more consumers, increasingly links up with myriad forms of entertainment and finds fascinating new ways to convey its images and tell its stories, it will surely reshape Hollywood in more ways than we can imagine.

CHAPTER FOUR

The People, Their Jobs and Their Salaries

W hen we think of Hollywood jobs, the most high-profile and high-paying positions usually come to mind: actor, director, producer, writer, studio head, talent agent, lawyer. Those are the people at the top, the movers and shakers who work under tremendous career pressures and become inordinately wealthy (at least the *successful* ones do) but they are only part of the picture.

Beneath that pinnacle, Hollywood is an anthill of activity, a bustling community in which more than a quarter of a million employees labor daily at specific tasks related to the development, production and distribution of motion pictures and television programming. They work on sound stages spread across the city; on shooting locations scattered throughout the county, state and beyond; at processing labs and editing bays crammed with technical equipment; at state-of-the-art special effects studios; in wardrobe warehouses smelling of musty old costumes; on mobile catering trucks steaming with meals for hungry crews; in cold rehearsal halls furnished with nothing but a long table and set of chairs; in

> 66 To survive in Hollywood, you need the ambition of a Latin American revolutionary, the ego of a grand opera singer, and the physical stamina of a cow pony. 99
>
> —BILLIE BURKE

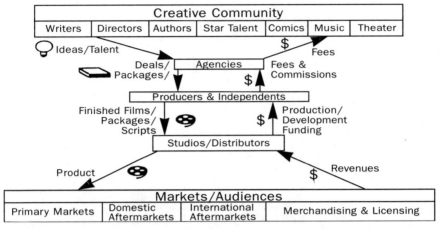

Flow chart of product, services and money in the entertainment industry. (Copyright Hugh Taylor, courtesy of Lone Eagle Publishing.)

file rooms crammed with thousands of scripts or actors' glossy 8 × 10s; in red carpet theater lobbies at star-studded premieres; in executive offices from the shabby to the lavish; and all manner in between.

It's not possible to examine *every* job in the industry, but this chapter will attempt to cover most of the key jobs, from the top rungs of the ladder to the bottom.

The Overall Power Structure

"Hollywood is a town divided into two camps: creative and business—each suspicious of the other," writes Mark Litwak in *Reel Power: The Struggle for Influence and Success in New Hollywood*. "Writers, directors and actors are members of the creative community. According to the businessmen, creative types are wonderfully talented people but, like children, cannot be trusted with money. On the other hand, says the creative community, studios executives, producers and agents are businessmen who are concerned only with making money and have no taste or artistic sensibility. Of course neither stereotype is accurate. Many businessmen can and do make artistic contributions to films, and many artists are shrewd businessmen. Nevertheless, rarely will a creative suggestion from a businessman be welcomed by a writer, director or actor; and almost never will a creative person attempt to negotiate a business deal himself."

Despite this division of purpose and sensibility, Hollywood's business and creative communities are joined at the hip (if not always at the heart), a symbiotic relationship that gives the town its shaky, constantly shifting power structure.

In the early 1990s, for example, Michael Ovitz, cofounder of the mighty talent agency, Creative Artists Agency (CAA), was frequently referred to as "the most powerful man in Hollywood" because of his relationships with so much top talent and his corresponding ability to package so many big motion pictures. As an agent, his control over moviemaking was said to be extraordinary, rivaling or exceeding that of some studio heads. Yet, even with all that wealth and power, like so many, he wanted to be "in production"—the true glamour and prestige position of developing, green lighting and producing motion pictures. So in 1995, he left CAA to become president and second in command to chairman Michael Eisner at the Walt Disney Company, following many other top agents who had moved into high-ranking production positions at various studios. After clashing with the (now) more powerful Eisner, Ovitz was out of a job after only fourteen months, a tradition known in Hollywood as "executive musical chairs" or "the revolving door."

When *Premiere* magazine published its annual list of "The 100 Most Powerful People in Hollywood" in 1997, Ovitz had fallen from the top ranks to the very bottom, at number one hundred (right after Ronald McDonald, representing the McDonald fast-food chain's profitable merchandising synergy with Hollywood). Rupert Murdoch, chairman of the ever-expanding multimedia empire News Corporation, was ranked number one (up from number four the previous year, with Disney's Eisner falling from number one to number two). Filling out the list were a variety of studio chiefs, agents, producers, directors, writers and stars (Tom Cruise was the top-ranked performer at number nine because of his long string of box-office successes and his producer's role on the megahit, *Mission Impossible*, while Paramount chairwoman Sherry Lansing, who had helped bring *Mission Impossible* and other successful films to fruition, was the highest-ranked woman at number thirteen).

Yet Ovitz could move quickly back up the rankings if he were to start or join a powerful agency or turn independent producer and put together one or two blockbuster movie deals. Likewise, a rising star like Will Smith, ranked seventy-nine in 1997, was certain to bound much higher on the 1998 list because of his back-to-back starring roles in two huge international blockbusters, *Independence Day* and *Men in Black*, and his newfound power in saying yes or no to movie projects. Two or three successive box-office bombs, on the other hand, would probably push Smith off the roster of "power players" and back to the ranks of well-paid but less important, name-brand actors.

The Ovitz Sweetheart Deal

When former agent Michael Ovitz left his post as president of the Walt Disney Company in late 1996 after barely more than a year on the job, he exited with a "golden parachute" that executive-pay experts valued at roughly $90 million.

His boss and close friend, Disney chairman Michael D. Eisner, had already made headlines when it was revealed that his own annual salary was nearly $9 million, with his company stock (part of his compensation package) valued at $184 million. (In 1997, Eisner exercised stock options at a reported profit of $565 million.)

Together, the compensation figures became symbols to many of Hollywood's extreme greed and imbalance of fortunes. The reaction of Disney stockholders to Ovitz's sweetheart deal was intense, along with the adverse publicity it generated, and within a few months, Ovitz made charitable donations totaling $25 million.

Many critics pooh-pooh *Premiere*'s annual Hollywood power ranking as journalistic gimmickry, yet many Hollywood insiders read it the moment it hits newsstands, particularly the hungry young executives on their way up who long to one day be included. That's because, in image-conscious Hollywood, the *perception* of power is almost as important as real power itself.

"Real" Power and the Fear of Failure

Where power ultimately resides is with those men and women who directly influence the production and distribution of motion pictures and television programming, getting big projects green lighted and out to the widest audience possible. It is measured to a great extent by the sheer volume of dollars they are able to generate through their business acumen, public popularity or both, and fortified by the relationships they develop and successfully maintain with other power players. It should be noted that a few players develop creative muscle and power of such legendary proportions—for example, writer-producer-director Francis Ford Coppola, writer-producer-director-actor Warren Beatty, producer-director-actress Barbra Streisand—that they are able to continue getting their projects financed long after their string of big hits has ended, often because studio executives are afraid to damage such treasured relationships.

For most, that kind of clout can change individually from year to year, month to month, even day to day, making Hollywood one of the most challenging, exciting and uncertain places in which to attempt a career. It is clearly not a place for the easily discouraged.

"If you're going to be in the business, you should become aware of that and accept it very soon because you will not survive [otherwise]," veteran entertainment attorney Richard Schulenberg told the *Los Angeles Times*. "If you can't weather the downside of this business, you should get out as quickly as possible because it will kill you one way or another—spiritually, emotionally, physically, the whole thing. . . . We're in a business where there is a great deal of pressure. People are always looking over their shoulder to see who's gaining on them. It is an industry fraught with rejection. The scary thing about our business is that so few actually succeed in it."

Adds film exec Chip Diggins, quoted in *The Hollywood Job-Hunter's Survival Guide*: "Getting your first job in the business may be the hardest thing you do. It is horrible, and frustrating and full of rejection. . . . It creates vast reservoirs of insecurity."

Perhaps that's why an adjunct industry has developed that is almost integral to the Hollywood workplace itself: "Hollywood shrinks," the dozens of psychologists and psychiatrists who specialize in entertainment industry clients. Linda Buzzell, for example, a psychotherapist who is quoted a number of times in this book, was a studio and television executive before founding the Entertainment Industry Career Institute, through which she offers counseling to those who are doing what she once did. Screenwriter Dennis Palumbo (*My Favorite Year*) is now a licensed psychotherapist specializing in creative issues and career transition at midlife, a serious personal issue for many in Tinseltown (see "Ageism and 'The Graylist'" in chapter eight). Dozens of other offices from West Hollywood to Beverly Hills to Westwood are occupied by psychologists and psychiatrists with similar specialties. (For more on this, you might want to read *Hollywood on the Couch*, by Stephen Farber and Marc Green.)

Before They Get Their Break

How people break into the film and TV industries depends to some extent on their background, goals and whether they are aiming for the creative or business side.

"I don't think there *is* a traditional [career] path in the entertainment industry," said lawyer Schulenberg. "It depends on luck—being in the right place at the right time—and who you know."

One does see some patterns and/or unavoidable truths, however:

- Men and women who hope to rise through the corporate executive ranks often bring with them a business or law degree and look for an opening at the assistant level in an established company or corporation. Internships are also becoming more and more common in the entertainment industry and are excellent ways to open doors, although interns are often unpaid and start with fairly menial work.

- Producer wannabes often start as lowly production company gofers, then look for an opening as a production assistant ("PA"), associate segment producer or other low-paying, labor-intensive position where they start learning the ropes and moving up.

- Many ambitious young people who want to see the television business from the inside, and make contacts, seek out the plum network "page" positions—short-term jobs as uniformed ushers who perform a variety of guest relations activities, from seating the audience members at live tapings to taking phone messages for important cast members. Numerous "big names" in Hollywood got their start as network pages.

- Aspiring agents, at least in the bigger agencies, traditionally start in the mailroom (it's a cliché, but a valid one) learning who's who and how the agency operates, while the agents up top scrutinize them, looking for future assistants and junior agents. Some move in sideways from the legal field. Many would-be agents, particularly those with fragile sensibilities, burn out in what is a tough, highly competitive, often cutthroat business.

- Future filmmakers—directors, producers or hyphenates of the two—often get their first technical training and make their first business contacts in film schools (though there are plenty of exceptions to this). (See list of film-TV Schools in the appendix.)

- Aspiring actors often hold jobs that allow them to work evenings or with flexible schedules (bartender, waiter/waitress, parking valet, switchboard operator, office temp) so they can make time for acting classes, auditions and accepting bit parts if they come. The keys to success for would-be film or TV actors is developing their skills and resumes by taking classes and appearing (often unpaid) in stage productions or student films, and, most importantly, *being seen* (by agents, casting directors, producers, directors and so on). If they're lucky, they'll have something special in front of the camera and get noticed. What a person does to earn a living in the meantime has no bearing on his or her career opportunities, with one notable exception: "acting" in the porn industry. Appearing in adult sex movies is an almost surefire way to sabotage a legitimate career (the

Hollywood's Notorious Nepotism

Nepotism is rife within the industry, with literally thousands of positions filled by friends or family members, sometimes regardless of their experience or skill level. While nepotism gets many friends and relatives "into the club," it rarely sustains a rise all the way to the top, where glaring ineptitude and failure are usually too costly to be overlooked because of bloodlines.

There is another reason so many relatives rise in the industry, besides the obvious doors that family relationships can open: They are born into and grow up around the business, feel comfortable in it and come to know early on how it operates and who the players are, sometimes on a first-name basis.

One sometimes hears exclamations of complaint about all the Jewish names on studio or network rosters or the end credits of movies and television shows, and there are a lot. But Hollywood was *invented* and *founded* by Jews (see "The Jewish Influence" in chapter eight), and many creative and professional traditions have been handed down through the generations as surely as the family silver, just as they have in non-Jewish families with names like Fonda, Coppola, Barrymore, Huston and Bridges. Hollywood is a labyrinth of power, politics and relationships, and those who come into the business understanding how it works have a head start on most outsiders.

The "club," of course, has traditionally belonged to or at least been dominated by white males. Nepotism, coupled with various kinds of prejudice, however conscious or unconscious, has tended to keep it that way, excluding many of those outside traditional social circles.

That's why "networking"—getting to know and build personal relationships with others in the industry—is so crucial here, especially for those who fit less easily into the club, whether it be for reasons of gender, ethnicity, nationality, religion, age, size or sexual orientation. (More on discrimination issues in chapter eight.)

few exceptions only prove the rule), though many go into the "sex industry" naively thinking it might be a path to mainstream work.

• Writers *write*. As with actors, what they do to pay the bills while they're getting started doesn't much matter. What counts, in both features and TV, are their *writing samples*—completed scripts—and who reads them. Patience, passion for their material, the ability to "pitch" a compelling story, a good agent and some luck also help. Youth is another valued asset; rightly or wrongly, very few screenwriters become established past the age of thirty-five or forty (see "Ageism and 'the Graylist' " in chapter eight). Most pros get started while living in L.A. It is extremely difficult to make the needed contacts and get one's material seriously considered while living away from the center of the action, though some have managed it. Although many successful film and television writers come from film-TV schools, perhaps just as many learn the craft on their own or develop it as an adjunct to another writing field, such as novels, the stage or narrative journalism.

• Crafts workers such as grips, electricians and carpenters usually bring with them a trades skill developed outside the industry and find a way in through a friend or relative who refers them to someone who can give them a job. This is particularly true of the crafts that come under the control of labor guilds, which are usually quite strict about who qualifies for a union card. (Because union wages and benefits are so much higher in California than in nonunion states, these are highly coveted jobs. Overtime is so pervasive and well-paying, especially in the film industry, it is not uncommon for certain craftspeople to earn annual incomes in the high five or low six figures.)

The Producer

Many people outside the industry have only the vaguest notion of what a producer is, and for several good reasons: (1) Anyone can adopt the term "producer," without legal restriction, whether or not they have ever been listed in film or TV credits in a production capacity; (2) even then, a person can have a "producer" credit, without having performed any tasks on the production; and (3) there are several kinds of "real" and legitimate producers, with varying levels of power and responsibility and sometimes overlapping functions, which can add to the confusion.

Basically, the genuine producers fall into two areas: creative and technical or "hands-on."

Creative Producers

Producer. Essentially, a producer is the pivotal deal-maker who puts a motion picture together, from the discovery of the script and often all the way through to its completion. This can include writing or optioning/purchasing a screenplay, getting a director or stars attached to the project, raising the initial financing (possibly all of it), budgeting the production costs, seeing the script through development, and hiring and delegating authority to key production staff for the shoot.

Such producers can range from extremely creative, even artistic, in nature, who spend literally years on a project determined to see their vision realized, to more commercially minded producers who try to package profitable deals, sometimes selling out their interest along the way to distributors or other financial parties. Most probably fall somewhere in between, though all producers are entrepreneurs at the core, combining their creative instincts with their zeal for business and salesmanship. There are no specific prerequisites—active producers range from MBAs to high school dropouts, and often come from the ranks of actors, writers, agents, lawyers and studio executives—but the most successful seem to have one trait in common: innate good taste in material, spotting a scripted story that has a good chance of translating well to the big screen and pleasing audiences or critics, if not both. Many Hollywood outsiders assume that being a good producer has to do with spotting trends, but it's actually the opposite; the best producers *start* trends by making highly original movies, while the less gifted producers follow. By the time it's a trend, the saying goes, it's already too late since movies generally take at least a year or two, and often longer, to make it from script to screen.

Like other above-the-line positions, the producer is also subject to age discrimination, although probably less so than for screenwriters and actors, and particularly if they have risen to the top of the profession with many hit movies behind them. Nonetheless, the producer's role is one than demands enormous energy and drive, and many very able producers get left behind as they grow older, pushed aside by the hustling young tyros coming up.

Coproducer. Either an equal partner with another top producer, the line producer or an associate producer who has a long relationship with the producer and is getting a title upgrade, although it is sometimes a hollow title handed out to a friend or associate.

Executive producer. This title is often conferred on someone who provides all or much of the financing, including, possibly, the studio executive who makes the distribution deal that finances the production; also handed out now and then to a star's agent or personal manager, along with a hefty fee. Generally regarded by Hollywood insiders as a suspicious or meaningless title. (This is less true in television, where the executive producer is traditionally the one who creates and oversees the show.)

Associate producer. Traditionally, this was the producer's top assistant and right-hand person, overseeing all production departments as well as the shooting schedule and overall budget. In recent years, it has been dispensed as a credit much more freely to writers, director's assistants, postproduction supervisors, even to spouses and lovers, as perks or favors. Again, another "suspicious" title, which, unfortunately, denigrates the true associate producers who actually fill work-intensive roles on some productions.

Technical or "Hands-On" Producers

Line producer (supervising producer). The true workhorse of the production, who manages the below-the-line employees (the "crew") and oversees the daily operations on the set, including the scheduling, budgeting and implementation of endless practical details. Often the busiest person on the production, up early and working late into the night; they work primarily in the office but generally visit the set at least once a day, sometimes several times daily.

Show producer (television). Also known as the "showrunner." The supervising producer on all of the episodes of a year's worth of shows, who is responsible for their production from the assignment of writers to final editing and technical postproduction. Often, but not always, a writer.

Segment producer (television). Creates segments of shows in the nonfiction field (documentary, news, reality, tabloid) under the supervision of the showrunner. Often includes research and writing, and sometimes supervision of editing. Such positions are often filled by sharp young people on their way up, and many women seem drawn to this career path stepping-stone.

Specialized Producers

Lastly, three specialized producing fields that combine the creative with the more technical:

Promo producer. Creates promos and trailers, including the writing and editing, for upcoming TV shows.

Trailer producer. Specializes in conceiving, writing and cutting trailers ("coming attractions") for feature films soon to be released. Similar functions are performed for various other formats by EPK (electronic or video press kit) producers, commercial producers, music video producers and so on.

---

66 The producer is like the conductor of an orchestra. Maybe he can't play every instrument, but he knows what every instrument should sound like. 99

—RICHARD ZANUCK

The "Producer" Glut

How do you become a Hollywood producer? Get a desk.
That's a joke that's been circulating around Hollywood for more than a decade, but it's rooted in a serious reality: So many producer credits are given out on motion pictures, the term *producer* has become almost meaningless.

"I'm tired of seeing producer credits when I know the people haven't made the movie," producer Steve Tisch (*Risky Business, Forrest Gump*) told a reporter for the *Wall Street Journal*. "Some people call themselves producers because they manage talent or because their best friend is a hot actor. It's a nebulous title in a sexy business."

The 1997 release, *G.I. Jane*, for example, listed no fewer than eleven people with production credits. A number of other films in the 1990s, such as *Radio Flyer* (1992), credited *ten* producers. A half dozen "producers" on a Hollywood movie is almost commonplace. One reason: With credits, egos are stroked and debts are paid.

"I give credits in lieu of money," admits producer Edward R. Pressman (*Wall Street, Conan the Barbarian*), "in lieu of all kinds of things."

Visual effects producer. A first cameraperson who specializes in a certain kind of shot or shots, with technical skills more akin to cinematography than producing. In essence, the director of photography of visual or special effects.

The Director

The director is the man or woman behind the camera who literally calls the shots. Directors can range from the artistic and independent-minded *auteurs*, who impress their personal style and vision on every aspect of the production, to more workmanlike directors who do little more than block the actors' moves, decide how the furniture will be positioned, order camera angles and keep the action moving smoothly and on schedule (more prevalent in TV and low-budget action pictures).

Directing successfully at the highest feature film level demands the ability to draw skillful or moving performances from actors, bring together the many visual techniques of filmmaking to create a "look" for a film, understand the various elements of narrative storytelling (structure, pacing, dialogue) and integrate them successfully using script and cameras, and have the management skills needed to act as a field general to a cast and crew that typically numbers 100 to 150—all under enormous creative, time, ego and budgetary pressures.

Actor Emilio Estevez is shown here taking on the role of director. (Copyright Touchstone Pictures.)

After the star, the director is the top glamour position in Hollywood, and often the highest paid, with numerous A-list directors now earning several million dollars per picture, and a few approaching the $10 million level.

A number of lower and less glamorous directorial positions include:

First assistant director. The director's right-hand person, whose duties are less creative and more akin to those of a line producer, as described above, with similar "field general" skills needed in a good director. This person is the set foreman who works with the department heads and the on-set crew to help the director get his or her vision on film. Sometimes directs scenes involving only extras.

Second assistant director. Essentially a coordinator or liaison between the production office, talent (including extras) and the first assistant director.

Second unit director. Handles nondialogue sequences, including inserts and scenic shots, and especially action scenes. Frequently also a stunt coordinator.

> **" "Anything is better than making a bad picture. " "**
> —DIRECTOR WILLIAM WYLER

Directors Guild of America (DGA) trainee. "Take a test with many other applicants at the [DGA]," advises Linda Buzzell in *How to Make It in Hollywood,* "and you may land one of these coveted internships."

Two directorial positions in the videotape field include the associate director, who assists the video director, and the technical director, who heads the light crew and works the switcher, a device that changes cameras quickly for varied angles and shots.

The Agents

The primary role of a talent agent is to procure work and negotiate compensation contracts for his or her clients, whether they be in the acting, writing, directing, producing or other creative fields. For this service, they generally take 10 percent of what a client earns.

Unlike producers, personal managers and other "players" in the business, who operate without special legal restrictions, agents are regulated by state law. "In the state of California," write Gail Resnik and Scott Trost in *All You Need to Know About the Movie and TV Business*, "the Talent Agencies Act in the labor code requires individuals who procure employment for artists in entertainment fields (except those that procure only recording contracts) to be licensed as talent agents by the labor commissioner. In addition, an agent must be franchised by the unions to represent union members."

Agencies come in a variety of sizes and shapes with varying degrees of power in the marketplace. For many years, the three dominant agencies in Hollywood have been Creative Artists Agency (CAA), International Creative Management (ICM) and the William Morris Agency, each with several dozen agents. Their clout has increased or waned through the years with the gain or loss of individual agents, many of whom leave to produce, take studio executive jobs or start their own agencies, and with the gain or loss of star clients. Yet all three maintain such large rosters of top talent in so many fields, each continues to wield considerable force, along with a handful of more recently-established "power" agencies that are challenging the big three.

Dozens of other agencies dot the Los Angeles landscape, from Encino to Culver City, ranging in size from respected, midlevel agencies with a dozen or so agents, to smaller, "boutique" agencies specializing in a certain kind of client, to one-man operations that may or may not be successful. Some clients prefer big agencies for the power they wield; others prefer smaller agencies for the

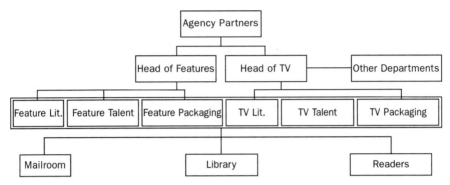

Chart of organization for a typical agency. (Copyright Hugh Taylor, courtesy of Lone Eagle Publishing.)

more personal attention they hope to get. (Top agents are notorious for ignoring their clients, especially in the matter of returning phone calls.)

What "Power" Agents Can Do

Resnik and Trost explain what the big agents do this way: "The top agents at the top agencies in town are some of the major players in the business. Their calls get answered, their demands get met, and they are just as important to the process as any person in Hollywood. Their power is based on the desirability of their clients, the collective clout of their agency, and the force of the individual personalities of the agents. . . . A powerful agent sets the pace for dealmaking in [Hollywood]."

By and large, they are a well-dressed bunch who drive expensive cars and eat at expensive restaurants, or at least the "in" establishments where the level of prestige is high and they can be seen by other players (see "Dining and Hanging Out," chapter seven). The biggest or most prestigious agencies tend to be located in Beverly Hills and Century City. Men have dominated the agency field for decades, but more and more prominent women are rising through the agency ranks, and a few have managed to wield nearly as much clout as their top male counterparts; if women are still in the minority, it is not by much. Because Hollywood is such a youth-oriented business, it is not uncommon to see many junior agents in their twenties and top agents in their early thirties, although most of the biggest "power" agents seem to be in their forties and fifties. A few, like the late Irving "Swifty" Lazar, are able to maintain relationships with top clients and players and work well into their "golden years."

Although an agent's job is to procure work for his or her client, it rarely works that simply. Most agents keep track of projects around town, know what jobs need filling and submit their clients for the right positions. The more connections and clout an agent has, the better chance he or she has of getting a client an audition (actors), set up with a pitch meeting or their samples read (writers), and so on. (Agents, it is often said, live and die professionally by their Rolodexes and personal relationships.) Their responsibilities also include negotiating contracts, following up with paperwork, seeing that the client is paid (checks come first to the agent, who takes his or her percentage and then cuts a check to the client), and other business details.

Yet the reality is, most agents spend the bulk of their time and energy on their established, big-money clients, while those just breaking in have to do most of the "getting around" and personal networking needed to jump-start a career.

How does one know if an agent is good or bad? You might check their client list and track record. Is the agent getting regular work for his or her clients? Does the agent have a high turnover rate in clients, or do they tend to remain loyal and stay through the years? Are they up to date on the guild minimums and other business details in the fields they represent? Do they know who the important players about town are, and do they know them on a first-name, handshake basis? Does the agent's office appear comfortable, clean, efficient and well-organized? Or is it shabby and in disarray? Does the agent frequently answer his or her own phone (a sure sign the agent isn't prospering or managing employees well), or are calls handled professionally and efficiently by a capable assistant? How would you rate the agent's attention span, stress level and ability to concentrate? Where do they eat lunch? What kind of car do they drive? How do they dress? And so on.

Ironically, as damnable as Hollywood agents can be for not returning phone calls, it is, at least, a sign that they are *busy*. Beware the agent that returns every call promptly and has lots of time to schmooze because that may be an agent who doesn't have a whole lot going on businesswise.

Hollywood is a place where 90 percent of the people live off the 10 percent who have talent.

—ANCIENT TINSELTOWN PROVERB

The Personal Managers

Personal managers are individuals who focus their attention on a single client or a few key clients, usually actors, and advise them on what professional moves they should make and what direction their careers should take. They also pick up the slack for agents, working continuously and aggressively to get their clients seen, noticed, auditioned and so on. For this, they take 10 to 20 percent of what a client earns, which includes all earnings, in addition to any commissions an agent takes from the same client.

Personal managers can range from highly effective and professional to sleaze-bag con artists on the make for needy, naive newcomers. The good ones have proven track records guiding the careers of actors from near obscurity to great success. Personal manager Delores Robinson nurtured the career of actor LeVar Burton (*Roots, Star Trek: The Next Generation*) from his days as a college drama student. Neil Koenigsberg, a former publicist, steered actor Mark Harmon into the roles that made him a television star and Jeff Bridges toward a variety of offbeat, challenging film roles. Harrison Ford, in sheer box-office dollar returns the most successful actor in modern movie history, has been with the same personal manager, Pat McQueeney, since early in his long career.

The better personal managers tend to be more relaxed than agents, less driven and image-conscious, more sensitive and nurturing. Some very successful personal managers even work out of their own homes, not because they cannot afford an office but because they prefer a more comfortable, hospitable atmosphere.

Yet for every personal manager who measures up to these, there are probably many more who are in it for the financial and sometimes sexual rip-off. These are the aforementioned con artists who convince naive actors that they will guide them to stardom, but hit them up for thousands of dollars in "expenses" without ever helping them get a job. They are the scumbags who "sign up" attractive actors or actresses as clients, then set them up sexually with friends in the business in exchange for money or favors, essentially serving as pimps. They are the frauds who send their clients again and again for a new studio portfolio of photos, secretly taking kickbacks from the photographer (also a common ploy of illegitimate acting schools and modeling agencies). And so on and so on. Every field has bottom feeders like these, uncaring sociopaths who leave in their wake broken hearts and shattered dreams. Hollywood just seems to have more than its share, perhaps because it's a unique place filled with so many dreamers.

Entertainment Industry Lawyers

Entertainment law is a highly specialized field that demands an understanding of how Hollywood works and the complicated nature of its contracts, and its practitioners can be found both inside and outside the networks and studios.

There are probably fewer than a hundred lawyers who specialize in handling the industry's creative talent, yet many are "players" in their own right, with a highly visible role in the deal-making process. Their basic purpose is to protect the long-range financial and legal interests of the client, which requires training and experience in intellectual property law as well as contracts unique to the entertainment industry. Some lawyers have come to play such a prominent role in their client's lives—the so-called "superstar" attorneys—that they are actively involved in putting together deals at the highest levels of the business, much like the most powerful agents.

"While most working actors use an agent, a manager and an attorney to promote and protect their career," write Resnik and Trost, "a small percentage of well-established actors will jettison their agents and managers and rely exclusively on their attorneys to act in all three capacities."

Lawyers are generally paid hourly ($100 to $600 per hour) or take a percentage of earnings (5 to 10 percent). In some cases, notably with screenwriters making their first deals, lawyers will "check contracts" and advise the writer for a flat fee, either in lieu of or, as an adjunct to, an agent.

Like agents, the top attorneys maintain offices primarily in Beverly Hills and the nearby business district of Century City. (More on geographical Hollywood in chapter seven.) Most are men, and they invariably work in elegant, if business-like, surroundings, and dress, drive and eat in similar fashion.

Actors: In a Realm of Their Own

Most jobs for Hollywood actors are in TV commercials (on-camera or voice-overs) followed by television programming and movies. Several other performing categories exist that may or may not involve acting: on-camera host, on-camera news reporter or anchorperson, show announcer, extra, stand-in and stunt person. (On the latter three, see "Industrywide Jobs/Descriptions," on page 112.)

Film and TV actors, however, are the performers Hollywood is truly about. They range from day players in bit parts or walk-ons earning a guild minimum of $540 per day to superstars who pull down tens of millions of dollars for a single role. Whatever their professional status, however, the peculiar nature of their work and the extraordinary heights of celebrity that some reach sets them apart from everyone else in the industry.

Why are the lives of actors so different?

More than anyone, actors give the movies their special magic. They are what everything in Hollywood revolves around, particularly as they become more successful—the camera lens, makeup artists, directors, agents, media and the deal-makers who need them so desperately to get their projects off the ground.

Actors are who the audience pays to see and truly cares about, the artists who bring characters to life, the fantasy objects of the lonely, bored and starstruck. With the exception of a few moguls and a handful of incredibly successful producers or producer-directors such as Steven Spielberg and George Lucas, the most popular actors are the highest-paid people in town. They are the kings and queens of Tinseltown, the most fussed-over, catered to and spoiled. At the same time, how they look greatly determines how much or what kind of work they will get, if any, and their images are under constant scrutiny. Frequently, before the camera and a crew of strangers, they must render themselves emotionally naked—sometimes even *physically* naked—knowing they will be seen that way by tens of millions of strangers around the world, in the sharpest close-ups and most penetrating light. They alone have the courage, perhaps the need, to expose themselves this way. Yet at the same time, they can be among the most self-conscious and insecure people in the business, addicted to attention but terrified of it at the same time.

Typically, actors are said to crave the adoration of the audience, but find love in more human, one-to-one terms more difficult; for some, it is probably true. They work in a world of fantasy and, more than anyone else, immerse themselves in it; more than a few seem to prefer the fantasy to the reality of everyday life lived by most others. It is also said that many actors are childlike, craving attention, needing supervision, unwilling to grow up and take full responsibility for themselves. Except for the minority who take charge of their careers and material as writers, directors or producers, the actors' craft is largely *interpretive* as they

---

66 [In L.A.] I felt like a hemophiliac in a razor factory. I worried about my career every day. 99

—ROBIN WILLIAMS

---

interpret and flesh out characters *created* by writers, under the *supervision* of parental directors.

These are archetypal descriptions, of course, and hardly apply to all actors. Yet those men and women who toil in the actor's trade, even the most mature and self-assured, all share similar experiences at some point, such as:

Facing the mirror. By their natures and the nature of their work, they seem the most narcissistic of Hollywood's creatures, obsessed with how they look, down to each falling strand of hair and new wrinkle, and alternately enthralled and appalled by what they see. The more well-known they become, the more they worry, lest they be seen or, worse, *photographed* in an unfavorable light or from an unflattering angle. Even those who attempt to foster a carefree image know the world is watching them once they step out the door.

Facing the camera's eye. From the still camera of the studio, where they are constantly updating their stock of glossy 8×10s, to the TV and movie lens they all hope to face, Hollywood actors have an intimate, ongoing relationship with the camera. It's partly a developed technical skill, partly instinct and crucial to their careers.

The search for an agent. In the beginning, they need an agent to help them get seen by directors, producers and casting agents. When they are stars, they need an agent to handle their multimillion dollar deals. In between, many actors, either dropped by an agent or not getting much work with their current one, fear they will never get a good agent again and that their careers may be over. The quest for an agent is one of Hollywood's more demoralizing but requisite activities.

Auditions. These can range from one-on-one meetings or readings for the director and any number of his or her associates, to the infamous cattle call, in which actors typically show up to find themselves waiting in line with numerous other actors, all dishearteningly of the same "type." Auditions are frequently adrenaline-producing, nerve-wracking affairs in which the more insensitive producers and directors have been known to stare absently out windows or pick their nose while actors perform difficult readings.

Learning lines, forgetting lines, flubbing lines. Memorizing dialogue is the first and most essential activity for a hired actor, an acquired skill that demands extreme concentration. Yet even the most adept at it will at some point feel the panic that comes with the memory's black hole or the hopelessly twisted tongue.

Sexual harassment. For the youthful and attractive of both sexes, being sexually objectified and physically pestered in casting rooms and elsewhere virtually comes with the territory. (See the sidebar "The Casting Couch," in chapter eight.)

Romance on the set. Actors are thrown together for weeks and months at a time, often on distant locations, frequently in the most intimate scenes, with attractive people of the same or opposite sex. Offstage, nature invariably takes its course, one reason many Hollywood marriages are so short-lived.

The gym. Many thespians fight it, particularly the New York-bred, "serious" stage actor, until they begin to get older, softer and employed by Hollywood less often. (The big stars, of course, often have personal trainers or head for high-priced fat farms.)

The lost part. Countless actors come close to a coveted or career-making role along the way, only to just miss out. The persevering, talented and lucky stay with it until they finally get their break. Of course, many actors just *think* they almost got the big part: It's not uncommon in Hollywood for a producer to let a number of actors down gently by telling them *all* privately that they were the director's "second choice." Many actors are happy to believe it, even when they keep hearing it again and again.

Rejection. It's the one sure thing every actor is destined to experience, not just once but over and over. Even the most successful, critically acclaimed stars get turned down for roles they covet. Hollywood history is littered with the suicides or near-suicides of failed or disillusioned actors; it's remarkable there aren't more.

Industrywide Jobs/Descriptions

Following is an alphabetized list of entertainment industry jobs that have not been previously covered, many of them "below-the-line" (crew member) positions:

Acquisitions coordinator/executive. Responsible for searching out, screening and acquiring projects that are completed or nearly completed for a network or distributor.

Animal trainer. Trains animals, both wild and domestic, to appear in television shows or movies. Often owns the animals and must adhere to Humane Society standards for training, safety and care while working on the set. (See also *Wrangler,* on page 118.)

Animator. Conceives and designs the visuals for an animated film and draws the characters. A position demanding extremely well-developed drawing and computer graphic skills.

Show Me the Money!
What the Actors (and Stars) Get Paid

Performers who are guild members working on union productions earn per-day minimums broken down by category: day performer (actor), $540; stunt performer, $540; stunt coordinator, $540; dancers (theatrical only, solo and duo), $540.

As actors become established and are hired on for more than day performer bit parts, they are usually able to command weekly salaries well above minimum. It is not uncommon for an established actor, who is known within the industry as a strong supporting player but whose name is unfamiliar to the public, to earn $5,000 to $15,000 per week, a rate that customarily rises if the actor is cast in a solid part in a hit movie. By the same token, certain supporting or character actors, or, more accurately, their agents, can price them out of work by demanding more than producers are willing to pay for their services.

Stars, of course, exist on another level altogether (for a history of "Superstar Salaries," see chapter one), and the astounding escalation of their salaries in recent years has become the subject of serious concern in Hollywood production offices.

In 1996, producer and talkshow host Oprah Winfrey was the highest paid television personality, earning an estimated $96 million, and in 1997, comedian Tim Allen ("Home Improvement") set a new high in weekly TV salaries, reportedly picking up $1.25 million per episode.

NOTE: Salaries for a wide range of other Hollywood jobs are listed separately on page 124.

Art director. Designs the sets for a movie and oversees their construction and selects the props. May help scout shooting locations outside the studio and select the costumes (depending on the role of the costume designer).

Best boy. The top assistant to the chief electrician or key grip (see *Gaffer*, on page 115).

Boom operator. Crew member responsible for maneuvering the overhead boom microphone above the actors' heads to pick up their dialogue clearly, but without getting into the frame of the camera shot.

Cable person (location sound assistant). Sets up the sound equipment and "mikes" the actors (attaches their radio microphones and makes sure the sound is clear).

Camera loader. Handles the "slate" (clapboard to signify a new take), keeps camera reports (on shots) and changes film magazines (canisters) during shooting. Also known as *second assistant cameraperson, second a.c.* or just *loader.*

Camera operator. Under the supervision of the cinematographer, handles the camera during shooting, including its movement to various positions and angles, and makes sure the image of the scene through the camera's viewfinder is correct.

Casting director (casting agent). This is the person, abetted by *casting assistants,* who studies the script and characters, then helps find suitable actors to fill the nonstarring roles, often giving the producer and director many choices for readings and auditions. The best casting directors spend much of their time searching out fresh talent and have sharp memories for names and faces, along with highly developed systems for keeping track of wide-ranging talent. They also assist in negotiating and closing some actor deals.

Composer. Working with the director's ideas and vision, creates the musical score for a film or TV show, writing original music for what is on the screen scene by scene. The *music editor* assists the composer technically and edits the music into music tracks for the final mix. Also selects and edits nonoriginal music to be used.

Costume designer. The head of "wardrobe," who researches and designs costumes to be used during shooting.

Costumer. Works under the costume designer procuring the clothing, costumes and accessories needed for a film production, and maintains their security, cleanliness and so on during the shoot. Procurement can be done through purchase, rental or borrowing (usually for an end credit to a store or designer), although actors sometimes wear their own clothes on very low-budget productions.

Costume supervisor. In charge of fittings, acquisition, inventory, maintenance and budgeting of all wardrobe as well as hiring the wardrobe staff.

Crafts services person. The person who supplies the crew with between meal snacks and refreshments and, secondarily, is responsible for keeping the set clean and tidy.

Development assistant. Assists a development executive or story department, reads scripts and sometimes works with writers on rewrites. Considered a good career track job for aspiring producers. (See *D-girls,* in the "Common Hollywood Slang" section of Appendix A.)

Director of photography (cinematographer). Also known as *DP.* Responsible for the film's "look" by lighting the set; setting up the general composition of the scene; thinking through the color images that will be produced; choosing the cameras, lenses and film stock; supervising the settings of the cameras and their movements; and integrating special effects. Much of this is done in consultation with the director.

Dolly grip. Crew member assigned to move the camera on special tracks for a moving "dolly" shot. (See *Grip* below.)

Editor. Selects the most effective footage captured on film, then arranges the individual shots, scenes and sequences into a narrative structure while technically integrating sound. A film editor may have enormous creative control in shaping a film, or considerably less, depending on the power and working style of the director.

Extra. Background or "B.G." person who appears in nondialogue role as an incidental figure during shooting, from passing by on the street to being part of a noisy crowd. May or may not be a member of an extras union, depending on the particular production.

Focus puller. Responsible for handling the camera, especially adjusting the focus, during shooting. Also known as *assistant cameraperson* or *first A.C.*

Foley artist. "Foley" is the process of creating special sound effects for recording and adding to a film's soundtrack. This is often done in unusual and creative ways, such as smashing a watermelon with a hammer to simulate a lethal blow to the head.

Gaffer. The chief electrician who oversees the required lights and power sources, from supplying the equipment to shutting down the set at the end of production. "Gaffer" is an old English term for boss dating back to the days of the big sailing ships. Known more often these days as the "chief lighting technician."

Greens person. The person in charge of gardening and landscaping on the set.

Grip. The "utility infielder" stagehand on the set who works an assortment of tasks, including setting up equipment, scenery and heavy items that "dress" the set; positioning equipment to diffuse the lighting; laying dolly tracks (tracks for the camera to roll on); and pushing the dolly during shooting. The term comes from the early days of the theater when a stagehand had to get a good grip on the heaviest sets for lifting.

Illustrator. An artist skilled at figure drawing and perspective who puts on paper the visual ideas of the script, director and production designer. (See *Storyboard Artist* on page 118.)

Key grip. Boss of the grips who takes orders from the director of photography.

Lead man. Directs the "swing gang" or set decoration crew to construct or "strike" (pull down) sets. Works under the set decorator.

Lighting director. Physically in charge of the lighting, working closely with the director and the director of photography. (See *Gaffer* on page 115.)

Location scout. Also known as *assistant location manager.* Searches out shooting locations needed for a film or TV production, ideally abetted by a vast and detailed knowledge of regional or city geography and special shooting sites. Works under the *location manager*, who is responsible for location needs being met, including securing proper permission and permits.

Makeup artist. Coordinates makeup schedules and the hairstylists as head of the makeup department. A *special effects makeup artist* is someone who specializes in creating creature or monster faces or more elaborate makeup work, such as wounds, corpses, and so on.

Matte painter. Computer designs and creates backgrounds for "matte shots," which utilize man-made backdrops to simulate large visual backgrounds such as the sky or mountains. This is known as computer generated imagery or CGI.

Music supervisor. Works for the studio keeping track of all music used on a film, including the clearance of rights. A complex job that involves administrative, library and some legal skills, as well as an extensive knowledge of the music business.

Negative cutter. Creates the pristine master negative from which all prints of a film will be duplicated ("struck"), a job requiring incredible precision and patience that is gradually being replaced by digital technology.

Postproduction supervisor. Responsible for seeing that every task is accomplished on time in the highly technical postproduction process, from supervising lab work deliveries to setting the sound mix.

Production coordinator. Liaison between the producer, unit production manager, assistant director, crew and performers. Distributes calls sheets (cast and crew scheduling information for specific shooting days) and manages the production office as well as other tasks.

Production designer. The person responsible for creating the look and design of the film, starting with creative meetings with the producer and director, followed by sketches proposing the look of certain scenes and their backdrops, sets, colors and so on. Often works closely with the DP and costume designer. In TV, known as the *scenic* or *set designer*.

Property ("prop") master. Procures, builds or reconstructs props for films and TV shows, and makes sure they are ready and available when needed for shooting.

Publicist. Attempts to generate or "plant" media coverage of a film or TV show, or coordinate related activities. A *unit publicist* is assigned the publicity campaign on a specific film and usually goes on location to act as liaison for the production with the press, to assist with interviews, to develop a press kit for later distribution and so on.

Script supervisor. Assists the director by keeping track of small details in each scene or take for the sake of visual continuity (e.g., What color tie was an actor wearing from one scene to the next? What did his hair look like? And so on). Also very useful to the editor regarding camera angles, lenses and timing the length of shots. An extremely detail-oriented job, with careful notes and a Polaroid camera as helpful tools.

Set crew. Term used for three key craftspeople: *construction foreperson, labor foreperson, paint foreperson.* They work under the *construction coordinator.*

Set decorator. Responsible for "decorating" the set with furniture, props, artwork and other ornamentation. Works closely with art director.

Sound mixer. The *production sound mixer* records sound during production; the *postproduction sound technician* or *supervisor* later handles rerecording for the final mix, which includes dialogue, effects and music.

Special effects supervisor. With his or her crew, produces explosions, fire, smoke, water (for rain), whatever is needed during filming, including the "squibs" that use small charges attached to bags filled with simulated blood to create the illusion of bullet hits and wounds. Must be licensed pyrotechnic specialists, with great technical and safety knowledge.

Stage manager. In television (with videotape), the person in charge of everything going on on the set, similar to the unit production manager or UPM in film (see below).

Stand-in. A person who physically resembles a star and literally "stands in" for that star during the adjusting of lighting and blocking of scenes, so the star is able to rest or attend to other matters.

Story analyst (reader). Someone who reads, synopsizes and evaluates submitted material, usually completed scripts. Entry-level work, often farmed out to freelance readers, although the networks and studios generally employ union members.

Story editor. At a studio, heads the story department, supervising the readers. On a TV show, an executive just below the producer and often a writer on the show, who hears pitches from freelance writers, coordinates story ideas and works on scripts.

Storyboard artist. Creates the storyboards, or painted cards, that depict a film's story line scene by scene, sometimes handled by the illustrator. Also used in TV commercials, animated cartoons and other visual mediums.

Studio teacher. Provides instruction for all school-age minors working on a production as required by child welfare laws, which mandate three hours minimum each day.

Stunt person. Either performs stunts as a *stuntman* or *stuntwoman* or serves as the *stunt coordinator* (usually a highly skilled and experienced stunt performer), who plans, choreographs and conducts rehearsals for stunts, with an emphasis on safety. Many stunt coordinators segue into the position of *second unit director*, handling action scenes.

Transportation captain. Runs the transportation department, which includes all vehicles from camera trucks to mobile dressing rooms. Next in line is the *transportation coordinator*, who oversees the maintenance and operation of all vehicles and works with the Teamsters Union, which provides all *drivers* by union contract (see "Hollywood Labor Unions" below).

Unit production manager (UPM). The person in charge of the crew, from hiring, setting contracts for crew and vendors, maintaining the budget and schedule and so on. Works under and sometimes overlaps the line producer.

Visual effects supervisor. In charge of such visual effects as mattes, model building and computer generated imagery (CGI), done in postproduction.

Wrangler. The person in charge of animals and other nonhuman creatures used during production, from horses to bugs to snakes and worms (i.e., the "worm wrangler"). Not the same thing as animal *trainer*, though the trainer sometimes functions as a wrangler.

Hollywood Labor Unions

Many of the specialized jobs described above are crew positions that come under the jurisdiction of various labor guilds, all of which have individual contracts with the studios and networks, as well as independent production companies known as "guild signatorees." Guild contracts cover a variety of issues, such as minimum wage, overtime, and working conditions, and differ to varying degrees from union to union (see "Pay and Salaries in Hollywood" on page 124).

Among the unions producers frequently deal with: Screen Actors Guild (SAG), Writers Guild of America (WGA), Directors Guild of America (DGA), Screen Extras Guild (SEG), International Alliance of Theatrical Stage Employees (IATSE), Teamsters, American Federation of Musicians (AFM),

Hollywood Job Hotlines

Networks:

ABC ....(310) 557-4222
CBS ....(213) 460-3000
Fox TV ....(213) 856-1111
NBC ....(818) 840-4397

Studios:

Twentieth Century Fox Film Corporation ....(310) 369-2804
Sony Pictures Entertainment ....(310) 244-4436
DreamWorks/SKG ....(818) 733-7000
Paramount Pictures ....(213) 956-5216
Universal/MCA ....(818) 777-5627 (JOBS)
Walt Disney Company ....(818) 558-2222
Warner Bros. ....(818) 954-5400

Theatrical State Employees Union (LATSE), Cinematographers Union, and the Costume Designers Guild.

In general, all studio movies must use union crews. Unit production managers, who handle the below-the-line employees ("crews"), work from "production books" that provide wage minimums and other guild stipulations for the various crafts. Virtually all hires are made by the supervisory workers in each craft, such as the key grip and the chief electrician (gaffer), and are often approved by the unit production manager (UPM). Generally, they hire men and women with whom they have worked before and find dependable, or new people personally recommended to them. Less often, in a jam, they might call the union to see who is on the "available list" (available to work), and hire in that way.

Some unions are easier to get into than others. An actor need not be a member of SAG, for instance, to be hired for a movie or television show, although he or she must be "Taft Hartleyed" in by applying for a union card to join a union shoot (being hired automatically qualifies them for membership). Likewise, one need not be a member of the WGA to sell a script (and is not required to join thereafter, though the potential benefits are significant). Other unions are considerably more strict about membership qualification and entry. The Teamster's Union, which provides all drivers, has perhaps the most stringent controls over who can and cannot work on a studio production, based on seniority, availability and other factors.

For more specific information about working with unions, including details of union contracts, consult *The Beginning Filmmaker's Business Guide*, by Renee Harmon. You'll also find a more complete list of entertainment industry guilds in Appendix B with information on how to contact each.

A Film Crew's Working Day

With the exception of night shoots, a crew member's typical working day begins between 7 and 8 A.M., depending on the projected start time for shooting, how much daylight shooting time is needed (if the shoot is outside or on location), the time of year and length of daylight hours, and so on. The caterer, hired independently to supply meals for the duration of the production, arrives about an hour before the crew to have breakfast ready half an hour before the crew call—hot and cold, from fresh fruit and doughnuts to french toast and bacon, and plenty of coffee. (Union crews in Hollywood are not only paid well, but generally treated quite well.) Crews customarily range in size from seventy-five to two hundred, depending on the scope and needs of the production.

A typical shooting day lasts about twelve hours, and overtime pay does not kick in until after ten or twelve hours, depending on the union contract. Crew members generally must be fed a meal every six hours, or the production suffers a "meal penalty," which means they will have to pay additional wages for the mealtime missed. Some shooting days last as long as twenty hours as producers attempt to get as much filming completed in a compressed time period, which cuts down on total shooting days and costs even with overtime. This has led to extreme exhaustion during many shoots and some highly publicized accidents, including at least one death in 1996 that some crew members attributed to the rigors of a nineteen-hour workday. Maximum work hours are currently the focus of debate between the unions and producers, with some guilds attempting to fix a maximum working day of twelve to fourteen hours, after which a production would have to shut down.

One often hears about downtime on a movie set, when much of the cast and crew has idle time on its hands. This is generally not due to anyone's laziness or lack of supervision on the set, but rather the structure of shooting itself. Filmmaking requires elaborate, painstaking repositioning and adjustment of equipment between shots to achieve a high technical quality—sometimes to the extent of moving all the equipment to the next location, and making careful adjustments for the change in light, shades of colors and endless other factors.

Juno Pix, Inc/New Line

Seven

Date: Wednesday July 26, 1995
Day 5 out of 9 Days

Juno Pix, Inc./New Line
825 N. San Vicente Blvd.
(310) 967-6818 (Office)
(310) 967-6707 (Fax)
Director: David Fincher
Producers: Arnold Kopelson/Phyllis Carlyle
Executive Producers: Gianni Nunnan/Anne Kopelson
Co-Producers: Stephen Brown/Nana Greenwald/Sanford Panitch
Line Producer: William Gernty

RPT @
4:30 A/7:30A*

CREW CALL

Crew Rpt Call: 4:30A/7:30A
Shooting Call: 5A

Sunrise/Sunset: 5:41A/7:57P
Weather: Hazy Sunshine/Ptly Cldy/80's

NO FORCED CALLS WITHOUT PRIOR APPROVAL FROM UPM

SET	SCENE	CAST	D/N	PAGE	LOCATION
*Note: Individual Crew Call Times Vary/Please check your call time					
I/E Helicopter POV's	122A	(Extras)	D		Company Bases @ 1st St/Alameda St.-LA
(Helicopter's POV: 3/4 Behind, watching Somerset's Car cross bridge/Peel Away over river at Washington St)					
Ext Helicopter - Air to Air Photography	123	5,7,9	D		(Please See Attached Map)
(Raking left side of helicopter. Sniper/California watch Somerset's car driving (can be poorman's process and shot in middle of day)					
I/E Helicopter-Air to Air Photography	124	5,7,9	D		
(Downshot traveling over river area. Chopper blasts through frame (left to right/away) tilt with it and follow as it peels left to right and flies					
into the setting sun)					
Ext Helipad	121	5,7,9	D		
(The SWAT team boards the helicopter and the helicopter lifts off)					
Note: To be shot over the course of the day by a 2nd Unit					
Int Somerset's Car (Ready @ 9A)	122		D		
(Cars POV of sign, indicating that they are leaving the city)					
Ext City Street	TBA	Extras	D		
(Cut Away - Passby of Somerset's Car) - 2nd Unit					
Ext City Skyline	TBA		MAGIC		
(Shoot Skyline) - 2nd Unit					
Please Note: Information forthcoming regarding early AM crew travel to Palmdale on 7/27					

ALL CREW REPORTING PRIOR TO GENERAL CREW CALL TO RECEIVE ND BREAKFAST

THIS IS A NO SMOKING SET

A film crew's day is organized and scheduled by a call sheet. This is part of a call sheet from the film *Seven*. Note that the weather forecast and times for sunrise and sunset are included on the sheet.

The relaxation level on a set, whether in a studio soundstage or out on location, varies from picture to picture, and depends to a great extent on the personalities of those who are producing, directing and starring. How the movie is proceeding also affects the day-to-day mood of the shoot. If a film is behind schedule, seriously over budget or beset with foul weather or other unforeseen problems, a shoot can become tense and anxious, from the producer on down.

A sense of easygoing camaraderie is common on film shoots, however, since crew members work together over a period of many weeks or months and often know each other from previous shoots. The smarter stars and directors learn to treat crew members with respect and equanimity because they are the worker bees who keep a production going. Some producers and directors even have open "dailies" each evening, when cast and crew members alike are welcome to view the previous day's footage. The relationship between the crew and the stars varies from star to star: some get along well with the crew, even like to "hang out" and engage in pranks, or provide the crew with gifts; others keep their distance. One rule that seems inviolable on film sets: below-the-line crew members do not make creative suggestions to the director, and certainly not to the stars.

Each night, when production wraps for the day, crew members are given a crew call sheet (specifying arrival times for the next workday) with a shooting call list (projecting when actual shooting is expected to start), usually accompanied by a map to the next day's location. In scheduling their crew members, unit production managers must take into account union rules about "turnaround" time—the number of hours of rest a crew member must be allowed before being called back for the next working day.

Crew conditions vary somewhat for television, particularly for indoor studio work, but many of the same rules and working patterns apply. However, TV crews are generally considerably smaller with TV shooting done at a faster, more economical pace.

In both films and TV, the producers usually throw a "wrap party" to celebrate the completion of film production or the TV season, a festive affair replete with food and drink to which cast and crew alike are traditionally invited.

Hollywood Biographies and Autobiographies

What follows is a select list of Hollywood autobiographies and biographies—some authorized, some not—that may prove useful in researching the lives of those who have lived and worked in Tinseltown.

Bogart, A.M. Sperber and Eric Lax

By Myself, Lauren Bacall

Cagney by Cagney, James Cagney

Cagney: The Actor as Auteur, Patrick McGilligan

Cecil B. DeMille, Charles Higham

Chaplin, Denis Gifford

Citizen Welles, Frank Brady

Crazy Sundays: F. Scott Fitzgerald in Hollywood, Aaron Latham

Dorothy Dandridge: A Biography, Donald Bogle

Down at the End of Lonely Street: The Life and Death of Elvis Presley, Peter Harry Brown and Pat H. Broeske

D.W. Griffith: An American Life, Croy Homer

Empire: The Life, Legend and Madness of Howard Hughes, Donald L. Bartlett and James B. Steele

Frank Capra: The Catastrophe of Success, Joseph McBride

Frank Capra: The Name Above the Title, Frank Capra

Fritz Lang: The Nature of the Beast, Patrick McGilligan

George Cukor: A Double Life, Patrick McGilligan

Goldwyn, A. Scott Berg

Hawks on Hawks, Joseph McBride

Haywire, Brooke Hayward

Hedda and Louella, George Eells

Hollywood's Master Showman: The Legendary Sid Grauman, Charles Beardsley

Howard Hawks: The Grey Fox of Hollywood, Todd McCarthy

Howard Hughes: The Untold Story, Peter Harry Brown and Pat H. Broeske

James Dean: The Mutant King, David Dalton

John Ford, Peter Bogdanovich

John Ford: The Man and His Films, Tag Gallagher

Keaton, Daniel Moews

Kid Stays in the Picture, The, Robert Evans

Legend: The Life and Death of Marilyn Monroe, Fred Lawrence Guiles

Life, A Elia Kazan

Marie Dressler: The Unlikeliest Star, Betty Lee

Marilyn: The Last Take, Peter Harry Brown and Patte B. Barham

Mary Pickford: America's Sweetheart, Scott Eyman

Mary Pickford and Douglas Fairbanks, Booton Herndon

Mayer and Thalberg, Samuel Marx

Pay and Salaries in Hollywood

(SELECTED LIST, COMPILED MID-1997)

ANIMAL TRAINER   Union minimums: $26.60 an hour for dogs; $30.72 an hour for stabled or wild animals.

ANIMATOR   Union minimum: $1,107 a week.

ART DIRECTOR   Union weekly minimums: $1,420 for taped TV; $2,223.46 for film.

CAMERA OPERATOR   Union minimum: $1,583.20 per week.

COSTUMER   Union weekly minimums: costume designer, $1,583.53; assistant designer, $1,293; sketch artist, $986.39.

DIRECTOR   Union weekly minimums: for films, a range from $6,406 to $10,193, depending on the budget and type of film (fiction or documentary), but these minimums are for extremely low-budget films; top feature film directors earn salaries in the millions. For network prime-time TV, a range per week from $15,358 to $73,024, depending on the length of the show (from half-hour to two hours). For non-network, non-prime-time TV, the minimums run roughly two-thirds less.

DIRECTOR OF PHOTOGRAPHY   Union minimum: $2,514.97 per week.

EDITOR   Union weekly minimums: apprentice, $856.91; assistant editor, $1,153.97; animation editor, $1,173.20; trailer editor, $1,328.92; sound/music editor, $1,446.86.

ELECTRICIAN (GAFFER)   Union hourly minimums: construction, $27.43; maintenance, $24.13.

EXTRA   Union per day minimums: general, $79; special ability, $89; stand-in, $102; choreographed swimmers and skaters, $244.

GRIP   Union hourly minimum: $24.

PROP MASTER   Union weekly minimum: $1,672.14.

SET DECORATOR   Union weekly minimum: $1,706.14.

SOUND TECHNICIAN   Union weekly minimum: $1,836.10.

Union minimums are determined during contract negotiations between unions and employers, and represent the minimum rates employers must pay union personnel during production. Top professionals in certain categories often earn considerably more than union minimums. For example, a favorite makeup artist requested by a top Hollywood star can command up to $3,000 per day, and a few top directors now earn several million dollars per picture and sometimes a piece of the gross.

Me, Katharine Hepburn

Mommie Dearest, Christina Crawford

Movies, Mr. Griffith & Me, The, Lillian Gish (and Ann Pinchot)

My Autobiography, Charles Chaplin

Nazimova: A Biography, Gavin Lambert

Norma Jean: The Life of Marilyn Monroe, Fred Lawrence Guiles

Open Book, An, John Huston

Orson Welles: The Road to Xanadu, Simon Callow

Ovitz, Robert Slater

Palimpsest: A Memoir, Gore Vidal

Pickford: The Woman Who Made Hollywood, Eileen Whitfield

Public is Never Wrong, The, Adolph Zukor (with Dale Kraner)

Steven Spielberg: A Biography, Joseph McBride

Wired: The Short Life and Fast Times of John Belushi, Bob Woodward

Research Suggestion

If you are a fiction writer who intends to create a one-shot or series character who works at a particular Hollywood trade, you might consider subscribing to a trade journal related to that field, such as *Written By* (see "The Screenwriter's Union: The Writer's Guild of America" in chapter five) or *American Cinematographer* (listed among more general trade publications in chapter six). You might also consult *Writer's Market* (Writer's Digest Books), which is available in many bookstores, or any number of useful library references, such as the *Gale's Directory of Periodicals, Reader's Guide to Periodical Literature, Magazine Index, Business Periodicals Index* or the *Directory of Newsletters*. You could also contact one or more of the unions listed above and in the appendix to inquire about trade publications they might be familiar with or could recommend in their particular field.

CHAPTER FIVE

From Script to Screen: The Screenplay Trade

I t all starts with the script."

That's a saying one hears a lot in Hollywood, although it may pertain more to the making of motion pictures, where the original "property" is the key to getting a project going, than to television, which tends to package its show concepts around stars before the scripts start to roll in. That's why we'll focus more in this chapter on the feature film script, and the journey it takes from its conception as an idea to production, a hugely important process that involves not just writers but agents, producers, studio executives, directors, stars and countless others. (Television writing will be explored a bit further toward the end of this chapter.)

Another saying you often hear in and around L.A.: "Everybody's writing a damned screenplay in this town." Decades ago, it was the dream of millions to write the great American novel—the notion, held by so many, that "I know I've got one good novel in me." Today, it seems like everyone is sure they've got one big blockbuster movie inside them that will make them fabulously wealthy,

> 66The most important part in filmmaking is played by the writers. We must do everything in our power to keep them from finding out.99
> —STUDIO EXECUTIVE IRVING THALBERG

or just a wonderful story that will find immortality on the big screen. And maybe they do.

What they have to do to get that terrific idea to the shooting stage, however, is another story all in itself.

Where Movies Come From

Many feature films have their beginnings outside Hollywood channels: as novels, stage productions, articles and nonfiction books ("true stories"), and even as songs (*Ode to Billie Joe*, for example, or *Alice's Restaurant*.)

Movies can also first take shape as an idea in the imagination of a producer, director, actor or studio executive that is assigned to a writer for development into a full script, a process that often involves a number of steps: an outline, a treatment, and a first draft, which may be followed by a rewrite and a polish, or turned over to another writer or other writers for such revision. These "step deals" usually allow the producer to pull out of the deal and change writers after each completed step, or bail out of the project altogether.

Perhaps the single greatest source of viable movie ideas is the collective community of screenwriters, those men and women who have actually written a screenplay and probably number somewhere in the tens of thousands, from the least experienced novices to the most seasoned pros.

Sometimes, a less experienced writer with a strong writing sample or two will land a paying contract to develop his or her idea into a script, especially if they have a good agent representing them. More often, though, the unestablished writer will have to write an "original screenplay" purely on speculation, on their own and without any money guaranteed, a situation known as "writing on spec," or writing the "spec screenplay."

If that original screenplay proves to be a highly desirable property within the Hollywood marketplace, a so-called "hot property," it is potentially much more lucrative than one written on assignment, since it is owned solely by the writer and gives him or her more leverage in negotiating a deal.

The Hot and Cold Marketplace

As noted in chapters one and two, the studio system dominated moviemaking in Hollywood during its first five decades. Like actors and other above-the-line talent, many screenwriters worked on contract, typically being assigned to one project and another at the whim of the studio production chief, with little or no creative autonomy. As the studio system disintegrated, above-the-line talent gained more creative and career independence in a more open marketplace, screenwriters included.

In recent decades, the screenwriting marketplace has tended to run in cycles. Original screenplays, for example, dominated much of the screenplay trade during the 1970s and early 1980s, following what has been reported as the first million-dollar deal to screenwriter William Goldman for *Butch Cassidy and the Sundance Kid* (1969). A bidding frenzy by studios and producers, engineered by various agents, drove the average price of spec scripts up dramatically, with deals in the mid-to-high six figures becoming almost commonplace in the early 1980s. Soon, many producers were making deals with writers based solely on a verbal "pitch" of their idea (more on "pitching" later). When many of the resulting screenplays generated this way proved inferior, even unproducible, the trend of making deals strictly from pitches cooled down. In the mid-1980s, the hot property got hotter than ever, thanks in part to the huge success of *Lethal Weapon* (1987), written as an original screenplay ("on spec") by a young writer out of UCLA named Shane Black. A wave of deals for spec scripts followed, fed by a flood of original material written during the Writer's Guild strike of 1988, with a number of writers pulling down a million dollars or more per script. Leading the pack was a savvy veteran named Joe Eszterhas, whose agent peddled his script for *Basic Instinct* (released in 1992) for $3 million, driving prices to all-time highs. When a number of these seven-figure purchases failed to be produced or resulted in box-office disappointments, including Black's *The Last Boy Scout* (1991) and Eszterhas's *Showgirls* (1995), that cycle also waned, though spec scripts are still being written and sold for very good money.

Throughout the 1990s, faced with costly flops and a wildly unpredictable marketplace, producers have tended to rely increasingly on "safer" source material: sequels to hit movies, remakes of classics, movie spin-offs from vintage hit TV shows, successful stage plays and, particularly, best-selling or critically acclaimed novels. This demand by Hollywood for "audience-tested" material also produced its share of expensive failures, with much of the problem blamed on egomaniacal above-the-line talent, bloated budgets and a generalized greed that was sweeping the industry. For many, the film debacle of *Bonfire of the Vanities* (1990), for which the novel's author, Tom Wolfe, was paid $750,000 for the dramatic rights, served as a metaphor for an era of moviemaking driven by ego, star power and wanton spending. (For more, see *The Devil's Candy: "Bonfire of the Vanities" Goes to Hollywood*, by Julie Salamon.)

Yet as the decade drew toward its end, millions were still being spent for the film rights to books by the likes of John Grisham, Michael Crichton, Tom Clancy and Stephen King, as well as for "hot" books by lesser-known authors.

Who adapts all this literary material for the screen? Generally, established screenwriters or newcomers with extremely strong sample scripts, which brings us back to another old Hollywood saying: "Your best script will probably never get made, but it could keep you working for years."

Making the Pitch

A "pitch" is a verbal presentation of a screenwriter's story, usually made to a producer or development executive or a combination of one or more of these people, in a scheduled "pitch meeting" that customarily takes place in the producer's or development person's office (though it can also be done on the wing, at a party or other social event, depending on one's connections and chutzpah).

Many producers prefer to hear a writer pitch to cut down on their reading time and to get a sense of the writer's personality, passion for his or her material, and level of professionalism (including grooming and general appearance, and what it might reveal about the writer). Pitching, therefore, is something of a craft in itself—numerous how-to books and workshops are devoted to it—and has become an integral part of the screenplay trade.

Pitching is essentially a sales job in which the writer attempts to interest or hook a producer fairly quickly, then spin the tale in a compelling manner, creating a sense of vivid main characters, their motivations and goals, key subplots or subtext, and hitting the major plot points ("turning points") within the story line, all performed with a sense of pace, timing and dramatic flair. Some writers are better at pitching than writing and vice versa. Many writers rehearse their pitches, much as actors rehearse a scene, and may use a tape recorder or a partner for feedback. Some prefer to "set up" their pitch with a "logline" description— a one-line story summary—while others choose to build the drama and suspense as they go rather than give too much away at the outset. Pitching styles are as varied as the personalities of the writers themselves, although succinctness and brevity are important, with five to fifteen minutes a common range.

The pitch meeting is both a coveted and dreaded event, an opportunity to interest a producer and initiate a deal but also a chance to strike out professionally, at least on this occasion. Going into a meeting, many writers like to have half a dozen story ideas or more fully developed in the event that one or more of their pitches fails to generate interest or proves to be too similar to a project the producer already has in the works. Ideally, for self-protection, the writer has developed these ideas at least in outline or treatment form and registered them with the Library of Congress (copyright) or the Writer's Guild of America (script registration), should any future legal questions arise regarding plagiarism or theft of idea. Some writers, however, do not bother to do this at this stage, and simply take their chances with the system.

Producers have notoriously short attention spans, especially for poorly presented pitches or story concepts they quickly realize they have no interest in. Some are more patient and considerate and will assist a screenwriter by holding phone calls, remaining attentive and even asking pertinent questions along the way. Others can quickly become fidgety, their eyes glazing over, or will rudely cut a writer off in midsentence and tell him or her to move on to the next idea or simply end the meeting altogether.

Perhaps the two worst mistakes a screenwriter can make in a pitch meeting are coming in with nascent, half-baked ideas and being long-winded. It's a sure way to turn a producer off, lower the stature of the writer in the eyes of his or her agent (who will invariably hear how the meeting went), and possibly close the door to that producer for future pitch sessions. If the pitch goes well, however, and the producer comes away from the meeting revved up for a particular concept, it could be the starting point of a lucrative writing deal, and with some luck, a completed feature film a year or two down the line.

Robert Altman's film *The Player* (1992), based on Michael Tolkin's novel and screenplay, presents a darkly comic look at Hollywood, and includes a "pitching" scene revolving around a frustrated but ambitious screenwriter and an incredibly shallow, superficial producer. While there is definitely some truth in this scene about the kind of mental shorthand and crass conceptualizing that can go on in these meetings, the reality is that pitch meetings are as varied as the screenwriters and producers themselves, which is all over the map.

I will offer three examples from my own experience, from pitch meetings (1) at the major studio level; (2) at a small production company with one well-received studio picture to its credit; and (3) with an experienced line producer hoping to move up to the level of full-fledged producer by acquiring a marketable script.

1. My partner and I met two high-level development executives at a major studio in a quiet, comfortable office on the lot; they were white males, in shirt and tie, cleancut, mid-thirties. My partner (there as the potential producer behind the script) and I sat in chairs facing the two execs as they sat in their chairs, with

glasses of cold bottled water provided by a secretary. The mood was generally amiable, if a bit awkward, though not tense. In this case, we were there to pitch one particular idea and, as the writer, I began the spiel. Our story was a romantic comedy, essentially straight but with strong gay overtones revolving around a zany situation of mistaken identity, and I did my best to tell it briskly and in entertaining fashion; if I faltered, my partner jumped in to help me out.

During my pitch, the executive facing me on the left smiled a lot, laughed now and then, and frequently nodded his head, indicating his approval. Once, thankfully, he burst out laughing when I hit the story's visual and comedic high point. In the end, he asked us a few questions to clarify story and character points, made a couple of suggestions and told us he thought the concept had possibilities, despite its sympathetic gay slant, which was not considered particularly marketable at the time. The other executive, the son of a very prominent producer and studio executive, remained dour and downbeat throughout the pitch; he never smiled, laughed or asked a single question, and would not have been out of place at a funeral. When my pitch was done, he said, perfunctorily, "I'll be frank. I don't like taking risks, and I don't believe the movie marketplace is a place to take risks. My idea of a good concept is *The Problem Child*." (The latter was a reference to a moderately budgeted film with a clear, if simplistic concept that was a surprising hit in 1990, though panned by many critics as crude and sophomoric.) The first executive then thanked us for coming in and told us he would get back to us. He did, a few days later, explaining that the idea was not "quite right" for the studio at this time.

2. I met with a producer and his partner, a former high-level agent, in their modest, cluttered offices; both were middle-aged men, extremely intelligent and fair-minded, with considerable industry experience and success behind them in other roles, although as producers, they had only one small feature film and one or two cable movies to their credit. I was alone this time, pitching several ideas; my best story among the bunch, I felt, was a dark suspense thriller that included strong romantic and action subplots, based on an original screenplay I was then rewriting. During my pitch, the two men were extremely attentive, frequently breaking in to ask questions and becoming more and more excited as the story progressed.

At the end of the pitch, we had a deal. After the money issues were worked out separately, they optioned my screenplay, and later exercised their option for a second term, making another payment, although the film was never produced.

3. I met with a man of foreign background in his comfortable home near Mullholand Drive, a legendary mountain ridge road with views of Hollywood on one side and the San Fernando Valley on the other. Then in his late thirties, he had served as a line producer and in other below-the-line producer functions on a number of moderately budgeted feature films, but wanted very much to be a true producer, rather than just a hired hand. I pitched a new story I had come up with, and which my partner (who had set up the meeting and was there as the potential coproducer) felt was my most commercial and surefire concept yet. Because the story was a complicated cat-and-mouse thriller with a stunning twist at the end, I had gone so far as to sketch out the major plot points and act breaks on paper in the form of a diagrammed arc, showing exactly how everything fit together and worked out.

The three of us sat on deep sofas in the line producer's living room, sipping wine and eating fruit and cheese; with us was a director who had already heard the basic premise as a logline description, and was sufficiently intrigued to hear the whole pitch. Assisted by my partner, I pitched with confidence and enthusiasm, and both the producer and director became equally excited. Out of the pitch meeting came a deal for me to be paid a flat fee to write the script, my first such deal, with payments worked out for a rewrite, polish and bonus payments if the film ever went to production, calibrated to the size of the final budget. A few days later, before a deal memo was issued to formalize things, the producer was offered a job with a small but up-and-coming television and film production company to head their feature film department. The company was not willing to pay me to write the script, as the producer had been; they wanted me to write it for free, on spec. I declined, and my concept remains on the back burner, like thousands of other viable ideas in Tinseltown.

The Life of the Struggling Screenwriter

As we mentioned in the previous chapter, what writers do for a living until they break into the industry has little or no bearing on their chances for success. A few successful screenwriters, in fact, have come to the trade after serving lengthy prison terms, using their lives of crime and punishment as source material for their scripts.

Ironically, those screenwriting excons had a certain advantage: by being incarcerated, they had plenty of "free" time on their hands to practice the craft, probably the most precious commodity to the screenwriting novice. Many would-be screenwriters have the notion that writing screenplays is easy (just a bunch of dialogue and action), or that they will land a lucrative screenwriting assignment because they've got a terrific idea for a movie. What they learn, in due time, is (1) they must write one or more quality spec scripts to have something to sell or as a sample of their talent, and (2) that screenwriting is considerably more difficult than it appears, demanding special skills and techniques unique to the craft of visual storytelling.

Very few, if any, screenwriters sell the first screenplay they write. More often, they write half a dozen or more as they develop a sense of the structure, pacing, use of scene "beats," effective dialogue and other techniques required of the medium. Sylvester Stallone became a superstar writer-actor-producer "overnight" when he appeared in *Rocky* (1976), which he also wrote; what many don't realize is that Stallone had written nearly three dozen scripts before he sold that first one. When asked the secret to becoming a successful screenwriter, writer-director Oliver Stone replied simply: "Keep your butt in the chair!" Another frequently heard adage: "You don't get paid to write—you get paid to *rewrite*."

Here are some other patterns and hard truths one often observes in the daily life of the struggling screenwriter.

Most screenwriters get their first breaks while living in L.A. It's extremely difficult to make the needed contacts and get one's material seriously considered while residing far from the center of the action, though a few have managed it. Even those successful "outsiders," however, must at some point come to L.A. to establish connections and get a sense of how Hollywood operates.

Many successful screenwriters are self-taught. Although many successful film and television writers come from film-TV schools, perhaps just as many learn the craft on their own, or develop it as an adjunct to another writing discipline, such as novels, plays or narrative journalism. Thousands seek the tutelage of self-proclaimed screenwriting teachers, who now comprise a cottage industry of their own. Another side industry: screenwriting how-to books and software programs. (See "Training Grounds: Where Screenwriters Study" on page 136.)

Writing is only half the game in La-La Land—the more successful screenwriters learn early on to socialize, network and take care of business. Some enjoy it, most don't. This daunting, sometimes demoralizing activity includes: selling yourself and your work to agents if you can get through to them; pitching to producers, if you or your agent can set you up with them; partying and schmoozing; handling Hollywood double-talk and deception; being well down the power scale and often treated with disrespect; and on and on. It is not a trade for the meek and overly sensitive.

Above all, one's material must get exposure to the right people. As one producer once told a gathering of aspiring screenwriters, "Unless you get your work to us and somehow get us to read it, we don't know you exist." To get noticed, frustrated screenwriters have held open readings of their work at cafes, or sent their scripts to production offices and agencies accompanied by boxes of expensive chocolates or other gifts. One aspiring scriptwriter turned her screenplay into a glossy folio that resembled a fancy magazine, and distributed it free to the offices of agents and producers, hoping they would open it up and start reading. Another adapted his screenplay into a stage play and mounted it at an Equity Waiver house, inviting producers to attend free—at a personal cost of $50,000! Then there is the long-circulating story of the comedy writer who was determined to get his screenplay read by Mel Brooks. Somehow he unearthed the filmmaker's home address and had his script delivered to Brooks's front door by a voluptuous young woman, who was topless. As legend has it, the usually jocular Brooks was not amused and did not accept the script.

By far the best way to get a script read by an agent is through a referral by a client or business associate of that agent. Again, networking—in classes, writer's conferences, seminars, film organizations and the like—can be a crucial career activity.

Right or wrong, youth is a valued asset. "Ageism is rampant," writes Del Reisman, former president of the Writer's Guild of America, west. "It is virtually institutionalized."

Very few screenwriters become established in middle age, and there have been instances of sixtyish screenwriters with distinguished track records overlooked for writing assignments specifically because they were considered too old for the job. (White hair is widely considered a serious career liability.) There is a widespread perception, especially among younger production executives, that older screenwriters are out of touch with and lack the sensibility to handle the youthful subject matter that dominates the feature film marketplace, where most of the ticketbuyers are under thirty-five. Reisman's own reasoning: "Young executives at studios and networks frequently are uncomfortable working with men and women who come from their parents' or even their grandparents' generation."

Whatever the cause, many agents feel it is more difficult to "sell" clients past forty who are not already well known, and see a writer's chances of sustaining a long-range Hollywood career diminishing at that point, whatever the level of their talent. When the WGA studied this situation some years ago, one agent privately admitted that he had decided against signing a talented new writer because the agency had a policy against taking on new clients over forty. (For more on this issue, see "Ageism and 'The Graylist'" in chapter eight.)

Rejection and creative frustration are endemic to the trade. Most screenplays that get written never get sold or optioned. Most that get sold or optioned never get produced. Most that get produced are first rewritten extensively by one or more other writers (or producers, directors, actors). Virtually all films are then further changed during the postproduction editing phase, and again during final editing, sometimes at the behest of the studio marketing department.

Clearly, screenwriting is not a medium for the writer who toils to see his or her story and vision reach the audience intact, as with publishing and the theater; it is a medium for the writer who is willing to sell away his or her work to others, who will then change it as they see fit (unless, of course, the writer is also the producer and/or director). In truth, most successful film and television writers spend their entire careers in relative obscurity, churning out scripts that directors and producers may consider little more than blueprints or outlines, suitable for massive revision. *Most screenwriters, in fact, make their livings not by selling original screenplays, but by rewriting the scripts of others, just as their own are being rewritten by someone else.* Even when the original writer is lucky enough to be kept on the project, it can be an arduous experience. Mike Werb and Michael Colleary, for example, who wrote the original screenplay for the 1997 futuristic thriller *Face/ Off,* describe the script's evolution this way: "*Face/Off*'s journey to the screen took almost seven years. In that time, we worked with two studios, three directors, fourteen producers, two dozen executives and wrote more than thirty drafts. We never left the project and continued writing and rewriting through postproduction."

The fact is, most aspiring screenwriters never achieve success, if success can be measured in terms of making a comfortable living consistently over many years. Many sell options on one or two original screenplays, or land a few rewrite assignments, but find that their careers never quite take off from there (as in my case). Many more never sell a thing or earn a dime. Most get burned out or simply give up after a few years and leave town, or move into related fields, such as writing for television, videos, commercials, animated cartoons, CD-ROMs and the like, or take publicity jobs.

That is not to show disrespect toward any of these fields, all of which demand their own kind of professionalism and craftsmanship, and in which many screenwriters get their starts. It's just that in Tinseltown, almost every writer secretly dreams of writing movies.

Training Grounds: Where Screenwriters Study

There are now so many aspirants to the screenwriting trade that an entire cottage industry has developed in Los Angeles (and elsewhere) offering to teach them how to write screenplays. These educational opportunities range from lofty university programs with rigorous qualifying standards to scam artists masquerading as experienced screenwriters or producers who prey on the naive dreamer. This wide-ranging group includes the following.

Film Schools

The two leading TV-cinema schools in the Los Angeles area are at the private and expensive University of Southern California (USC) and the public and more affordable University of California at Los Angeles (UCLA); both have turned out many of Hollywood's leading screenwriters, directors and producers. Richard Walter is currently the colorful cochair (with Lew Hunter) of the UCLA School of Film and Television, dubbed by *Variety* "the Jewish mother of screenwriting" because of his personal Hollywood connections and the many careers he has nurtured among his own students while they were still enrolled in his classes. USC takes a different approach, with guidelines that prohibit instructors from putting students in touch with the industry prior to graduation, considering it a potential conflict of interest and detriment to serious study.

USC also runs a noted business graduate school for aspiring producers, the Richard Stark Producer's Program. At UCLA Extension, the university's continuing education arm, the Writers' Program offers a wide range of television and screenwriting classes taught by professional writers, as well as its annual Diane Thomas Screenwriting Award, named in memory of a former student who died not long after writing the original screenplay for *Romancing the Stone*. A number of other colleges in the area also offer classes and/or degrees in film and TV writing, and the American Film Institute and the Sundance Film Institute both offer highly respected screenwriting programs. On the East Coast, New York University offers a highly regarded film program. In between, across the country, dozens of film schools turn out thousands of would-be screenwriters and filmmakers every year. (See also "Schools and Study Programs" in Appendix B.)

Screenwriting teachers. A number of individuals in Hollywood have carved lucrative niches for themselves by offering weekly classes or weekend workshops, lecturing large groups of people on how to write screenplays. Their emphasis, not surprisingly, is on the understanding and craft of screenplay structure. A few of these "screenwriting gurus" have legions of satisfied students, including many very successful writers and producers who testify to their teaching skills and value to the screenplay trade. I've personally met or observed many of these teachers in action, and certain traits seem to be shared by several of the better-known, including a penchant for self-promotion, an arrogant and self-important manner and a tendency to inflate their own screenwriting credits. One refers to himself as a "screenwriter" in his promotional material, but lists no specific credits, a dead giveaway that he has little or nothing to list. Another claims to have "sold" nearly a dozen screenplays over the years, when, in fact, most of those were actually *options* going back many years and all unproduced. Still another boasts to audiences that his is the superior "method" for creating the ideal movie screenplay, although his own (rather paltry) credits are limited to TV. Teaching in this area can be quite profitable: Robert McKee, one of the best known and most highly regarded, has become a millionaire lecturing to several thousand students annually at (currently) $450 a head, while still nurturing his hopes of one day seeing a screenplay of his own produced.

Workshops. A number of unaccredited film writing programs offer courses for aspiring screenwriters, such as the Hollywood Film Institute, Writer's Boot Camp and the Writer's Connection. Many others have come and gone.

Minority and writing intern programs. Various guilds, studios and TV networks offer programs to train and encourage access to women, African-Americans, Hispanics and members of other minority groups (for a list of minority organizations in Hollywood, see chapter eight).

Instructional books. Hundred of books have been written on the craft of storytelling in general, and screen and TV writing in particular, and they sell faster in L.A. than chicken-and-bean burritos. But one sees a number of key books again and again on the desks and bookshelves of ambitious screenwriters around town. They include *The Art of Dramatic Writing*, by Lajos Egri; *The Hero With a Thousand Faces*, by Joseph Campbell; *Screenwriting Tricks of the Trade*, by William Froug; *Adventures in the Screen Trade*, by William Goldman; *Techniques of Screen and Television Writing*, by Eugene Vale; *Writing the Script*, by Wells Root; *Screenplay*, by Syd Field; *Making a Good Script Great*, by Linda Seger; *Lew Hunter's Screenwriting 434*, by Lew Hunter; *Screenwriting: The Art*,

Craft and Business of Film and Television Writing, by Richard Walter; *Story*, by Robert McKee.

Software programs. Dozens of computer software programs are now on the market to assist writers in formatting their screenplays, offering plot inspiration, or otherwise improving content and quality. Among them: Scriptor, Collaborator, Final Draft, Movie Master, Movie Magic Screenwriter, Scriptware, Script Thing, Script Wizard.

From Submission to Production

Each year in Hollywood, thousands of scripts are submitted to producers, mostly by agents. Into each production office come hundreds, sometimes thousands of these submissions.

Those sent by the more respected or successful agents generally get read first, but producers try to respond to *all* agented submissions, since their relationships with agents is crucial to their receiving a continual flow of material. Few producers accept submissions directly from writers for two reasons: taking submissions only through agents enables producers to screen out the weaker material, and it protects them from possible later charges of idea theft or plagiarism. Even those producers who say they will read unsolicited submissions tend to put them aside in a slush pile where they remain unread for weeks, months—sometimes forever. (Many agents do the same with scripts that come in without a referral from a top client.) Most producers who accept unsolicited submissions will require the writer to sign a release form or waiver, which absolves the company from any obligation to read or return the material and limits their liability in any possible future legal actions regarding a similar project they might produce.

How these scripts are physically handled varies from office to office. Some offices are well-organized, with efficient database systems for logging and filing incoming material and moving it through the reading process, from readers to development executives to producers at the top, if the script should get that far. Other offices, particularly the smaller, financially marginal operations, are often sloppy and inconsiderate in dealing with submissions, sometimes literally stacking them up willy nilly on side tables, or tossing them into cardboard boxes in corners, where they get read in no particular order, if they get read at all.

The more professional and efficient production companies prioritize incoming material for reading and try to respond within two weeks. With the majority of these companies, a script or other property will pass through a number of steps.

Coverage

A "reader" reads the script and prepares a "reader's report," or "coverage." The coverage customarily identifies the script by genre; compresses the story line to a logline description; provides a plot synopsis and thumbnail descriptions of the main characters; offers a fairly detailed evaluation of the material (usually a page); and may include a final set of evaluation boxes to check, such as *recommend*, *maybe* and *pass*, or even a place to recommend the writer for an availability file or assignment on another project if the material shows strengths in a particular area (structure or dialogue, for example). The exact nature and format of the reader's report will vary from company to company, as will the individual reader's influence in how a script is received higher up, but most readers' reports serve only as the first stopping off point for a script.

This may seem to diminish the purpose and importance of the reader's work, but in a busy production office, studio or agency, it is vital for both legal and administrative reasons. It provides development executives with a concise, efficient way to track and deal with the constant flow of written material, and well-organized records of when it was received, who read it and responded to it, and when it was returned, should that ever become an issue down the road. (Plagiarism and copyright infringement lawsuits are common in the movie industry. Most of these lawsuits are dismissed, and most of the rest are settled for relatively small sums out of court. Now and then, however, writers who feel their story lines have been unfairly ripped off bring strong, well-documented cases, prove them in court, and win sizable settlements, sometimes in the millions of dollars in the cases of very successful films. These are generally paid, at least in part, by special studio insurance policies.)

The Next Reading

Readers come in all types, from envious and mean-spirited to intelligent and fair; some will never amount to much career-wise, while others will go on to be top development executives, producers, agents or even screenwriters. Development executives are aware of this disparity in the quality of reader coverage and read it accordingly, rarely accepting a reader's evaluation at face value. The development executive is primarily looking for a *type* of story the company might be interested in that looks reasonably well-written in the reader's eyes. If the reader's report indicates a script is not remotely something that would interest the company—a dark, erotic thriller submitted to a company that produces light-hearted family films, for example—the development person may not bother to read the script. Good production companies try to have *every* submission read beyond the entry-level reader stage, although some busy executives sometimes rely on coverage or a development person's evaluation in lieu of actually reading the script, even when negotiating for it. (I once saw this happen right before my eyes with coverage I had written, as my boss paraphrased my evaluation over the phone as if the words were his own.)

The Story Meeting

The better readers are both literate and understand the movie marketplace, and are thrilled when they find that gem of a script among the hundreds of mediocre or inferior screenplays they must read. They know that writing good coverage on a script that eventually is purchased and becomes a hit movie can be important to their careers. (Many others, of course, are timid and weak-willed, fearful of recommending a script the boss might not like.) In some companies, a reader will be in a position to champion a script he or she particularly likes in a "story meeting." In turn, a development executive will take up the cause for a particular script he or she favors, supporting and "selling" it to the upper executives, both for the desire to develop a good movie and the career advancement that is built on such successful choices.

The Pass Stage

The fate of many scripts is decided in the story meeting, where scripts are either retained for further reading, discussion and possible deal-making (the lucky few), or rejected outright (the great majority). Scripts are turned down either by phone (the "telephone pass") or mail (the "pass letter"). As a rule, producers try to pass on projects gently, out of kindness using euphemisms and vague excuses rather than the truth, but also to avoid alienating agents or writers they may want to work with again. (Rarely will a copy of a reader's report reach the hands of the agent or writer, unless through close inside contacts.) It is then up to the agent or writer to try to get another reading for the script from another producer (or the agent of a star who might be interested, if that's warranted). These meetings tend to be held in a room convenient for all, and move along at a fairly brisk pace, since everyone in Hollywood is always behind schedule (especially in their reading), late for the next appointment, or coming in late from the last one.

Worth noting: In Hollywood, meetings are cancelled or postponed by over-scheduled executives almost as often as they are announced.

140

The Deal Memo

If a company decides it wants to become involved with a particular property—treatment, original screenplay, published novel—negotiations take place between the production company and, ideally, the agent and/or lawyer representing the writer. These meetings range from easy and cordial to tense and filled with a certain amount of gamesmanship and tough talk. Frequently, there is a lot of give and take regarding money, guaranteed rewrite fees, net point participation and the like, as producers try to hammer out the best deal they can for themselves and agents try to do the same for their clients. (For an inexperienced writer to negotiate with a producer is like a minnow sitting down for lunch with a great white shark. Ideally, writers will focus on the creative aspects of a writer-producer relationship and leave the dirtier business of deal-making to agents and lawyers, which is what they get paid to handle. As a rule, writers try to *never* talk money with their producers.)

If negotiations are successfully concluded, the producers will either "option" the property for a specific period (usually six months or a year, with clauses for option renewal) or purchase it outright. The producer's lawyers will then issue a "deal memo," a shortened version of the proposed contract, which serves as a legal contract until the more detailed contract can be worked out and drawn up, something that may take months. In some cases, with a less-established writer, the producer will seek a "free option," working with the writer on a handshake basis, with no money changing hands, to see if a viable script comes out of it that mutually benefits both parties. (For an excellent and highly detailed breakdown of this entire process, see *The Hollywood Job-Hunter's Survival Guide*, listed with other recommended books on page 148.)

With a "done deal," the property now goes into development.

In Development

Depending on the terms of the deal, the writer can either be dismissed and replaced by another writer at this point, or, more likely, be retained for at least one rewrite of the script (*every* script will be rewritten to some extent) that often begins with an "outline" or "treatment" for the proposed new draft. Typically, this process will not proceed easily, with the script moving quickly and smoothly toward production. More likely, the property will enter into what is known in Hollywood as "development hell," a period of many months or even years that involves creative meetings with the producer on changes or new directions for the screenplay, notes (comments and suggestions on the script) from the

141

producer or development executives, input from stars who may become attached and then unattached to the project, and so on. It is common during this period for the writer to work with an assigned development executive, who serves as a creative guide and liaison for the above-the-line talent involved on the project. It is also quite common for the producer to drop the original writer along the way, replacing him or her with a writer the producer feels might handle revisions more productively, or bring in a specialty "script doctor" to work on specific areas of the script, such as dialogue or action scenes. (For a deeper and more detailed look at this process, see John Gregory Dunne's nonfiction account, *Monster*.)

For many writers, development hell is an exasperating, even humiliating process, as they attempt to give the producers what they want, while trying to salvage their own creative vision and personal integrity. Writers frequently blame insensitive or semiliterate producers and studio executives ("suits") for much of their misery. Some years ago, for example, a well-known novelist who also worked in films found himself in a high-level meeting with a production executive at a major studio, listening to the exec complain about his adaptation of a famous novel the studio had purchased. As the "suit" railed on about all of the problems in the script and how it failed to reflect the quality of the book, the writer began to suspect the executive had read neither the novel nor his screenplay, but was relying solely on a reader's coverage. He tested the executive by asking if he felt such-and-such a character in the script needed more work, naming a character that did not actually exist. When the executive replied enthusiastically in the affirmative, the frustrated writer stood up and screamed, "You have the cranial development of an eggplant!" He was escorted off the lot and told never to return; the movie has yet to be made.

Some development situations proceed more productively, however, and result in a screenplay the studio green lights for production.

Preproduction

It is during this stage that most of the hiring is done, from the director and cast (the above-the-line talent) to the key members of the production crew (the below-the-line talent), as described in chapter four. Just because a project goes into preproduction is no guarantee it will ever reach its projected start date. Signing the right cast members is particularly crucial and may hinge on yet more script revisions, and countless other vagaries of the marketplace. While development hell is a drawn-out, agonizing process that tests patience, preproduction is a tense period in which the studio can suddenly pull the plug, shutting the project down. Countless screenwriters have seen their projects on the brink of production, only to have a star pull out of the project (or even die), a new studio chief take over and cancel the movie at the last minute, and so on. Since the most successful screenwriting careers are built on a succession of produced movies with a hit now and then along the way, getting that first script into production can literally make or break a career, especially if it goes on to become a critical or box-office hit.

In Production

If everything falls into place, the movie goes into production. The original writer may or may not still be involved at that point. Depending on the deal, if the writer is due production bonus money—significant payments hinging on the start of production—that money becomes due the first day the cameras roll. Some writers are welcome on the set and may be involved with revisions all the way through production. Others may be less welcome or even banished from the set and any involvement, depending on their relationship with the producer and other above-the-line talent at that point. Many directors are uncomfortable having the original writer around, particularly if other writers have been brought in for revisions, which is so often the case.

If a writer is lucky enough (or wants) to be invited on the set, he or she is likely to be treated with an indifference bordering on disrespect (though this varies from production to production). At this point, the director is in charge of an enormous, mutating, nearly unmanageable enterprise, and writers are often looked upon as nuisances and distractions. Screenwriters lucky enough to still be involved at the production stage learn to stay out of the way and to speak only when it's necessary—at least until they become big shots, at which point they will probably be producers themselves.

The Screenwriter's Union: The Writers Guild of America

The eight-thousand-member Writers Guild of America, with branches on the West and East Coasts, is a labor union that represents film and TV writers as well as writers in other new, emerging technologies.

The WGA has its origins in the Screen Writers Guild, a social club formed in 1921 by motion picture writers. In the 1930s, its members began to address such issues as the protection of writers' rights and economic conditions.

Following the 1937 Supreme Court decision upholding the constitutionality of the National Labor Relations Act, the guild became certified as the collective bargaining agent of all motion picture writers and began collective bargaining with producers in 1939. Over the next fifteen years, the guild went through various organizational changes and became affiliated with guilds representing writers in other mediums, such as radio and television. It finally set up dual branches in 1954, as the Writers Guild of America, west, and the Writers Guild of America, East, with the Mississippi River serving as the jurisdictional dividing line.

The WGA is an extremely active and powerful organization that at times has gone on strike against the producers over wages and other issues, forcing producers to the negotiating table (the last time in 1988). It is considered to have one of the most attractive wage and benefits packages among the entertainment industry unions. WGA wage minimums are based on such factors as the length, format (half hour, hour and so on), medium of distribution (network, syndication, cable, feature film), budget range and other factors; the breakdown is complicated. If you need current minimums for your research, contact the WGA.

Among the other WGA member services are the monitoring, collection and distribution of millions of dollars of residuals (payments for the reuse of film and TV programs) annually; the determination of writing credits for feature films and TV shows; and the enforcement of rights set forth in labor agreements with production companies, as well as individual contracts. The WGA also sponsors many writer-related events throughout the year, including seminars and panel discussions, and actively works on the behalf of writers in the areas of legislation, international agreements and public relations.

There is a common misconception that a writer must be a member of the WGA to sell a screenplay or work within the industry. This is not the case; virtually every day, non-WGA writers sell or option scripts or get hired for writing assignments or staff jobs. However, one must join the guild to take advantage of many of its benefits. To qualify for membership, a writer must earn twenty-four units of credits during a three-year period, based on work completed under contract or upon the sale or licensing of original written material with a company that has signed a WGA Collective Bargaining Agreement. For example, the sale of a feature length screenplay to a guild signatory company is worth twenty-four units, a rewrite earns twelve units, a polish three units and so on.

Membership in the guild hardly guarantees wealth and success. Only one percent of the WGAw's membership, for example, consistently earns more than a million dollars a year, and half the active members make less than $75,000 annually. Many members make only a marginal living, if that.

Among the WGA's other services, available to both members and nonmembers:

- A script registration service that provides a dated record of the writer's claim to authorship of a particular piece of material should any issues arise concerning ownership or originality. The WGAw registers some thirty thousand scripts and treatments each year; members, $10 per registration; nonmembers, $20 (213/782-4540).

- A variety of programs designed to encourage access and career opportunities for writers who are African-American, Latino, Asian/Pacific Islander, American Indian, women, over forty, disabled or freelance (213/ 782-4648).

- An agency list to assist writers in contacting literary agents who have signed the WGA Agency Agreement (cost by mail, $2.50; 213/782-4502).

- The James R. Webb Memorial Library, which houses a large collection of scripts, videotapes, books, photos and other items related to the screenwriting trade, is open to the public for research purposes Monday to Friday, 10 A.M. to 5 P.M. (closed for lunch 12:30 to 1:30 P.M.). Located at the new WGAw headquarters (see address below) (213/782-4544).

- A monthly magazine, *Written By*, which includes interviews with noted member screenwriters, writing tips, guild news and other features of interest to scriptwriters. (For subscription information, call the toll-free number: 888-WRITNBY).

- A World Wide Web Site (http://www.wga.org) with WGA news, writing tips, interviews and so on.

- For a free WGA *general information booklet*, which includes a list of other WGA informational publications and their prices, as well as details on all of the above subject areas, contact the WGAw, 7000 West Third St., Los Angeles, CA 90048. (213/782-4500); fax (213/782-4803).

Writing for TV

One often hears that breaking into feature film writing, as much of a challenge as it is, is fundamentally easier than getting a foothold in network TV. This is due in part to the sudden career cache that can come with a single, sought-after screenplay, and also because of the unique technical demands of the TV medium.

The great bulk of TV movies, for example, are assigned to established writers

HOLLYWOOD'S GREATEST STUNTS

Timing Sheet

Show #202 / 58081 / EP #5

	ITEM	ITEM RUN	ACT RUN	SHOW RUN	office use
	ACT ONE				
1	COLD OPEN	0:01:12	0:01:12	0:01:12	
2	MAIN TITLES	0:00:25	0:01:37	0:01:37	
3	TERMINATOR2/SCARECROW & MRS. KING	0:08:24	0:10:01	0:10:01	
4	TEASE/BUMPER	0:00:12	0:10:13	0:10:13	
	BREAK ONE				
5	*COMMERCIAL POSITION #1*	0:03:00	0:03:00	0:13:13	
	ACT TWO				
6	AGAINST ALL ODDS/RACE TRAILERS/	0:09:13	0:12:13	0:22:26	
	MAKING OF GRAND PRIX/FIT FOR A KING				
7	TEASE/BUMPER	0:00:10	0:12:23	0:22:36	
	BREAK TWO				
8	*COMMERCIAL POSITION #2*	0:02:30	0:02:30	0:25:06	
	ACT THREE				
9	RETROACTIVE	0:08:05	0:08:05	0:33:11	
10	TEASE/BUMPER	0:00:11	0:08:16	0:33:22	
	BREAK THREE				
11	*COMMERCIAL POSITION #3*	0:02:00	0:02:00	0:35:22	
	ACT FOUR				
12	ADRENALIN	0:06:00	0:06:00	0:41:22	
13	TEASE/BUMPER	0:00:13	0:06:13	0:41:35	
	BREAK FOUR				
14	*COMMERCIAL POSITION #4*	0:03:30	0:03:30	0:45:05	
	ACT FIVE				
15	BLOODMOON/HONG KONG STUNTMEN/	0:09:15	0:09:15	0:54:20	
	OLD MOTORCYCLE STUNTS				
16	TEASE/BUMPER	0:00:10	0:09:25	0:54:30	
	BREAK FIVE				
17	*COMMERCIAL POSITION #5*	0:01:45	0:01:45	0:56:15	
	ACT SIX				
18	WRAP/FLED	0:03:08	0:03:08	0:59:23	
19	CREDITS/LOGOS	0:00:30	0:03:38	0:59:53	
	TOTAL RUNNING TIME			0:59:53	
	TARGETS - PROGRAM 47:00 - TRT 59:45				
	ACT 1 MUST END 8:00 - 18:00				
	ACT 4 MUST END 37:30 - 47:30				

10/29/96   3:59 AM

This is a typical timing sheet used by writers, producers, directors and editors to plan and time a television show. The timing sheet is a crucial document during the final editing phase.

who have demonstrated a proficiency for handling the formulaic structure required for made-for-TV movies (multiple act breaks for commercials). Most of these writers work their way up from dramatic episodic writing and understand the special demands of the medium; one sees many of the same names again and again in made-for-TV movie credits.

Most of the network TV writing assignments, of course, are in the series format. A series writer is hired by a story editor or producer who has read samples of the writer's work, and feels he or she is particularly well-suited to write for that show's situation and established characters. These samples usually come to the producer through an agent, though not always.

Frequently, the writer is first asked to pitch ideas for episodes. If the producer or story editor likes an idea, the writer is usually assigned to develop it into a story outline, then a treatment and, if it reaches that stage, a script. This is a "step" process carefully structured under Writer's Guild guidelines, with payments due at each step. Obviously, if a writer is working for a non-network, nonguild show, and there are many, the union rules do not apply and financial arrangements have to be worked out show to show, company to company, project to project.

When hired, the writer becomes part of a team of writers who develop and write individual episodes, or segments within episodes (in the case of reality and documentary programs). Frequently, series writers are also the producers of the show, with a great deal of creative control as well as a sizable financial stake in writer payments and residuals. Consequently, finding an open, nonstaff position on a series TV show has become extremely competitive, and the freelance (nonstaff) series writer something of an endangered species. Because a TV series depends on its consistency from week to week for its success, it demands an extremely cooperative spirit and resilient personality on the part of the show's writers.

"All scripts are tabled," explain the authors of *All You Need to Know About the Movie and TV Business*, "i.e., literally brought to a big table with regular series writers and producers and eventually the actors. The script is read in this open forum and 'improved' by the input of everyone at the table."

In addition to the unique technical and structural aspects of series TV writing and the team approach inherent in the work, a television writer must also learn to handle the varying demands of stars, producers, directors, network executives, advertisers, outside pressure groups and others who influence or attempt to influence a show's content. And all this must be done under the most demanding time pressures. It is not uncommon on a situation comedy, for example, for revisions to be made right up to the start of a live taping, with more revisions hastily scribbled during the dinner break before the second taped performance. Series writers, it is said, learn to eat, sleep and live with the show during its production months, although they are extremely well paid for their long hours, with top writers earning $200,000 to $300,000 for a season's work, not counting the lucrative future residuals.

At times, weekly television production takes on a factorylike feel, with scripts and shows being churned out on the series assembly line, and original material so rehashed by so many writers as to be almost unrecognizable by the time the show airs.

Recommended Books on How Hollywood Works

At this point, you've worked your way through a history and overview of Hollywood (chapter one), taken a deeper look at the separate film (chapter two) and television (chapter three) industries, been apprised of dozens of job categories and descriptions (chapter four), and followed the process of a script from idea to production.

Still confused by the complexity of it all?

Here are a dozen books of varying types (some already mentioned in passing) that may help outsiders better understand and find their way through the "Tinseltown maze."

All You Need to Know About the Movie and TV Business (Simon and Schuster), by Gail Resnik and Scott Trost, entertainment attorneys who also have extensive experience at the creative end, is an excellent, "nuts 'n bolts" survey of what happens before and behind the camera.

The Hollywood Job-Hunter's Survival Guide (Lone Eagle Publishing), by production executive and Harvard MBA Hugh Taylor, was written to provide "an insider's winning strategies for getting that (all-important) first job." It lays out just how Hollywood works, top to bottom, in concrete, well-organized, easy-to-understand terms, with helpful charts and other graphics. Excellent resources appendix.

An excellent companion title, *Breaking and Entering: Land Your First Job in Film Production*, by April Fitzsimmons, has recently been published by Lone Eagle, which specializes in books, directories and software for the entertainment industry. For a catalog, contact Lone Eagle Publishing at 2337 Roscomare Road, Suite #9, Los Angeles 90077-1851 (310) 471-8066; http://www.loneeagle.com.

From Script to Screen: The Collaborative Art of Filmmaking (Holt), by Linda Seger and Edward Jay Whetmore, is a highly informative account—based on interviews with leading writers, directors, producers and others behind the scenes—tracing the journey of several notable feature films from conception to completion.

Opening the Doors to Hollywood: How to Sell Your Idea: Story-Book-Screenplay (Random House), by Carlos De Abreu and Howard Jay Smith, is a serious, solid, step-by-step guide through the complex world of commercial moviemaking.

The Insider's Guide to Writing for Screen and Television (Writer's Digest Books), by Ronald Tobias, provides a wealth of concise, practical, authoritative information and advice for the hopeful scriptwriter.

How to Make It in Hollywood (HarperPerennial), by Linda Buzzell, a psychotherapist and career counselor, is on the lighter, less concrete side, emphasizing success tips and coping skills. Contains a very good resources appendix.

Adventures in the Screen Trade (Warner Books), written in the early 1980s by Oscar-winning screenwriter William Goldman, remains a classic insider's account of "the movie biz," still highly recommended to anyone considering screenwriting as a profession.

Hello, He Lied, and Other Truths From the Hollywood Trenches, written in 1996 by Linda Obst, a former journalist and a successful studio producer (*Sleepless in Seattle, Contact*, etc.), is a frank, entertaining, insightful account of working and surviving in the movie industry from a woman's point of view.

Reel Power (Plume), by Mark Litwak, is a perceptive, deeply revealing look at how Hollywood works from someone on the inside who writes, quite accurately, that "it's just about impossible to succeed in Hollywood without a thorough understanding of its ways." First published in 1986, but still very useful.

The Studio (Simon and Schuster), by novelist-screenwriter John Gregory Dunne, is an anecdotal, darkly humorous nonfiction account of a year in the life of Twentieth Century Fox. Written in the late 1960s, and considered a classic of its kind. Even more current is Dunne's *Monster* (Random House), which chronicles his involvement as a screenwriter in the making of the movie *Up Close and Personal*.

For a more detailed list of resource and reference books on Hollywood, see Appendix B.

CHAPTER SIX

Hollywood Hype

If Hollywood is the entertainment capital of the world, much of its "stature" is due to its own remarkable efforts at self-promotion. Madison Avenue notwithstanding, where else do you find such intense, costly, crass campaigns to promote its products, people and images, carried out with such unbridled restraint? When it comes to sheer *hype*, Hollywood is pretty much in a league of its own.

Thousands of men and women owe their livelihoods to the work they do generating media coverage of movies and television programs and, particularly, their stars. Collectively, they comprise an enormous publicity machine, ranging from the highest-paid publicity executives, who command their forces from bustling, high-rise suites to the lowliest, independent "flacks," who work out of cluttered, one-person offices, scrounging for clients and trying to "plant" items anywhere in the press they can.

For all this self-promotion to succeed, the publicists need the media, just as the media needs celebrities to liven up its pages and programs, put some glamour on its covers and in its TV promos, sell more copies and draw more viewers. They exist in awkward symbiosis—a love-hate relationship in which each is dependent on the other, yet mutually distrustful. Frequently, they see each other as the enemy: one side trying to limit or control press coverage, even distort or suppress the truth, if it serves the client's purpose; the other determined to unearth and print the most revealing facts (or rumors) it can, no matter how damaging, and sometimes with an irresponsible disregard for fairness or accuracy.

To be sure, there are competent, respected professionals working on both sides of the fence, performing their services honorably. And no one can deny that Hollywood deserves serious coverage: It is a company town that supports a multibillion dollar industry that exports its product to a voracious, worldwide audience, reflecting America in the process. The images and stories Hollywood manufactures and the messages they carry help to shape the consciousnesses and perceptions of countless millions. As these visual mediums—movies, television, videos, computer-generated programming and so on—occupy more and more of our attention and time, they continue to have a profound impact on reading habits and learning skills, literacy levels, communication between individuals and within families. Given all this, Hollywood cannot and should not be ignored by the media, and there are serious editors and reporters working within the ranks of the entertainment press covering news and issues of substance and importance.

Yet most of the Hollywood coverage is pure fluff, blatant hype or tawdry gossip, and the public cannot seem to get enough of it. Feeding off one another, the Hollywood publicity juggernaut and the vast entertainment press produces a wave of "information" so relentless and voluminous it sometimes seems to overwhelm the coverage of more important issues and events. Surrounded by wealth and glamour, living and working in the world's brightest spotlight, suffocated by their own, self-serving verbiage, these mutually dependent purveyors of "entertainment news" often act as though Hollywood is the center of the universe and nothing else really matters all that much. (I write as someone who has worked extensively in the entertainment press.)

In this chapter, we'll examine this massive and unending effort to keep Hollywood in the public eye: how it works, who the players are and what their daily lives are like.

Why is it worthy of an entire chapter? Because this is the way most writers outside Hollywood come to "know" it, and it's important to understand how that information reaches them, and the larger public, if they are to write about Hollywood in an intelligent, accurate and reasonably fair manner.

The Publicists

Whatever term you use for this professional category—publicist, press agent, public relations officer, flack or, in *Variety* slang, "praiser"—it is occupied by a special sort of person who operates under a special set of rules.

The jobs in publicity are generally filled with energetic young people, from their midtwenties to late thirties, who are bright and alert to current events and thinking. They remember one's name and face, and particularly what status a person holds in the media they simultaneously serve and try to manage. They are always alert to opportunities to introduce one acquaintance to another. They tend to be fit and well-groomed, and to dress for success, yet they don't want to dress so well that they "show up" the stars they may represent. Many come from journalism backgrounds or with journalism degrees, since gathering information, giving it some thought and writing it up is an important part of the job.

To Hollywood outsiders, publicity positions may seem glamorous, but at entry level, they are relatively low-paying and labor-intensive. Countless junior publicists live in debt (and small apartments) trying to keep up with the payments for the decent automobile and attire that is expected of them, but that their lower five-figure salaries fail to cover. Nonetheless, there is always room for the motivated to move toward the top, where it's possible to earn a comfortable living. $60,000 per year is not uncommon for union publicists, with senior publicists earning in the $75,000 to $80,000 range. Scales at the major film studios may run higher than that, with a director of publicity falling into the $90,000 to $100,000 range. Senior vice presidents can earn from $200,000 to $250,000, and department presidents considerably more.

This kind of pay comes with a price, however, particularly in the lower echelon positions: The job requires a unique sense of serving the client or production, which means courting media representatives. Even when these press people are rude, combative, or simply wrong, they must be treated delicately and with deference because they may be needed again on the next movie, show or star client. Publicists are also typically used as "scapegoats and doormats," as one Hollywood veteran puts it. If something goes wrong, the lowly publicist is the one who often gets blamed, with the blame frequently coming from the more powerful publicity execs who have risen to the top. The job also demands great attention to detail, as well as long and often gruelling hours filled with pressure and a certain sense of not being much appreciated. Traditionally, the publicity ranks have been filled with a disproportionately large number of women and gay men. Many women, shut out of the "old boy's network," may see publicity as an opportunity to rise in the industry; many gay men may be drawn by the Hollywood glamour (my apologies to the PC Police), and the chance to find their niche in an industry dominated at the top by straight white males.

Writing in the *Los Angeles Times*, freelancer Hilary de Vries risked the wrath of the Hollywood publicity community when she referred to "the classic publicist's curse: low-self-esteem-fueled fawning." Yet it might also simply be a special sensitivity many men lack. Explained a veteran Hollywood publicist (male): "Stars are unusually anxious people. They relate better to women—as hand-holders, as 'mommies.' A lot of men just can't do that very well."

Peggy Siegal, a high-profile personal publicist on the East Coast, once told a magazine writer that to be effective, publicists must "be very supportive and calm with their clients but they have to be much tougher with the press. They switch back and forth between the feminine and masculine sides of their person-alities [all the time]."

For all the demands and stress placed on publicists, however, most seem to bring a special passion and devotion to their work and to think of their business almost as a calling.

The Studio Publicists

As previously discussed in chapter four, studio publicists are responsible for gen-erating free media exposure for their movies and their stars, while the marketing people are planning and "buying time" for their TV and cable spots (commer-cials) and "buying space" in magazines and newspapers as well as other media.

The studio publicists fall into two categories (although their assignments often overlap): Staff publicists generally work on the studio lot, while unit publi-cists (with reference to the filming "unit") are frequently freelance publicists who are hired to work "on location," wherever the movie is being filmed. Among their basic tools:

Press Releases

These are issued at various times during the preparation and production of the filming and sent to all possible media. They contain basic facts about the movie, such as star casting, hiring of a director and production start date. The writing is invariably bright and concise, emphasizing only the positive while ignoring or glossing over any problems that might come up—budget overruns, production delays, union disputes and the like. Before being issued to the press, these re-leases are carefully screened by the director of publicity, producers of the film, and possibly the director and the stars, or their personal publicists, agents or managers, who may ask for changes (and invariably get them). By its nature, a press release is not necessarily intended to be an accurate, truthful document, but rather a public relations tool designed to serve the client. Smart reporters and editors know this and use them accordingly.

Press Kits

During the "shoot," or filming of the movie, the unit starts the process of pro-ducing the printed press kit. Some films also put out a "behind-the-scenes" electronic press kit, or EPK, for use by the electronic media; it is often produced by a freelance specialist who can handle on-camera interviews, video scripting and so forth.

The printed press kits, which are distributed to reporters, editors and reviewers for their background use, include a list of all the credits on the film and several pages of history and credits on each of the stars as well as the major creative staff of the picture. They also provide a history of the production, synopsis of the plot, several features related to the production and the stars, and a set of still photographs (sometimes slides) of the stars and scenes from the film. Like press releases, press kits are carefully tailored and sanitized to suit the studio's needs and create a positive image of the movie and the stars.

The EPK is distributed to television and cable outlets, and includes "clips" (selected scenes or sequences) from the film as well as brief comments ("sound bites") about the movie by the stars and director. These are designed for entertainment producers who can use pieces of the EPK to create their own segments.

Unit publicists tend to be a different breed from the permanent, staff publicist who works primarily on the studio lot and in and around town. Because most units are freelance, moving from assignment to assignment, sometimes to exotic or far-flung locations for weeks or months at a time, they tend to be more independent, carefree and resilient. They often build careers by becoming friends with certain stars, directors or producers, or simply because they are known as extremely dependable, with good media contacts and relationships. A unit can earn $1,000 a week and up, plus per diem expenses of $35 to $50 per day, and some of the more in-demand units can make $2,500 a week or more while assigned to major films with major stars.

During the shoot, they have a variety of duties, including preparing the press kit, meeting with local media and coordinating interviews and photos the media might require. They sometimes hold a formal press conference with local media as the cast and crew assemble to start shooting, and customarily organize interview schedules for reporters and photographers visiting the set from out of town, and accompany the stars during the interviews (if requested), handling any related problems that might develop. The classic nightmare for the unit is being caught on a "troubled production," when he or she must field endless questions from inquisitive media while trying to protect and placate the production's demanding above-the-line talent ("damage control"), and keep the studio bosses happy back home. As a rule, unit publicists are valued more for their people skills than their writing ability.

Fielding Press Requests

From the time a film is conceived, if "major players" are involved, press requests start coming in. These might range from confirmation that a particular star has been signed to a salary or budget figure, and countless other details that reporters feel they need for an item or story they might be working on. Frequently in the early stage of a film, especially preproduction, the studios like to reveal as little as possible, the theory being that less publicity is good publicity until the details are "firm" and the picture is a definite "go."

As the picture moves toward and then into production, some press inquiries or requests for interviews may be uncomfortable for the studio (regarding script rewrite problems, for example, or star tantrums). In situations like these, the publicist's role becomes one of running interference or practicing crisis management as he or she attempts to deflate the scope of the problem or discourage (even subvert) tough inquiries. As publicists negotiate with reporters over what kind of facts they might get, for example, or to whom they might be given access for an interview, they develop relationships with the press that may be crucial at a later date, when exposure for the movie *is* desired and the publicists need the press on their side. Consequently, much of what the publicist does as the movie makes its long way toward its release date is a delicate game of diplomacy, with the publicist caught between the filmmakers and the media, though with his or her allegiance always on the side of the producer and the studio.

Setting Up Interviews

In general, the one-on-one interviews reporters most covet are with major stars, ideally the "exclusive" in their area of the media. For example, NBC's "Today" show may want to interview a certain star in conjunction with a new movie, but only if it gets the interview exclusively among the morning news shows or at least ahead of a major competitor, such as ABC's "Good Morning America." For many years, the *Los Angeles Times* reportedly had a policy of running profiles of major stars only if the *Times* had its interview in print before its chief competitor, the now-defunct *Los Angeles Herald-Examiner*. This kind of competition and these kinds of demands put studio publicists in a constant quandary, since their goal is to generate as much positive exposure for the movie as possible, timed close to its release date. On the other hand, for a much sought-after star, publicists are in the catbird seat, and able to bargain—for more airtime, say, or for multiple segments carved out of a single interview, or even which reporter will conduct the interview (with the publicist angling for the "friendly" interviewer, of course). Publicists must also weigh and prioritize press requests and decide which should be granted based on such things as whether the publication, TV show or reporter is hostile or friendly, or "important" enough to warrant the investment of time. After that, the publicist must work out any number of details and ground rules: how much time and personal access to the star a reporter will have, where the interview(s) will take place, if certain questions will be off limits, if the reporter is willing to "check quotes" for verification and/or approval. All this must be done with careful attention to schedules, since it is the publicist's responsibility to see that everyone is in the right place at the right time with the information they need to move the story forward.

When a star is profiled on an important TV magazine show such as "20/20" or "60 Minutes," or in a widely read national magazine such as *Vanity Fair* or *Entertainment Weekly* (particularly as a cover story), the publicist who engineered and set up the interview has scored what may be a career-building coup (although the boss at the top will probably grab the credit). On the other hand, if the story turns out badly for the star and studio, it's often the publicist who gets blamed and sometimes fired.

The Press Junket

One of the more productive publicity tools is the press junket, which involves bringing in dozens of reporters and freelance writers from across the country to do mass interviews of key participants in a film. These are usually the stars, the director and the producer or producers, but sometimes others are included if their roles on the film have been significant, such as animal trainers or makeup specialists.

These junkets are scheduled one week to several weeks prior to the film's release date to maximize "opening date" publicity, but with enough time to allow the media to make their deadlines. They are generally conducted over a two- or three-day period, when the studio flies in roughly fifty to one hundred reporters or freelance writers representing newspapers, magazines, radio and television stations, and syndicated shows, putting them up in cushy hotels and often paying travel and hotel expenses. It is not uncommon for a studio to spend from $100,000 to $200,000 on a junket, and sometimes competing studios will join to "piggyback" their films during the same event, spreading the cost. Because of the obvious conflict of interest possibilities, many media companies will not allow reporters to accept such "freebies" and will cover the expenses of its reporters or reimburse the studio.

Some of the major media outlets—*Los Angeles Times*, *New York Times*, *People*, *Entertainment Weekly*, *TV Guide*, *GQ*—shun junkets entirely, and the herd mentality and atmosphere that comes with them; using their clout, they attempt to arrange private, more exclusive interviews on their own, when they are able to ask more probing or wide-ranging questions. Junkets tend to be favored by the smaller publications or television outlets, or less discriminating and demanding freelance writers, called "junket whores" in some circles, who are happy to get their few minutes with a star, follow the rules and ask only the more polite questions. One Warner Bros. film executive sees the arrangement this way: "It's the one opportunity you have to cover middle America from both the TV and the newspaper perspective with some very high-level talent that they would not ordinarily meet."

Studio publicists run junkets with military precision, carrying pagers and walkie-talkies to monitor the arrivals and departures of their stars. Typically, reporters encamp in a "hospitality suite," which, in effect, serves as the junket's war room. There, they receive press kits and are invited to partake of a hot-and-cold buffet. Other freebies might also be handed out, such as T-shirts bearing the film's logo, a novelization of the film or posters.

There are basically three types of junket interview sessions, all run rigorously by the clock:

The TV interview. Usually one day is set aside for these sessions, which are conducted at exact, six-minute intervals. A star is placed in a hotel room that is set up with a camera and lights. The interviewer is ushered in, introduced to the star, asks his or her questions and receives a videotape copy of the interview for their station on their way out. A few "more important" media outlets, such as *Entertainment Tonight*, get perhaps twenty minutes with a star.

The one-on-one print interview. A few newspapers with larger circulations, such as the *Chicago Tribune* or the *Washington Post*, are allowed one-on-one interviews that typically run from fifteen to thirty minutes, with the time agreed to well beforehand, often after some negotiating between reporter (or editor) and publicist. The reporters are asked to arrive a half hour prior to the interview. At the appointed time, the publicist escorts the reporter to the hotel suite set aside for these interviews, makes the introductions and leaves the reporter alone with the star for the scheduled time. In some cases, if the star is unusually sensitive or needs tending, or controversy is swirling around a particular film or role, the publicist will wait in a nearby room in case they are needed, or even sit in on the conversation if the star requests it.

Buena Vista Pictures Marketing

In order to insure that you are properly reimbursed for any incidental
expenses you might incur on the **1997 LOS ANGELES AUGUST FILM PRESS
JUNKET**, we ask that you itemize those expenses and submit this form by
September 5, 1997:

> Georgia O'Connor
> Vice President, Field Marketing
> Walt Disney Studios
> 500 South Buena Vista Street
> Burbank, CA 91521-1387

Date   Nature of Expense   Amount

_____

_____

_____

_____

PLEASE ATTACH RECEIPTS   Total: _____

*ONLY INCLUDE RECEIPTS FOR THE *A THOUSAND ACRES* JUNKET

Signature: _____

Name (Print): _____

Affiliation: _____

Social Security Number: _____
(Accounts Payable must have in order to make reimbursement for expenses)

Mail check to the following address:

_____

_____

_____

_____

CHARGE #3N 651 7403 KT23 2048 (1997 LOS ANGELES AUGUST FILM PRESS JUNKET)

This is a standard media expense reimbursement report used by studio marketing
departments for "press junkets" and other studio-sponsored press events.

The round-robin. With this approach, a large room, such as a hotel ballroom, is set up with several tables used to individually seat the stars and other persons to be interviewed. Typically, a group of eight to ten reporters (most armed with tape recorders) gather around a table, tossing out their questions. After about thirty minutes, the interview subjects move to another table to face a new set of reporters and questions. A variation on this is to have the interview subject move to a series of hotel rooms, with a new group of reporters in each.

For the interviewees, of course, the assembly-line junket can be numbing and exhausting, as they are often asked the same question or questions again and again. Actor Nicholas Cage, for example, did fifty-four one-on-one interviews on a single Saturday when he was promoting *The Rock* in 1996. Some media-shy or less cooperative stars refuse to submit to these junkets, but many stars accept them as part of their high-paying jobs or are required by the terms of their contracts to participate. Tom Hanks, while doing a junket for *Forrest Gump*, was asked when he would judge himself a success. He replied good-naturedly, "When I don't have to do these interviews!"

The Publicity Tour

For reporters in distant cities who are unwilling or unable to attend a press junket in Hollywood, the studio may elect to stage a city-by-city publicity tour, transporting their stars to interviews. These are customarily conducted in a restaurant or hotel suite, with the reporters allowed considerably more time than they would be during the fast-paced, compressed press junket. Depending on their level of stardom, the stars customarily get top-of-the-line accommodations during these trips, including first-class air flights and limousine service. For television stops, they are usually attended to by hairstylists and makeup personnel, often their personal favorites. The pace is invariably hectic as the publicists try to wedge in as many appearances as possible each day.

Press Screenings

Studio publicists are also responsible for setting up multiple screenings for the media in Los Angeles and New York, sometimes at a screening room at the studio or in small rented screening rooms, for certain television programs and print magazines in consideration of their early deadlines. These screenings may be for reviewing purposes, but also to allow producers and editors to determine if, in their eyes, an upcoming film warrants coverage, or how much coverage and what kind. Often, because the film may not yet be technically finished, the media representative may be shown a "rough cut" of the film, with the tacit understanding that it is still in the postproduction stage.

General press screenings of the finished movie are held close to its release date for a wide range of media people who review or report on film. On some occasions, the studio rents a movie theater or one of the special theaters around town, such as those at the Academy of Motion Picture Arts and Sciences, the Writer's Guild or the Director's Guild, all of which seat five hundred or more. On special occasions, a press party follows, replete with food and drink.

Premieres

This is the evening event set aside to showcase a film in glamorous and festive fashion, usually held at one of the area's more attractive theaters shortly before the film's official release date. This gala, which often benefits a charity, comes complete with klieg lights sweeping the night skies, limos arriving out front delivering stars, and a red carpet that leads dozens of arriving celebrities up "the line." This refers to the roped-off area where the celebrity photographers, or paparazzi, attempt to snap the photo that may be worth hundreds, even thousands of dollars if they capture just the right expression that gives their "pic" more marketability (see "Hollywood's 'Buzzing Insects'" on page 173). Next comes the gantlet of media reporters, including some with camera crews. Publicists are on hand to lead the film's stars from one reporter to the next; each has only a few seconds to elicit the usable quote or sound bite before the star is led away. After the premiere, some stars make themselves available to comment on how wonderful the movie was. (The rule at such events is: If you don't have something nice to say, keep your mouth shut or lie.) Then they drift off to a lavish private party, to which only a select group of reporters is invited, if any.

Exploiting the Internet

This is the latest tool in the publicist's arsenal, as studio publicity departments spread the word about their movies via the World Wide Web. The first studio to take such advantage of the Internet, according to some reports, was MGM, on behalf of its 1994 science fiction adventure, *Stargate*. The movie, which starred Kurt Russell and James Spader, was a surprise hit, and other studios began to follow MGM's lead. "It was a hard sell at first," recalls a Universal publicist. "But a Web-developing firm offered to set up three sites for us for only $20,000. It was amazingly cheap. What's not to try?"

"What's the Buzz?"

J ust as Wall Street brokers tune in to 'the word' on the street," writes Giselle Benatar in *Entertainment Weekly*, "so Hollywood spin doctors nervously measure the pitch of industry 'buzz.' "

Buzz is one of the least tangible, least definable, least explicable of all Hollywood phenomena, yet it's as vital a part of the Tinseltown experience as Army Archerd's *Variety* column or lunch at the Ivy. It's so much a part of the L.A. scene that it even has a trendy city magazine named after it. So just what is it?

EW offered this:

"*Definition of Buzz*: Hot gossip about an upcoming film.

Usage: 'Project X has good buzz,' casually dropped at pitch meeting.

Term for dealers: Buzz merchants.

Rule of operation: Nobody starts the buzz, but everyone in Hollywood traffics in it."

Buzz, then, is a kind of ephemeral, industry word-of-mouth, perhaps conceived and generated by the buzz merchants, perhaps not. Studios attempt to encourage the buzz when it's positive, stifle it when it's negative. At some point, it seems to take on a mysterious momentum of its own, like gerbil stories and rumors of dead Beatles.

Universal subsequently promoted its Arnold Schwarzenegger comedy, *Junior*, with what it called "the world's first interactive movie premiere," and the studio now regularly uses the World Wide Web for a variety of promotions, as do virtually all the studios. Numerous celebrities also have their own web sites, several independent publicists specialize in Internet promotion and star "chats," and use of the medium by publicists is expected to grow as the Web becomes more mainstream.

The Rise of the Personal Publicist

Historically, personal publicists were low-profile people who were loathe to have their names mentioned in the media; with a few notable exceptions, these independent press agents preferred to let their clients shine, while remaining quietly and anonymously in the background, pulling the publicity strings.

Through the 1970s and 1980s, as the power in Hollywood continued its shift from the studios and producers to the stars and their increasingly enormous salaries, and the media began to take a more aggressive approach to reporting on Hollywood, the entertainment community witnessed the dramatic rise in the visibility and influence of the personal publicist. By the 1990s, a handful of extremely successful press agents (almost exclusively women) represented many, if not most, of Hollywood's top stars and forged for themselves and their clients unprecedented power in the area of media relations. It has led to a cold war between the media and the most controlling publicists, as summed up in this *Los Angeles* magazine title over an article written by a veteran husband-wife Hollywood reporting team: "Flacks Fatales—They're Rude, Hormonal and Power Hungry—And They're Out to Control Everything You Read and Hear About Hollywood."

How do they wield this power? Let us count some ways:

1. They are often able to dictate what studio publicist and unit publicist is assigned to a film in which their client is starring, which can end up with the media focus on the star, rather than on the film itself.

2. They frequently "demand the cover," that is, insist on the placement of their star's face on a magazine cover in exchange for granting the interview.

3. They are sometimes able to demand approval of the writer who will interview and profile their client, and, quite naturally, select someone known for writing kinder profiles ("puff pieces"), or who has been friendly on past assignments involving the star.

4. They frequently select the photographer who will shoot the pictures, as well as demand approval of any photos used, taking these decisions out of the hands of editors.

5. They are sometimes able to influence what kind of coverage their client will be given, and how a profile will be slanted by putting certain questions or subject areas off limits during the interview.

6. Some personal publicists play "chicken" with editors, offering access to a major star only on the condition that one of their less famous clients also gets coverage.

Because magazines need star faces on their covers to maintain high newsstand sales, only the most fiercely dedicated editors oppose such demands. This influence over the media by certain personal publicists (and some studio publicity departments as well) has become a heated issue in Hollywood journalism circles. It came to a head in 1992, when superstar publicist Pat Kingsley issued a "consent decree" to reporters on behalf of her clients, Tom Cruise and Nicole Kidman, while they were participating in a press junket for *Far and Away*. The consent decree was a legalistic form that, in effect, was a loyalty oath that placed restrictions on the interview, particularly on when and how it might be used (see reproduction on page 164).

Many media outlets capitulated and signed the agreement, including "Entertainment Tonight" and CNN's "Showbiz Today." Others, charging "manipulation" and "extortion," refused to go along. Kingsley, who had risen from the position of a secretary at a PR agency to become the most powerful publicist in Hollywood representing more major stars than any other single person, stood her ground, with this explanation: "We object to the new journalism, where a reporter does an interview for one publication and then turns around and sells it to a tabloid." She and Cruise were no doubt also sensitive to the practice of many TV producers who insert old sound bites into new stories, sometimes out of context.

To many publicists, it is the press that has too much freedom and power to cause harm to their clients, either through inaccuracy or irresponsibility. They see their role as a check and balance to an aggressive, sometimes unfair, media that seems to become less restrained and less sensitive with each passing day. One male Hollywood publicist likens Pat Kingsley to a mother lion protecting her cubs: "You go after one of them and you're dead." The *Los Angeles Times* claimed that "her ruthless control of media access to these stars has changed the nature of celebrity." Another publicist says, "A good publicist does whatever has to be done to protect the image of the client. That's their job, pure and simple."

Some publicists take their responsibility so seriously that they act as impenetrable screens between their clients and the press, even making decisions about access and interviews without relaying press requests or consulting their clients. More than one publicist has deliberately lied to the press, thereby disseminating false information to the general public. A few make dictatorial demands as if they, not editors and producers, are in rightful control of the media. Such strong-arm publicity tactics can backfire, of course; magazine covers can be lost and articles canceled by editors tired of the intimidation. Some stars, realizing the importance of good press relations, do not like the hard-line approach and have been known to fire publicists for attempting to muscle and muzzle the press. Yet more and more, the biggest stars seem to be as concerned about protection from the press as the coveted exposure it can give them.

The Network Publicists

Network publicists tend to be a different breed than studio or personal publicists. They generally keep more regular hours, and lead simpler, saner (and

UNIVERSAL PICTURES MARKETING, 100 UNIVERSAL CITY PLAZA, UNIVERSAL CITY, CALIFORNIA 91608

CONSENT AGREEMENT

This consent agreement is made with respect to interviews done for the Universal Pictures film "FAR AND AWAY," for use by _____. In consideration of the promises and agreements made herein and for other good and valuable consideration, receipt of which is hereby acknowledged, it is agreed as follows.

1. The interview may be printed only in _____ as part of its regular publication and for no other purpose. _____ may not print excerpts of the interview as part of another publication or with other materials not related to the subject of the interview, and no portion of the interview may be distributed to or used in connection with the advertising or promotion of any publication without the express written consent of Universal Pictures and Nicole Kidman.

2. Each segment of the interview may be printed only during or in connection with the Initial U.S. theatrical release of the motion picture "FAR AND AWAY."

3. The interview or any rights with respect thereto may not be licensed or assigned to any person or entity for any purpose.

4. In the event of any breach by _____ of the consent agreement, Universal Pictures and Nicole Kidman shall have the right to revoke all permissions herein granted, and in the event of any such revocation, _____ shall thereafter have no rights in or with respect to the interview.

By: _____

Title: _____

Date: _____

Publicist Pat Kingsley created a controversy when she issued this "consent decree" to the media to "protect" her clients Tom Cruise and Nicole Kidman. The document, issued in 1992, became a symbol of the rising power of the personal publicist.

considerably less glamorous) lives. Network flacks are generally amiable and helpful to a point, but notoriously noncommittal or simply unavailable when reporters come to them with investigative or negative slants. They know that, regardless of a serious media request, the next show and the next season, like their jobs, will go on and on, pretty much on schedule. Likewise, the life of the network publicist has traditionally been determined by the calendar:

- In late May, the networks announce their coming autumn schedules, including new series.
- In July, the networks showcase the series and other programs for the nation's TV critics. Each year, the Television Critics Association organizes a period of interviews spanning roughly three weeks for as many as two hundred reporters at the Ritz-Carlton Huntington Hotel in Pasadena. These take the form of massive press conferences for network executives, producers and stars of the new shows, some notable returning series or made-for-TV movies. To help writers, transcripts of the taped sessions are provided to the attendees. Some reporters write their articles day by day during the event; others write their articles in the fall, or whenever the program is scheduled to begin airing.
- In September, the traditional network TV season opens with orchestrated hoopla, including the shipping of videotapes of the new programs to critics around the country for their advance reviews.
- In succeeding days and months the most crucial competitions take place, especially the three "sweeps" months of November, February and May, in which the ratings help determine advertising prices.
- During two weeks in January, the networks face the critics again to present the "second season"—the new series that replace the failed shows of the first season.

With the dozens of new cable networks that have appeared on the market in recent years, as well as the emergence of upstart broadcast networks like Fox and others, the rigid structure and predictable parameters of network publicity have loosened up and changed somewhat. Nonetheless, creativity, imagination and chutzpah seem less in demand from TV publicists than from their movie studio counterparts. TV publicists tend to be rather passive, their jobs more routine and predictable like the medium of television itself. At their networks, they invariably occupy smaller offices than studio and personal publicists, and much of their time is spent churning out endless press releases demanded by the routine of TV series programming. Because television must reach such a broad, common-denominator audience, their key targets are the mass media outlets that extend into the heartland, such as *TV Guide*, "Entertainment Tonight," and the family newspaper.

Network publicists are under constant pressure from TV producers and stars for more—and more *distinctive*—coverage, but face the problem that TV shows and stars are seen in tens of millions of American homes week after week, making them less interesting as subjects to both reporters and readers alike.

Unless, of course, scandal or tragedy crops up—which brings us to the entertainment press.

The Entertainment Press

The armies of media that watch Hollywood's every move fall into two broad categories: the trade press, which focuses on significant business and technological developments and serves those who work in the industry (see "The Trade Publications" on page 175); and the consumer press, which is usually more interested in stories about stars, dynamic new projects and the like, for the consumption of the general public.

The basic consumer outlets include the following.

Newspapers

Entertainment coverage within a major newspaper can take a number of forms, including news reports, movie box-office figures and TV ratings, business articles, feature stories ("soft" articles as opposed to "hard" news pieces), profiles, investigative articles, "backgrounders" and analysis pieces (commentary usually assigned to the more veteran and insightful reporters or critics). A few major newspapers, such as the *Los Angeles Times* (see the sidebar, "The Mighty *Los Angeles Times*" on page 168), will have individual beat reporters as well as numerous freelance writers to provide most of this material; most newspapers, especially those with audiences less interested in the daily goings on in industry, will pick up a good deal of their Hollywood coverage from the news wire services ("off the wire") or syndicates.

Working the entertainment beat can be an odd, exhilarating, sometimes perplexing experience, in which relatively unseasoned journalists can suddenly find themselves thrust into a world of glamour, fame and high-finance. Many younger entertainment reporters or freelance writers, who might be making anywhere from $300 to $1,000 per week, find themselves dealing with senior publicists making up to $250,000 per year or interviewing actors making $20 million per picture. The reaction of a reporter can range from awed and starstruck to envious and resentful, or a mix of such feelings. As these reporters gain increasing knowledge of and contacts within the film and TV industry, many find themselves aspiring to jobs in the industry they cover; inevitably, some slip into conflict of interest situations as they continue to report on (or review) the very people they would like to work for or sell their screenplays to. One can usually recognize the weakness setting in as their reporting goes from "tough" to "puff," from balanced to fawning and they carefully avoid taking on serious investigative assignments. Many reporters and critics do, in fact, join "the industry," most often as screenwriters and production executives, sometimes as publicists.

Those who stick with journalism must deal with the fact that they labor in a relatively low-paying trade and be careful that their reporting doesn't become motivated or tainted by spite. When it does, the result is often the nasty, unfair, one-sided "hatchet job" that seems to be written for no reason except tearing down someone the reporter once admired and built up. There are many serious, respectable journalists working the entertainment beat, yet it's rare to find the reporter or critic who hasn't at some point secretly coveted a career on the other side.

Syndicated Columnists

In the 1930s and 1940s, Americans devoured Hollywood gossip like the air they breathed, and Hollywood gossip columnists attained unprecedented power and influence within the media, including radio. Walter Winchell, Hedda Hopper and Louella Parsons could make and sometimes break careers, and struck terror in the hearts of publicists and studio moguls alike with their often righteous revelations about the private lives of Hollywood's biggest or rising stars. Others followed in later years, carving lucrative careers for themselves either in print or on TV: Sheilah Graham, Dorothy Kilgallen, Sidney Skolsky, Joyce Haber, Rona Barrett, a few others.

Today, with the public more accustomed to celebrity naughtiness and various TV shows breaking the most notable celebrity news, the syndicated columnist is something of an endangered species. There are still columnists in major cities, several in New York and Chicago, including the sprightly "Page 6" column in the *New York Post*, and Mitchell Fink in *People*. But only two syndicated columnists plow the field with much influence these days: Liz Smith from the East Coast (carried in sixty newspapers) and Marilyn Beck and Stacy Jenel Smith (who work together) on the West Coast (carried in 110 papers), with the

The Mighty Los Angeles Times

Once, when I was starting out as a freelance writer and having lunch with a Universal Studios publicist, I mentioned that my current assignment was with the *Chicago Tribune Sunday Magazine*. "It's nice that you're writing for the *Trib*," the publicist said, "but I'll be honest with you. The only newspapers studio publicists really care about are the *New York Times* and the *Los Angeles Times*, because they're the only papers their bosses see."

Among those two publications, which I also wrote for at various times, the *Los Angeles Times* occupies a unique position as the only major newspaper left in Los Angeles, with daily and Sunday circulations of more than a million readers. The *Times*'s last serious local rival, the impoverished *Herald-Examiner*, closed down in 1989, and the smaller *Los Angeles Daily News* primarily serves the Valley. Founded in 1881, the *Times* is housed in a massive, concrete-and-marble structure, which occupies a full square city block at First and Third Streets downtown across from City Hall, befitting the largest and most influential newspaper on the West Coast. In the eyes of many publicists, the *L.A. Times*, as it is known locally, is "the only game in town." As Hollywood's hometown newspaper, it probably carries more coverage of the film and TV industry than any other daily newspaper in the world.

Until the late 1970s, most of the *Times*' entertainment coverage amounted to comfortable stories about the stars and the movies, with emphasis on the cultural rather than the business aspects. Seldom did a hard news story in its pages emanate from Hollywood, and no writers were assigned to regularly deliver probing reports on the industry. That changed in 1977, with the so-called "Begelman scandal" or "Hollywoodgate." For some time, word had been leaking out that the authorities were looking into business "irregularities" involving celebrated agent-producer David Begelman, an inveterate gambler who was then president of Columbia Pictures, and one of the top movers and shakers in Hollywood. The *Times*, however, failed to seriously pursue the story, which was broken first by the *Wall Street Journal* and other major *Times* competitors. Begelman, who got caught forging a $10,000 check made out to actor Cliff Robertson, was ousted from his studio job after admitting to forging company checks and embezzling $61,000. Getting scooped on such a big hometown story by its out-of-town rivals thoroughly embarrassed the *Times* and its top editors, and a new policy gradually took effect that deepened and sharpened the paper's coverage of the industry in the daily and Sunday Calendar sections. In the 1980s, this led to a certain amount of friction with the studios and entertainment publicists, who had grown accustomed to the *Times*' studio-friendly manner of reporting.

Today, most of the harder industry coverage is handled by a number of excellent reporters in the business section and its "Company Town" column. Yet the entertainment industry pervades almost every section of the paper, with the life and style section running features on the fitness regimens of the stars, the legal briefs column devoted largely to Hollywood-related lawsuits, and so on. Even the Sunday real estate section runs a regular front-page column, "Hot Property," which reports on the costly homes that are bought and traded by Hollywood's elite, complete with prices and descriptions, right down to their spas, screening rooms and tennis courts.

As numerous media watchers have observed, it's the kind of column that could only originate in L.A.—and only in the *Los Angeles Times*.

Beck/Smith column the more reportorial of the two and considerably lighter on gossip. All three women also turn up in various TV venues.

Consumer Magazines

In the modern era of star coverage, the landmark date is March 4, 1974—the first official issue of Time, Inc.'s *People Weekly*, which hit newsstands for thirty-five cents with actress Mia Farrow on the cover. Editors had always known that the right face on the cover could boost sales, but *People* was devoted to front-to-back "personality" coverage, a concept that met with astounding success. Before long, celebrities also began to dominate the covers of a wide range of consumer publications, from news weeklies like *Time* and *Newsweek* (whose coveted covers subsequently lost much of their prestige), to men's magazine's like *Esquire* and *GQ* and most of the women's magazines, which had once been the domain of fashion models. *People* had spawned the "celebritization" of the magazine world.

Throughout the 1990s, *People* consistently topped most magazines in total revenues, and continued to have a ripple effect on the publishing industry. The magazine's most popular personality through the years, however, was not a Hollywood figure, but English royalty. Princess Diana appeared on the cover a record forty-three times prior to her death in 1997, causing sales to escalate each time.

While *TV Guide* had been around for decades as one of the largest-circulation magazines, the 1980s and 1990s also saw the rise of other publications devoted to the exclusive coverage of Hollywood subjects, including *A&E Monthly*, *American Movie Classics Magazine*, *Black Film Review*, *Cinefantastique*, *Cinefax*, *Daytime T.V.*, *Discover* (The Discovery Channel Magazine), *Disney Channel Magazine*,

Entertainment Weekly, Fangoria, Filmfax, Movieline, Premiere, Satellite TV Week, Satellite Choice, Sci-Fi Entertainment, Soap Opera Digest, Soap Opera Weekly and *Total TV/Pay-Per-View*.

The Electronic Media

May 28, 1982, is another day that will live in the hearts of Hollywood press agents. That was the premiere date for the daily syndicated TV show, "Entertainment Tonight." Suddenly, publicists could blanket the country with their promotional stories or interviews, reaching tens of millions of viewers at once on a program that was notoriously "soft" and devoted to celebrating stars. It gave publicists a leverage they didn't have before; they were now able to bypass or ignore reporters or other media outlets they didn't want to deal with, or make unprecedented demands, knowing they had "ET" in their back pocket, ready to give them national exposure.

Just as *People* had a ripple effect on the magazine industry, the success of "ET" in syndication gave rise to a wave of TV celebrity coverage, including shows like "Showbiz Today," "Access Hollywood" and "E! Extra" on the E! cable network, which continue "ET's" tradition of largely celebrity-friendly coverage.

There is a simple reason for TV's generally soft approach: unlike the print media, TV needs footage to make its stories work, particularly star interviews and film and TV clips. To gain access to the stars or permission to use the clips, TV producers and reporters must be extremely careful about what they report and how they report it. And, since TV is part of Hollywood itself, with some of the shows owned by large entertainment companies that also produce movies and other television programming, the tendency is to ignore or soft-pedal the more problematic Hollywood stories. As a news editor on the now-defunct "Entertainment Daily Journal," a Fox Entertainment News show that attempted harder-edged entertainment reporting, I saw numerous serious pieces shot down or abandoned because it was impossible to clear the rights to the visual material we needed to help tell the stories. In print, we would have gone ahead with the stories in a heartbeat, relying on words, not images, to get the job done.

How Coverage of Hollywood Has Changed

The first fan magazine, *Photoplay*, made its debut in 1912 to exploit and satisfy the voracious appetite for personal information about the stars who appeared in the fascinating new medium of motion pictures. *Photoplay* was the seed for a long line of "fanzines" that extended into the 1930s and 1940s, and bore such names as

Movie Mirror, Screenland, Modern Screen and *Screen Romance*. While they probed a bit into the less seemly aspects of the private lives of certain celebrities, they took an approach quite gentle by today's standards and never went too far; after all, they depended on the cooperation of the powerful studios for access to the stars and their photos. Indeed, with a few exceptions, the fanzines of that era acted almost like public relations organs for the studios and Hollywood's press agents, not unlike much of the mainstream press in general. This included printing deliberate falsehoods to protect images or cover up "unacceptable" behavior, such as homosexuality, unwed pregnancy, infidelity, spousal abuse and alcohol or drug addiction.

That all changed in the 1950s with the appearance of a new, less kindly brand of Hollywood reporting, in such notorious "scandal sheets" as *Confidential*, *Insider, Lowdown* and *Whisper*, whose sole purpose was to dig up and publish "Hollywood dirt." By then, the studio system was on the way out, and with it the studio's formidable influence over much of the press.

The rise of the supermarket tabloids over the ensuing decades brought celebrity coverage to a new peak of boldness and outrageousness, with almost no aspect of a celebrity's life considered off-limits. The exception for many years was homosexuality (most of the time), but even that taboo fell at the end of the 1980s, when the phenomenon of "outing" closeted gay celebrities and public figures made its way from certain factions of the gay press into the "tabs" and even into the mainstream press itself. (See "The Outing Trend," page 172.)

It was also at the end of the eighties that the popularity of supermarket "tabs" peaked, when they were collectively selling twelve to fifteen million copies each week, led by the *National Enquirer* and the *Star*. (The *Enquirer's* record was 6.6 million copies sold in 1977, when it published a clandestine photo of Elvis Presley's bloated corpse in its casket, snapped secretly at his funeral.) By the late 1990s, the sales figures of the tabs were down by more than half, in part because much of the novelty of shock reporting had worn off. Another factor, however, was the tabloid-style reporting that had crept into much of the mainstream media, as reported by the *Los Angeles Times* in 1997: "There are tabloid TV shows, cable talk shows, mainstream newspapers, entertainment magazines, the eleven o'clock news, the Internet and scores of other outlets to satisfy the celebrity news appetites." The *Times* also noted that the World Wide Web "is full of sites devoted exclusively to celebrities, such as CelebSite, an indexed site that lists extensive details on stars' lives." More and more, in the 1990s, the line between the mainstream and the exploitation media became blurred.

The "Outing" Trend

For decades, one of the unwritten rules for film and television stars was: It's OK to be gay as long as you don't flaunt it, publicly acknowledge it or get caught at it. By and large, the press went along, either discreetly avoiding the discussion of the private lives of certain celebrities, or tacitly cooperating with stars and publicists by printing accounts of heterosexual feelings and relationships the reporters and editors knew to be false. It was understood that to reveal a star's homosexuality in print was tantamount to destroying his or her career, and many stars lived out their lives and careers in secret shame, abetted by a cooperative press.

Then came "outing"—the practice of publicly exposing the homosexuality of closeted celebrities and public figures against their wishes and their will. It followed by four years the 1985 AIDS death of closeted film icon Rock Hudson, beginning as a gay political tactic within a segment of the more militant gay press, which felt more gay visibility and honesty was needed in the fight for gay rights and against the AIDS epidemic. Within a year, seeing an opportunity to jack up supermarket sales, the tabloids jumped on the bandwagon, naming names of some of Hollywood's biggest stars or their gay children, even paying former same-sex lovers for their tape-recorded accounts, as well as personal photographs, which were published in sensational style.

There was a tremendous outcry against the practice from many in the gay community, who contended that coming out or remaining closeted should be a personal and private decision, and likened outing to a new kind of McCarthyism. Publicists also decried outing, declaring that much of a star's success was built on his or her ability to appeal to the public's largely heterosexual fantasies, and that the American public was not ready to accept actors as romantic leading men and women if they knew them to be privately homosexual.

No celebrities who were directly "outed" filed lawsuits, however, and none suffered noticeable career damage. Outing, along with the continuing impact of HIV and AIDS, has clearly had an impact, both on the media and Hollywood itself. Since the trend went into full swing at the start of the decade, a number of television and film actors have come out on their own (see "The Gay Factor," in chapter eight), as well as many other notable entertainment figures, without apparent harm to their careers. Still, at this writing, no major American film star has publicly acknowledged his or her homosexuality, and it remains to be seen when, or if, that will happen.

The Special Role of the Critics

Since film reviews began appearing regularly not long after the turn of the century, they have become a part of the national consciousness and another part of

Hollywood's "Buzzing Insects": The Paparazzi

Prior to the 1950s, professional photographers generally behaved with deference and courtesy toward celebrities; it was standard practice to ask permission before shooting their photographs. That changed with the emergence in the fifties of the Italian "paparazzo," the aggressive, tabloid-style photographers who chase after stars, made famous in director Federico Fellini's film, *La Dolce Vita* (1960). Paparazzo literally translates as "buzzing insect," an apt description for the packs of cameramen (relatively few are women) determined to get the photos they want, no matter what.

In the 1960s, Ron Gallela defined the new breed of paparazzi as he became something of a celebrity in his own right, devoting much of his time to stalking and shooting pictures of the John F. Kennedy family, particularly the President's wife, Jackie. In addition to photographs of Jackie, later Jacqueline Kennedy Onassis, the most sought after exclusive photos in recent decades have been those of Elvis Presley, Elizabeth Taylor, Princess Diana, Michael Jackson and Madonna, each of whom seemed to generate a peculiar and particularly intense fan worship that makes photos of them especially valuable.

While a highly prized celebrity photo might have brought a few thousand dollars in the 1950s, by the late 1990s, a single, revealing photograph of the right star at the right moment could sell for as much as several hundred thousand dollars. At one point, a shot of actress Brooke Shields alone was selling for about $100; with fiancé and tennis star Andre Aggasi, the price went up to $100,000. TV actress Pamela Anderson Lee, married to rock star Tommy Lee, reportedly sold photos of their baby for a total of $450,000 to various tabloids. One enterprising paparazzo rented a house on a hilltop above Madonna's home for nine days at a cost of $5,000 a day, and got pictures with his telescopic lens of the performer that he sold for more than $150,000. In 1997, the most coveted photo by far was that of Michael Jackson's baby; he sold it to the newspapers himself, reportedly for half a million dollars or more.

Dozens of paparazzi roam the streets of Beverly Hills, West Hollywood and other L.A. neighborhoods by car and motorcycle, as well as many other major cities around the world and popular celebrity vacation spots like Aspen. They typically stake out driveways, restaurants, party sites, film premieres, and airport terminals. It's common to see the paparazzi yelling, waving and calling out the names of celebrities as they point their cameras, hoping to get the stars to look directly into their lens, which makes the resulting photo considerably more valuable.

The reputation of paparazzi reached a new low on August 30, 1997, when the high-speed pursuit of Princess Diana in Paris by a pack of celebrity photographers ended in a horrific car crash that claimed her life and those of two others. There was a worldwide outcry against the "buzzing insects" and, at least for a time, most of those in Hollywood were on their best behavior.

the love-hate relationship between Hollywood and the media. When the reviews are negative, Hollywood dismisses the importance or authority of critics; when the reviews are raves, the studios reproduce the most quotable sections in newspapers and on television screens across America as if the critics are brilliantly perceptive.

A number of critics have achieved their own kind of fame: Pauline Kael of the *New Yorker*, Bosley Crowther of the *New York Times*, Andrew Sarris of the *Village Voice*. But for all the attention paid them, no print critic has ever begun to equal the clout of two Chicago newspaper writers who, in the early 1980s, took their debates on films to television as a team—Gene Siskel and Roger Ebert, the duo known as Siskel & Ebert. Entertaining sparring partners, relentless self-promoters, with a syndicated TV audience in the tens of millions, they have acquired such a high profile and vast following that their "thumbs up" and "thumbs down" judgments on movies can send millions flocking to theaters on opening day, or staying away. (Even then, the studios are able to maintain some control by selecting the best clips from the movie for airing with the televised review, knowing that pictures often speak louder than words.)

In general, film critics aren't required to have any special credentials. Many come with college film degrees or film reporting backgrounds, but just as many have started as young writers who had a passion for movies and happened to be in the right place at the right time when an editor needed someone to "write up a movie." It's an odd, somewhat lonely occupation, with much of the time spent in dark screening rooms or theaters, or back at the office, writing up review after review. (Producers and studio marketing people prefer that critics see their film with a large audience, particularly in the case of comedies, where the laughter is such an important part of the moviegoing experience.) The average critic may review as many as a hundred movies a year; for some of the larger newspapers, it might be as many as 200 to 250 of the estimated 450 to 500 movies released each year. Major newspapers usually have a pecking order of critics, with the senior or top film critic assigned to the most important releases, and the bottom rung critic forced to sit through and review the worst of the dreck. Burnout is one of the occupational hazards.

The ideal film critic is a serious student of the form, with a deep knowledge of cinema, particularly the work of the master filmmakers, and an understanding of the film production process. Yet more and more, anyone is able to call himself or herself a "critic" simply by getting their byline atop a review or their face on camera as they read their opinions off a TelePrompTer. In recent years, a new breed of "reviewing whore" has appeared on the scene—"easy" critics who gush over almost every movie that comes out, creating quotable catch phrases in praise of the film, thus ensuring that their blurbs and names will be widely reprinted in studio ads for the movie. Some reviewers have even been exposed as frauds after earning money to write positive reviews for use by the studios, and fabricating or exaggerating their credentials or affiliations with the media.

With hundreds of critics plying the trade around the country, a number of regional and national critics associations have formed to give awards and deal with professional issues. Among the more prominent are the National Society of Film Critics, the National Board of Review, the New York Film Critics Circle, the Los Angeles Film Critics Association, the Chicago Film Critics, the Boston Society of Film Critics, the Independent Film Critics Association, the New York Independent Film Critics, the Newspaper Film Critics of America and the Television Critics Association.

The Trade Publications

For those who toil in Hollywood's film and television industry or make their living covering it as reporters, "must" reading includes the two major trade publications: *Variety*, including both its daily and weekly editions, and *The Hollywood Reporter*.

Variety was launched first as a weekly in 1905 by Sime Silverman, a disaffected show business critic on the *New York World Telegram*, who was irate because he wasn't allowed to write a negative review of a vaudeville act if the theater's ads were running in his paper. So he started his own trade publication, *Weekly Variety*, which came to be known as "the Bible of show business." It also became famous for its breezy use of language and slang headlines, such as the legendary Stix Nix Hicks Pix (rural audiences reject films with farm settings). Other typical *Varietese*: "boffo" (for big at the box-office), "yawner" (boring movie), "oater" (Western movie) and "tenpercenter" (agent), all used routinely in the paper until they caught on in everyday Hollywood conversation and, to some extent, with the general public. (See "Common Hollywood Slang" in Appendix A.)

W.R. Wilkerson started *The Hollywood Reporter* as a daily in mid-Depression 1930, and three years later, the New York-based *Variety* started a daily edition in Hollywood. Although the "trades" carried some columns of gossip and social chitchat, they were first and foremost business journals that covered the deals, trends and dollars and cents figures of the industry, bolstered by numerous, no-nonsense reviews.

Over the decades, the reputations of the two papers have been up and down, with both taking heavy criticism at times for frequently publishing press release material unchecked. Their chumminess and commercial symbiosis with the industry they cover—all that trade advertising—is perhaps their most serious weakness. Nonetheless, they remain indispensable resources for staying on top of the daily goings-on in the business, and have shown marked improvement in recent years. In 1989, Peter Bart, a former *New York Times* reporter and later a Hollywood producer and studio executive, took over at *Variety* as vice president and editor-in-chief. The two editions of *Variety* (which consolidated in 1987) beefed up their reporting, and Bart's own commentaries were delivered with a sharp edge, although he has also been accused at times of playing favorites with his former cronies. The *Reporter* is run by editor-in-chief and publisher Robert J. Dowling, who comes from a trade publishing background and has expanded coverage, including an international edition.

To contact the trades: *Daily Variety* (5700 Wilshire Blvd., Suite #120, Los Angeles, CA 90036; 213/857-6600); *Weekly Variety* (475 Park Ave. S., New York, NY 10016; 212/779-1100); *The Hollywood Reporter* (5055 Wilshire Blvd., Los Angeles, CA 90036; 213/525-2000).

Other trade publications that may prove useful for research include:

American Cinematographer (1782 N. Orange Dr., Hollywood, CA 90028; 213/876-5080)

Billboard (5055 Wilshire Blvd., Los Angeles, CA 90036; 213/525-2300)

Broadcasting (5700 Wilshire Blvd., No. 120, Los Angeles, CA 90036-4396; 213/549-4100; fax: 213/937-4240)

Broadcasting and Cable Yearbook (R.R. Bowker, 121 Chanlon Rd., New Providence, NJ 07974-1541; 908/464-6800)

Electronic Media (6500 Wilshire Blvd., Los Angeles, CA 90048; 213/651-3710)

Entertainment Law and Finance (111 Eighth Ave., 9th Floor, New York, NY 10011; 212/463-5522)

Film and Video (8455 Beverly Blvd., Suite #508, Los Angeles, CA 90048)

Filmmaker Magazine (Independent Feature Project, 110 West 57th St., 3rd Floor, New York, NY 10019; 212/581-8080)

Independent (Foundation for Independent Video and Film, 304 Hudson St., 6th Floor N., New York, NY 10013; 212/807-1400)

Interactive Update (38 East 29th St., 10th Floor, New York, NY 10016; 212/684-2333; fax: 212/684-0291)

Millimeter (1775 Broadway, Suite #730, New York, NY 10019; 216/641-5265)

New Media Magazine (901 Mariner's Island Blvd., Suite #365, San Mateo, CA 94404)

Video Business Weekly (345 Park Ave. S., New York, NY 10010)

Video Magazine (460 West 34th St., New York, NY 10001)

Video Review (902 Broadway, New York, NY 10010)

Video Software Dealer (5519 Centinela Ave., Los Angeles, CA 90066)

Video Week (475 Fifth Ave., New York, NY 10017)

WIRED (covers the Internet) (520 Third St., 4th Floor, San Francisco, CA 94107; 415/222-6200; fax: 415/222-6209; info@wired.com

Paul Kagan Associates (126 Clock Tower Pl., Carmel, CA 93933; 408/624-1536; fax: 408/625-3225) publishes a number of newsletters reporting on the broadcast and cable TV industry.

Also see Appendix B for Hollywood Web sites and databases that offer computer access to wide-ranging information on the movie and television industry.

CHAPTER SEVEN

Geographical Hollywood

I n this chapter, we will take a tour not only through Hollywood, but also the outlying communities that have strong Hollywood ties or flavor, and are linked in various ways to Tinseltown. For those writers who need a broader knowledge of Los Angeles and Southern California for their background material, an immense subject in itself, we will recommend some excellent resources.

An Overview of the Region's Physical and Cultural Characteristics

To understand this area in a physical sense, an outsider needs to be aware of several key characteristics:

Immense Physical Sprawl

Los Angeles County is comprised of eighty-eight incorporated cities, of which Los Angeles is one, covering 4,083.21 square miles. The city of Los Angeles, at 465 square miles, is the nation's largest. (Hollywood is not an incorporated city but a district within the city of Los Angeles.) Most of the city's districts and adjacent communities are located within a largely flat basin between the ocean (to the south and west) and mountains (to the north and northeast), with vast arid, desertlike terrain to the east. This is commonly known as "the Los Angeles basin."

The Area Teems With People

L.A. County is the state's most populous, with 9.24 million people in 1996 (at least those that were counted; many immigrants and homeless persons were surely missed). More than a third of those, roughly 3.5 million, reside within the Los Angeles city limits, making it the nation's second largest city. While some smaller "apartment communities," such as West Hollywood, are among the densest in the state, the overall population per square mile in the city of Los Angeles—6,830—is relatively low. (The number of inhabitants per square mile in New York City, for example, is 23,494.) However, an influx of nearly 28 million business and tourism visitors each year causes the population to swell (New York gets about 25 million). Recent calculations by the U.S. Census Bureau project that by 2025, California's population will have grown by 18 million, from 31.6 million (in 1995) to more than 49 million, akin to absorbing the entire current population of New York state. According to the study, half these will be immigrants, both legal and illegal, and millions are likely to settle in Southern California.

Cars Dominate the Culture

On any given day, close to five million cars travel the streets and freeways of Los Angeles, causing widespread gridlock. Although the city has encouraged carpooling, including a special freeway express lane ("the diamond lane," marked by diamond-shaped insignia) for cars carrying two or more passengers, each day 1.7 million citizens drive to work alone.

Morning and evening commuting is a driving nightmare that becomes worse as the population increases; it is not uncommon in some sections of the city for a fifteen-mile commute during the peak rush hour to take an hour or more. (Even at midday and on weekends, many of the city's streets are sluggish with traffic.) Among the most clogged intersections: Wilshire Boulevard and Veteran Avenue in West L.A. (near UCLA), and Highland Avenue and Sunset Boulevard in Hollywood (near the Hollywood Freeway on- and off-ramps), each of which is crossed by 128,000 cars every twenty-four hours. Dozens of other city intersections register 100,000 or more cars passing through each day.

This situation has led to such intense frustration on the streets and freeways ("road rage") that numerous shootings from and between cars occur here each year, as well as screaming matches, fistfights and the like. Parking is equally bad,

> " Hollywood is 72 suburbs in search of a city. "
>
> —DOROTHY PARKER

179

L.A.'s "Car Museum"

For a historical look at automobiles in Southern California, consider a visit to the Petersen Automotive Museum on L.A.'s "Museum Row," which includes period landscape and building re-creations among its many exhibits (6060 Wilshire Blvd. at Fairfax Avenue; 213/744-3314).

---

with some parking structures in tonier business districts charging up to $13 to park, some street parking meters requiring a dollar or more per hour, and a number of hotels demanding $20 for off-street parking, with the prices going up all the time. Developing communities in Southern California are now designed first and foremost to alleviate parking and traffic flow problems.

The city bus system is barely adequate and no longer cheap (the basic fare in 1997 was $1.35, higher for express buses, with transfers costing a quarter); the primary riders are the poor (largely nonwhite), the elderly and students. Taxis are costly and used infrequently (especially compared to more centralized cities like New York and Chicago) and primarily by the affluent. The aboveground Metro Rail system, only a few years in operation, has yet to catch on as a major source of transportation. The subway connecting downtown, Hollywood and the Valley has been beset by mammoth budget overruns, construction accidents and deaths, alleged incompetence, financial scandal and endless delays. When (and if) the subway finally opens, it may take time to build customer confidence, since many residents are apprehensive about riding an underground train system—part of which tunnels beneath the Hollywood Hills—that has been plagued by so many construction and engineering snafus in earthquake-prone L.A.

Other than traffic congestion and the basin's notorious smog (improved but still a serious health concern), the most obvious example of the automobile's impact on L.A. is the proliferation of drive-up, drive-in and drive-through businesses, a phenomenon that began in the 1920s and has grown to include drive-up bank ATMs, drive-in churches (using former drive-in theaters) and, more recently, drive-through cappuccino bars.

While the automobile has brought enormous personal freedom and geographical access to millions of Southern Californians, it has also caused immeasurable anxiety, physical discomfort, health problems and ecological damage.

The Freeways Connect Almost Everything

To move around Southern California, one needs to know which freeways go where, where they connect and so on. Except for the middle section of the city's west side—the Beverly Hills/West Hollywood area, which is located several miles from the nearest freeway on-ramp—and certain suburbs (particularly the beach cities), drivers jump on and off the freeways to get around the way New Yorkers hop on and off the subways.

Perhaps the most famous and photographed freeway interchange in the world is the dramatic nexus of the 101 (Hollywood Freeway) and 110 (Harbor and Pasadena Freeways) in downtown Los Angeles. Completed in 1953, it was the world's first "four-level grade separation," with seventeen miles of tiers criss-crossing and undercutting in a cloverleaf effect. Today, the "Four Level," or "Stack," as it is variously called, serves nearly half a million cars daily that spin off in eight directions along its lanes. (For an excellent overview map of the Los Angeles freeway system, see the current *Frommer's Los Angeles*.)

Palm Trees Are Everywhere

Although dozens of varieties of palms can be seen throughout virtually every area of Southern California, there is only one true native: *Washingtonia filifera*, better known as the Washington or California palm. This is the tall (fifteen to eighty feet) palm with the slim but sturdy shaft and crown of shaggy fronds whose fruit served as a food source for the local native Indians of the eighteenth and nineteenth centuries. Thousands were planted along Los Angeles area streets during the 1920s and 1930s, and many continue to dominate the street-scapes of Hollywood, West Hollywood, Santa Monica and other communities, emblematic of the region and of Hollywood in particular. As one aspiring actor said after arriving by freeway: "When I saw the palm trees, I knew I was in Los Angeles."

Mild Climate

"A harmonious merging of latitude and the influences of seashore and mountains," write Leonard Pitt and Dale Pitt, in *Los Angeles A to Z*. "The combination

---

❝A great place to live if you're an orange.❞

COMEDIAN FRED ALLEN

---

produces a nearly perfect human environment that over the years has attracted huge numbers of settlers and tourists from less hospitable climes." The Pitts point out that Southern California has two seasons: ". . . a long, dry, moderately warm spell from May to November, and . . . a wet, moderately cool, but never bitter spell from November to May." Because of the varied terrain within the county, including mountains, valleys, desert and seashore, a wide variation of weather exists within this generally temperate zone. In winter, the thermometer rarely drops below 40° in Los Angeles, and is more often in the high 50s and 60s; in summer, it rarely rises above 100° and is customarily much cooler, especially toward the ocean. Studies have shown that the only reasonably pollution-free air is close to the beach, where the ocean breezes drive the smog inland; much of this "bad air" is forced through mountain passes into the sprawling, suburban communities of the San Fernando and San Gabriel valleys, where the pollution sometimes reaches dangerous levels during the warmer months.

> Hot winds that felt like the devil's breath blew into Los Angeles from the desert, rattling through the shaggy eucalyptus trees like a dry cough.
> FROM THE NOVEL *SIMPLE JUSTICE*, BY THE AUTHOR

The Santa Ana Winds Blow Hard
The region's famous "Santa Anas," which are hot, dry winds that blast in from the northeast deserts, generally in late summer and early fall, get their name from Orange County's Santa Ana Canyon, through which many of these sirocco-like winds pass. Mystery novelist Raymond Chandler termed them "red wind." While they are helpful in clearing the skies of pollution, they also generate a strange, edgy tension among many residents, and often find their way into *noirish* descriptions of the city.

Natural Disasters Strike Frequently
Earthquakes, flooding, mud slides, prolonged drought and wildfires are all common to the region. Much of this is cyclical: During the hot, windy weather of summer and early fall, the wildfires ravage the dry brush; with the brush and roots gone, the winter rains loosen the hillsides, sometimes causing monstrous mud slides (hundreds have been killed over the decades by walls of mud crushing houses and automobiles). Following the rains comes new growth, which will

grow dry again with summer and feed the next wildfires, continuing the cycle. Consequently, brush clearance, both private and public, is a major activity here, and smoking is forbidden on many hillside and mountain roadways.

Earthquakes, of course, continue to pose an enormous threat, with dangerous fault lines running under many sections of the Southland, including downtown Los Angeles; the certainty of more major earthquakes gnaws at the subconscious of many residents. The Northridge earthquake of January 17, 1994, which registered 6.7 on the Richter scale at nearby Cal Tech University, has been deemed the single, costliest natural disaster in American history. It caused some $20 billion in damage, killed an estimated sixty persons, left twenty thousand people homeless and millions of residents with jittery memories of the predawn tremor that ruptured the earth and caused whole buildings to collapse. Minor earthquakes and aftershocks (measuring 5.0 or less) are now so common in Los Angeles that most are ignored or taken in stride. After some "shakers," many people pause in what they are doing, jokingly estimate the Richter size of the shock, then go back about their business. The threat of another "big one" is quite serious, however, and after the Northridge disaster, thousands of uneasy residents left the city for good.

Crime Is Rampant

To some extent, Los Angeles developed as a brawling, boozing, thieving frontier town, and though it has grown to become one of the most important cities in the world culturally and economically, it is still plagued with widespread criminal activity, from white-collar corruption to street-level thuggery. Although many cities rank higher than L.A. in overall violent crime, the murder rate here in the early 1990s was grim, with roughly half a dozen murders being committed within the county each day—more than two thousand a year—and more than a third of them gang-related.

Several factors were at the heart of the city's alarming rise in violent crime in the 1980s and 1990s: The proliferation of violent gangs, their almost casual use of automatic and semiautomatic weapons, and the introduction of crack cocaine, all of it exacerbated by inner city unemployment and poverty. To this day, certain gangs control entire neighborhoods, marking them (and many outlying communities) with spray-painted gang graffiti, and terrorizing residents through cowardly drive-by shootings ostensibly carried out for intimidation or revenge, but which often cause the deaths of innocent bystanders. (News reports of another child killed or seriously injured by gunfire occur almost daily here, and in many sections of the city, children are not allowed to play outside.) While the majority of gangs in the city are African-American or Hispanic, gangs also exist that are Asian, Anglo, Pacific Islander and, more recently, Russian immigrant. Gangs have also figured in the sale and use of crack, a cheap, highly addictive form of cocaine that has created a new generation of desperate junkies in all parts of the city, but has ravaged the black community in particular and caused a ripple effect on the overall crime rate.

Robbery, especially, has been affected. For several decades, Los Angeles has been known as the "bank robbery capital of the world," thanks in part to the easy access to so many freeways, aiding escape by automobile. (Many bank tellers now work behind bullet-proof Plexiglas.) But more recently, two newer types of robbers have emerged here: carjackers, who pull drivers from their cars at gunpoint and steal the vehicles, and ATM bandits, who stake out ATM machines and rob customers as they withdraw cash. In some instances, cold-blooded murder accompanies both types of robberies, adding yet more crime and violence to the evening news and helping to crank up the tension of daily life.

That anxiety diminished somewhat with the dramatic drop in violent crime rates that began in the mid-1990s, due in large part to an increase of police officers on the streets, updated police equipment and methodology, more community-based law enforcement, attempts to diminish or control gang activity and a self-imposed truce among a coalition of large gangs. Nonetheless, a nine-month rampage of gang warfare that began in late 1996 claimed fifteen lives in a two-square-mile patch of South Central Los Angeles, reminding everyone, but especially those in the poorest neighborhoods, that bloody violence was still an indelible part of L.A. life.

The Mexican Influence Is Pervasive

Until the mid-1700s, the area that is now Los Angeles city and its environs was a natural paradise in which native Indians made their homes and roamed freely. It was first "settled" in 1781 by forty-four dark-skinned colonists from Mexico as a Spanish pueblo. Thereafter, until this Mexican city was annexed by the United States, Spanish was the chief language and Mexicans were the predominant residents, landowners and leaders. The first missions were run by Mexican priests; the first newspapers printed in Spanish; the first streets named after prominent Mexicans from the fields of business, education, philanthropy and politics. The area remained Mexican until 1850, when California entered the union, and *pueblo de Los Angeles* was incorporated as a U.S. municipality, following prolonged, bloody warfare waged with Mexico. Consequently, one finds a pervasive Mexican influence, not just in Los Angeles, but throughout the region in the ethnic makeup of the people, the names of cities and major streets, the architecture, food, music, fashion and so on.

Diversity Is the Norm

Los Angeles has often been described as the most ethnically and culturally diverse city in the world. It has been reported that one can hear nearly eighty languages spoken by city residents, who have moved here from more than 140 foreign countries. Exact ethnic measurements are difficult because of so many uncounted immigrants, but in the late 1990s, the population broke down roughly this way: 42 percent Latino, 36 percent Anglo, 12 percent African-American, 10 percent Asian. More Mexicans, Armenians, Koreans, Filipinos, Salvadorans and Guatemalans live in Los Angeles County than in any other area of the world outside their homelands, and the largest concentrations of Japanese, Iranians and Cambodians in the U.S. are found here. More than a million adults and children speak English as a second language, and more than fifty foreign-language newspapers are published within the county, with seventeen languages other than English heard daily on the radio. (For the past several years, FM Spanish-language K-LVE, devoted to Spanish-language ballads, has topped the audience rating charts.) Spanish is by far the most frequently heard non-English language, but it is not uncommon to overhear conversations spoken in Vietnamese, Hmong, Cantonese, Tagalog, Hebrew, Russian, Korean, Armenian, Cambodian and Farsi. Dining out on Mexican, Italian and Chinese food has been second nature to most Angelenos for decades, but now Thai, Japanese, Caribbean, Persian, Cuban, Ethiopian, South American and other ethnically flavored restaurants dot the city's landscape. Countless book and video stores, movie theaters, museums and other cultural venues further reflect the wide range of backgrounds found here.

The impact of illegal immigration on the local culture and economy has become a major political issue in Southern California in the 1990s. To be sure, undocumented workers make up a significant part of the work force; the "underground" economy (such as unlicensed vendors and domestic workers paid in cash) is widespread; and thousands of men and boys gather daily in bunches in various sections of the city hoping to be picked up for day labor jobs, while many of the women board buses for jobs as domestic workers and other positions that may not require documentation. Racial and cultural tensions also exist in other

185

Despite sometimes precarious topography, developers have built a great many homes in the Hollywood Hills, shown here. (Photo by Nyla Arslanien.)

social sectors, often erupting into violence and, even at least two devastating riots. To a great extent, one sees ethnic pockets and communities forming, and often corresponding economic ghettos, rather than widespread racial assimilation. "White flight" has resulted in some areas, with many affluent caucasians (and some affluent nonwhites) fleeing to the more comfortable, crime-free west side and outlying suburbs, or to adjacent Orange County.

Yet one also sees many of these ethnic groups revitalizing and bringing a new sense of identity and pride to economically plagued or neglected neighborhoods. Others spread out individually, particularly the second and third generations of immigrant families, finding their rightful place in literally every community in the region, many of which were once considered strictly white enclaves. In truth, for all the ethnic division, racial tension and economic disparity that exists here, day in and day out one sees a dazzling array of ethnic diversity in places of work, dining, socializing, recreation and worship. Tom Bradley, an excop from a black sharecropping family, served as the city's mayor from 1973 to 1993 (elected by a primarily white and Latino constituency) and during most of the 1990s, the city's police department has been run by one of two African-American chiefs.

186

Currently, the fifteen-member city council includes elected officials, both male and female, who are black, Hispanic, Jewish and openly gay.

While the city and its surrounding areas may not be the ideal "melting pot" some might have hoped for, they do comprise the country's modern day Ellis Island, and every economic and occupational strata reflects this remarkable ethnic and cultural influx. For writers to portray the Los Angeles of the 1990s as a strictly ghettoized city, or to relegate its nonwhite residents to traditional stereotypes or roles, would be naive, grossly inaccurate and unfair.

The Districts and Neighborhoods

Again, to cover the entire Los Angeles area in this book would be impossible, but we will introduce you to those districts and neighborhoods with the strongest Hollywood influence and connections. They include central Hollywood, West Hollywood, Beverly Hills, Century City, Westwood Village, Bel-Air, Santa Monica, Pacific Palisades, Malibu, the San Fernando Valley and Culver City.

To think that these are the only communities where Hollywood people live, eat, play or hang out would be a serious misjudgment, however; "Hollywood types" are spread far and wide across the Los Angeles basin and beyond, from the desert resort city of Palm Springs to the southern shoreline communities of Manhattan Beach and Hermosa Beach to distant northern seaside havens like Montecito, some sixty miles away. (Again, it's important to realize how sprawling a region this is, and how much the automobile impacts personal lifestyles.) Actor John Leguizamo (*Spawn, A Brother's Kiss, Body Count*), for example, who hails from New York's lower east side, keeps his West Coast home in Echo Park, a largely working class, Latino community situated in the hills between Hollywood and downtown Los Angeles. "I hate being in the Hollywood ghetto," explains Leguizamo, "where everyone's rich and deep into mortgages and Mercedeses. In Echo Park you have Silver Lake [with sizable Latino, gay and artistic communities] and Chinatown and Thai Town nearby, the best of everything where all cultures meet."

That attitude captures perfectly the way many men and women in Hollywood's creative community choose to live, away from the glitter, glamour and excessive social whirl—the "Hollywood" the public rarely sees or reads about.

Hollywood

When we speak of Hollywood as the entertainment capital of the world, it is in the figurative and symbolic sense. Although many postproduction houses and other film industry support companies are located in Hollywood, along with several major record companies, only one major studio, Paramount, remains. Most of the wealthiest and most successful creative people in the industry left Hollywood decades ago as it began to change from a picturesque residential, creative and tourist mecca into a seedy, crime-ridden urban zone replete with tacky tourist shops, drug dealers, panhandlers, runaways and prostitutes, a bleak situation that bottomed out toward the end of the 1980s.

Located roughly eight miles west of downtown, Hollywood is still the most famous piece of real estate in the world and has been rebounding economically and aesthetically since the early 1990s. Ironically, severe damage during the 1992 riots and the 1994 earthquake had some positive effects by generating massive federal relief funds that helped the revitalization effort. Crime is down 21 percent overall since 1993, the streets are noticeably cleaner and more attractive— swaying palm trees and filmstrip crosswalks have been added—and business is significantly up. In 1996, the area reportedly attracted some nine million visitors, who spent roughly a billion dollars during their stay.

Reviving Hollywood has become a top political priority in the office of the mayor and the district's councilwoman, and a number of landmark sites on or near Hollywood Boulevard, such as the historic Egyptian Theater (6712 Hollywood Blvd.), are undergoing restoration. This follows the earlier renovation by the Walt Disney Company of the El Capitan Theater (6838 Hollywood Blvd.), a legendary picture palace that had fallen into disrepair but is now Disney's showcase theater in L.A. and the highest-grossing, single-screen theater in the United States. Some two dozen other projects are in the works, including the new Hollywood Entertainment Museum and the Museum of Hollywood History, to be opened in the refurbished, historic Max Factor building (1666 N. Highland Ave., just south of Hollywood Boulevard). Still, it remains to be seen if the historic heart of Tinseltown will be able to make a complete comeback.

In addition to Hollywood Boulevard itself, the fabled "street of dreams" that is now an official national historic district, a number of other locations, landmarks and institutions help define Hollywood. These include:

The Hollywood Sign. Hollywood's most recognizable symbol was erected in 1923 with thirteen letters spelling out HOLLYWOODLAND to advertise a real estate subdivision; the last four letters were dropped during a renovation in the late 1940s. The sheet metal letters rise fifty feet and stretch more than 450 feet across; once illuminated with several thousand high-wattage bulbs, the sign now rests in darkness at night in deference to the cost of lighting and the wishes

The most famous landmark in the area is the Hollywood sign, which sits near the top of Mount Lee in the Hollywood Hills. The letters, which are fifty feet high, are made of sheet metal. (Photo courtesy of Hollywood Chamber of Commerce.)

of nearby residents. The sign is situated on cactus-strewn Mount Lee at the top of Beachwood Canyon, accessible (with difficulty) via Durand Drive near Beachwood Drive, but well viewed from the corner of Sunset Boulevard and Bronson Avenue nearly two miles below. The base of the sign is fenced off and protected by motion detectors against vandals, who have plagued the landmark for decades. In 1932, a failed actress named Peg Entwistle gained immortality when she leaped to her death from atop one of the letters; most sources say it was the "H."

The Hollywoodland Gates. The sandstone gates, with modest arches and towers that suggest a gothic, fairy-tale quality, were originally erected as the entrance to the Hollywoodland subdivision. Now worn down by time and weather, they are located approximately a mile up Beachwood Drive from Franklin Avenue at Westshire Drive, in the quaint village of Beachwood Canyon.

The Walk of Fame. This is the three-and-a-half mile stretch of more than 2,500 bronze medallions set in granite stars that pay tribute to Hollywood's famous (and, in some cases, long forgotten). They can be found along Hollywood Boulevard, between Gower Street and La Brea Avenue, and along Vine Street, between Yucca Street and La Brea Avenue. The sidewalks are cleaned six days a week; one weekend out of every month, a group of volunteers, the Star Polishers, gets down on hands and knees to individually shine the stars. The Hollywood Chamber of Commerce (213/469-8311) oversees the Walk of Fame and currently charges celebrities or their fan clubs or supporters $4,000 for the honor. Dedication ceremonies usually take place at noon on the third Thursday of each month, and the public is welcome to watch the hoopla.

Some of the more popular star locations: Rudolph Valentino (6164 Hollywood Blvd.), Greta Garbo (6901 Hollywood Blvd.), James Dean (1719 Vine St.), John Lennon (1750 Vine St.), Louis Armstrong (7000 Hollywood Blvd.), Marlon Brando (1765 Vine St.), Mickey Mouse and Barbra Streisand (both at 6925 Hollywood Blvd.), John Wayne (1541 Vine St.), Ronald Reagan (6374 Hollywood Blvd.), Sammy Davis, Jr. (6254 Hollywood Blvd.), Michael Jackson (6927 Hollywood Blvd.), Harrison Ford (6667 Hollywood Blvd.), Clark Gable (1610 Vine St.), Tom Cruise (6912 Hollywood Blvd.) and Johnny Carson (1749 Vine St.). Because of unexpected sinkage caused by the underground subway construction along Hollywood Boulevard, more than two hundred stars are being temporarily removed for their protection, including those of Marilyn Monroe (6744 Hollywood Blvd.) and Elvis Presley (6777 Hollywood Blvd.). A complete map with star locations is available from the Chamber of Commerce.

At least three other "walks of fame" can be found in the Los Angeles area: *Hollywood's Rock Walk* (7435 Sunset Blvd.), which pays tribute to rock 'n roll legends; the *Hollywood Walk of Stars* (7734 Santa Monica Blvd., actually located in West Hollywood), which displays handprints and footprints of porn icons in front of the gay Tomkat Theater (formerly the straight Pussycat); and the *Latino Walk of Fame* (East Third Street and South Broadway, downtown Los Angeles), which pays homage to such legendary stars as Pedro Armendariz, Dolores Del Rio and Cantinflas, outside the Million Dollar Theater, one of the opulent picture palaces left over from Broadway's movie exhibition heyday. (After many years of economic decline, today Broadway is a vibrant, bustling commercial district serving a largely Hispanic and Spanish-speaking clientele.)

The Chinese Theater (6925 Hollywood Blvd.; 213/461-3311). This opulent and outlandish movie palace, designed in the form of a fanciful Chinese temple, originally opened in 1927 as Grauman's Chinese Theater. With a change in ownership in modern times, it is now officially Mann's Chinese Theater, part of a chain, but still retaining its distinctive charm. Each year, several million visitors crowd the theater's entry court to examine and take pictures of the 160-plus celebrity handprints, footprints and signatures that have been imprinted in concrete squares through the decades. Marilyn Monroe, Humphrey Bogart, Bob Hope (a *nose* print), Frank Sinatra, Paul Newman, Elizabeth Taylor, Ginger Rogers and cowboy star Gene Autry (his horse's hoofprint) are among those represented.

The Hollywood Wax Museum. Modeled after Madame Tussaud's Wax museum in Paris, the Hollywood Wax Museum (6767 Hollywood Blvd.; 213/462-8860) recreates famous movie events and stars with lifelike wax figures. It is not a serious, historical museum in the real sense, but an unabashed tourist trap (with varying admission charges) that particularly appeals to kids.

Hollywood Studio Museum (2100 North Highland Ave.; 213/874-2276). This museum of movie stills and other exhibitions is housed in the horse barn used as an office and studio by Cecil B. DeMille when he shot *The Squaw Man* in 1913, thought to be the first feature ever shot within the borders of Hollywood. It originally stood at Selma and Vine Streets, and was later moved to the Paramount Studios backlot by DeMille, who had it declared an historic landmark in 1956. Paramount, with expansion plans, removed it in 1979 and it sat forlornly on a vacant lot until reaching its present site in 1985 across from the Hollywood Bowl, thanks to Hollywood Heritage, an organization dedicated to preserving historic Hollywood buildings.

Musso & Frank Grill (6667 Hollywood Blvd.; 213/467-7788). Opened in 1919 and reputedly the oldest restaurant in Hollywood, Musso & Frank was a favorite of such writers as Faulkner and Fitzgerald in the 1930s and 1940s, as well as many stars and directors, and remains popular with the film industry crowd. With a lengthy menu of simple, old-fashioned food, served by no-nonsense waiters, Musso & Frank features cozy booths on the west side, a long counter in the middle for solitary diners and a more elegant dining room on the east side, all wood-paneled and virtually unchanged since its last remodeling in 1937. For many, it is like stepping back into a bygone era (not the prices, though).

Frederick's of Hollywood (6608 Hollywood Blvd.; 213/466-8506). This is the famous art deco, purple-and-pink lingerie shop opened in 1947 by Frederick Mellinger, the inventor of the push-up bra, which has spawned more than two hundred Frederick's stores in thirty-nine states. In addition to a wide assortment of lingerie on display and sale, Frederick's also offers its free "lingerie museum," which includes famous show business bras worn by a wide range of stars, from Milton Berle to Madonna, as well as other undergarments of the stars. Many vintage items were lost to looters during the 1992 riots, but Fredericks remains a popular Hollywood attraction.

Max Factor Museum of Beauty (1666 North Highland Ave. at Hollywood Blvd.; 213/463-6668). Another art deco landmark, this building served as the headquarters of Russian wig and cosmetics artist Max Factor after the Russian immigrant made his initial fortune providing fine makeup for many of Hollywood's top directors in Hollywood's early years. (He came to America in 1908 and died thirty years later.) Antique cosmetic samples, John Wayne's toupee, a vintage dressing room and movie stills are part of the museum's campy tour through movie makeup history. Admission is free.

The Janes House (6541 Hollywood Blvd.). Constructed in 1903, this Queen Anne-style Victorian house is the last surviving example of the mansions that lined the boulevard until the 1920s. Saved from demolition, it now houses the Hollywood Visitors Information Center (see "For More Information on Geographic Hollywood," on page 212). For decades, set back from the street and surrounded by commercial buildings, it sat in disrepair, an oddity to passersby but home to the elderly and reclusive Janes sisters. According to Richard Alleman in *The Movie Lover's Guide to Hollywood*, rumors have long persisted that Henry Farrell, author of the novel, *Whatever Happened to Baby Jane?* on which the 1962 film was based, patterned the two main characters in his story after the Janes sisters. Alleman points out that in the film, the former child star portrayed by Bette Davis was named Jane Hudson. The Janes house looks across Hollywood Boulevard to Hudson Street. Writes Alleman: "Author Farrell, however, denies any connection."

Hollywood and Vine. This intersection of Hollywood Boulevard and Vine Street is a venerable symbol of Hollywood's glamorous heyday, though it hardly looks glamorous today. The Equitable building, on the northeast corner, housed a number of agents who represented such stars as Clark Gable, Greta Garbo and Loretta Young. The Taft Building, on the southeast corner, also housed some powerful agents, was the broadcast site of Ronald Reagan's radio show and was the headquarters for the notorious Hays Office (see "Censorship and the Production Code" in chapter one). Decades ago, when it was the hub of the radio and movie industry, it was dubbed "Little Paris." A few vestiges of that era remain, if not at the corner itself then nearby, with such landmarks as the ornate Pantages Theater (6233 Hollywood Blvd.) and Palace Theater (1735 N. Vine St.). For the most part, however, this part of town is drab and rundown, with no better example than the fabled original Brown Derby restaurant (1628 N. Vine St.), which has been demolished and turned into a parking lot.

Grave Line Tours (213/469-3127). Created by a former mortician, this macabre but campy tour conducted in a converted hearse offers customers a two-hour trek past the homes where stars have died, committed suicide or been murdered. (To conduct your own celebrity death and burial tour, you might consult Ken Schlessler's *This Is Hollywood* or Richard Alleman's *The Movie Lover's Guide to Hollywood,* or go on-line with Find A Grave.com at http://wee.orci.com/personal/jim.)

Hollywood Memorial Cemetery (6000 Santa Monica Blvd.). It's here that you'll find the crypt of Rudolph Valentino (number 1205, Cathedral Museum, far left-hand corner), visited annually by the devoted and mysterious "Lady in Black" (actually in her third incarnation as the tradition is passed on to new generations). Other dead luminaries resting here include Cecil B. DeMille, Douglas Fairbanks, Sr., Peter Finch, Peter Lorre, Tyrone Power and Marion Davies. The cemetery, located in an area that has gone from glamorous to seedy over the decades, has been in bankruptcy since 1995 and has stopped selling plots. (Some visitors come here expecting to find the grave of Marilyn Monroe, who is actually buried at the *Westwood Cemetery,* 1218 Glendon Ave., in West Los Angeles.)

Farmer's Market (Third Street and Fairfax Avenue). Technically located in the "midtown" district of Los Angeles, this popular shopping mart is commonly thought of as a "Hollywood attraction." Originally opened in 1934 with eighteen food stalls where farmers sold their fresh produce, Farmer's Market today has more than 160 stalls, shops and cafes offering a wide range of ethnically diverse merchandise and cuisine. Immediately to the north is CBS Television City (at Beverly Boulevard), and across the intersection on the southwest corner is the Writer's Guild of America, west, the headquarters for the screenwriting trade on the West Coast (for more on the WGA, see chapter five).

West Hollywood

West Hollywood is situated between Hollywood and Beverly Hills with a geographical shape that has been variously likened to a key, a tommy gun and a tongue sticking into the ear of Hollywood.

> ## *"Hollywood by the Sea"*
>
> Since the early 1990s, Hollywood has witnessed a dramatic migration of entertainment companies westward, with perhaps the greatest concentration found along Colorado Avenue between 20th and 26th Streets in Santa Monica—what *Buzz* magazine refers to as "Hollywood by the Sea."
>
> Basking in fresh ocean breezes, such diverse firms as MGM/UA, Sony Music, MTV, Savoy Pictures, Playboy Studios West and Langley Productions (Fox TV's "Cops") have migrated from other parts of the Los Angeles area and coexist in a thriving creative and business atmosphere. The west side positioning puts entertainment executives and producers closer to Los Angeles International Airport (a few miles south), further from the worst traffic congestion and smog, and within minutes of the trendy beachside area of Santa Monica and its upscale amenities, where creative Hollywood-types like producers Oliver Stone and Jerry Bruckheimer have opened offices. It also makes for a shorter commute for those who live in nearby Beverly Hills, Bel-Air, Malibu and Pacific Palisades, all traditional residential enclaves for Hollywood's elite, *Buzz* points out.
>
> If Steven Spielberg's DreamWorks/SKG builds a studio in nearby Playa Vista, as it hopes to, it would be the grand jewel in the west side crown.

With a population of about thirty-six thousand covering 1.9 square miles, it is one of the state's densest cities as well as one of its most colorful. Because West Hollywood existed as an unincorporated pocket administered by the county until 1984, when it became an independent city, individuals and businesses within its borders were able to operate with fewer restrictions and less police control than those who came under city jurisdiction elsewhere. That sense of personal freedom and tolerance, even a touch of lawlessness, still flourishes today. "With its booming nightlife and progressive government," writes Gil Reavill in *Hollywood and the Best of Los Angeles*, "West Hollywood is more Hollywood than Hollywood itself, and one of the liveliest communities in Los Angeles."

This reputation is due in part to the city's large gay and lesbian population and the active gay social and cultural scene along Santa Monica Boulevard (nicknamed "Boy's Town" by many), and the famous Sunset Strip club scene a few blocks up the hill. In addition to its ten to fifteen thousand gay and lesbian residents, thousands more flood into the city nightly to patronize the clubs, restaurants, coffee bars, bookstores, gyms and boutiques that cater to a largely homosexual clientele. The city's annual Halloween night celebration, once an informal street party of gay club patrons outfitted in outlandish costumes, has now become an official and rather commercialized event that attracts tens of thousands of Southland residents, including many families with children. The annual Christopher Street Gay Pride Parade and fair, held each summer, draws even greater numbers.

All this excitement comes with a downside, of course, with drugs, prostitution and a continuing HIV crisis figuring in the equation. Hundreds, perhaps thousands, of the city's residents have died since the AIDS epidemic first gained attention in the early 1980s. Actor Sal Mineo was murdered by a robber in the carport of his West Hollywood apartment (8563 Holloway Dr.). The overdose deaths of actor River Phoenix and comedian John Belushi both took place at Sunset Strip locations, amid reports that drug use along the Strip was rampant. Although he was not arrested, comedian Eddie Murphy was stopped by deputies in 1997 after he picked up a transsexual prostitute along a stretch of Santa Monica Boulevard notorious for its cross-dressing street hustlers. The impact on residential neighborhoods around the more popular clubs has become a heated issue within the city, with complaints ranging from increased traffic and parking problems to loud drunkenness and lewd conduct. Gay-bashing is another serious problem as carloads of young men from outlying communities sometimes cruise known gay areas late at night looking for victims; a number of gay men and lesbians have been severely beaten or killed in recent years.

The city is by no means all nightlife. It is also home to a large population of the elderly and retired, including many of Jewish heritage. It was this group, seeking rent control, that formed a coalition with gay activists to forge cityhood in 1984. West Hollywood then elected the nation's first gay majority city council and was dubbed "America's First Gay City." In recent years, "WeHo," as some refer to it, has become a growing haven for Russian Jewish immigrants. Just as "gay rainbow" flags and other symbols of gay solidarity decorate many businesses, one sees increasing Russian or Hebrew lettering in working-class neighborhoods, particularly in West Hollywood's middle section along Santa Monica Boulevard between Fairfax and LaBrea Avenues.

Many celebrities make their homes in West Hollywood and nearby Beverly Hills, and it is not uncommon to see famous faces at the Pavilion's supermarket at Santa Monica and Robertson Boulevards, in the boutiques or galleries along Melrose Avenue, browsing for gay and lesbian book titles at A Different Light bookstore, sipping coffee at Starbucks or the Abbey, or dining at any number of the city's "in" restaurants. (See "Dining and Hanging Out" on page 207.)

West Hollywood has a number of noted landmarks, but perhaps none more visible or dramatic than the Pacific Design Center, which serves the interior design trade. The massive structure, plated with a blue glass exterior and known for years as "the Blue Whale" after its opening in 1975, is situated on Melrose Avenue just east of San Vicente Boulevard. A nine-story extension with an equally striking green glass exterior has since been erected on the sixteen-acre site, where it catches the eyes of drivers passing along nearby Santa Monica Boulevard, which serves as the main artery through the city.

The Sunset Strip

This mile-long stretch of Sunset Boulevard between Crescent Heights Boulevard and Doheny Drive is considerably tamer today than in decades past. Speakeasies, gambling casinos and elegant nightclubs proliferated in the 1930s and 1940s, with three—Ciro's, Mocambo and the Trocadero Cafe—reigning as the grand showplaces where Hollywood's greatest stars regularly dined, drank and danced the night away. (To see them recreated, rent the 1991 gangster film *Bugsy*.)

As the studio system began to erode and Hollywood glamour started to fade in the 1950s, strip joints sprouted up along the Strip and heavy boozing and prostitution became rife. In the 1960s, free-spirited "hippies" and hard-living rock 'n rollers moved in; repeated clashes with deputies culminated in a violent rampage one night that spawned a cheap exploitation movie, *Riot on Sunset Strip* (1967). In the 1970s, as the disco era boomed and dozens of popular clubs opened elsewhere, the Strip went into serious decline, with shuttered businesses, teenage runaways, drugs and prostitution becoming more visible. (The elite **Sunset Plaza** pocket seemed to be immune to these problems; tony eateries like **Le Dome** (8720 Sunset Blvd., still a power-lunching and nightly stargazing spot) and **Nicky Blair**'s (8730 Sunset Blvd., no longer in business), continued to attract Hollywood stars and power players, and was a favorite hangout of camera-flashing paparazzi). When West Hollywood became an independent city in 1984, it found a new sense of identity, as well as new energy and leadership from its own city hall, and other sections of the Strip began to rebound.

Today, the Sunset Strip is an eclectic mixture of live music and dance clubs, comedy clubs, restaurants and shops ranging from funky to fashionably posh. Thousands flock here at night, particularly on Fridays and Saturdays, and it is not uncommon to find celebrity limousines trapped in the ensuing gridlock. Looming over it all is a glut of advertising, from painted plywood rock stars

The faded but still popular Chateau Marmont Hotel serves as the unofficial eastern gateway to the Sunset Strip in West Hollywood. Rich in history and cultural lore, and a favorite among less flashy celebrities and filmmakers, it is also the death site of comedian John Belushi. In the late '90s, it opened the much trendier Bar Marmont, an immediate "in" spot. (Photo by John Morgan Wilson.)

rising several stories atop always-busy *Tower Records* (8801 Sunset Blvd.) to eye-catching, customized billboards touting movies and record albums (known in the industry as "vanity boards") to the gargantuan images of entertainers like Tina Turner and Julio Iglesias hawking hosiery and other merchandise on the sides of high-rise buildings that have been turned into towering vertical billboards ("tall walls"). Like Hollywood itself, the Sunset Strip is a strange hybrid of creativity and commerce, but always with the accent on selling and promotion.

Among the more notable locations along the Strip, moving from east to west:

The Chateau Marmont Hotel (8221 Sunset Blvd.). Erected in 1927 to resemble a Norman castle, the "Marmont" is legendary for its faded elegance, charm, privacy, celebrity assignations and star clientele. Among the more famous residents: Greta Garbo, Boris Karloff, Paul Newman, Marilyn Monroe, Dustin Hoffman, Robert DeNiro, Jim Morrison, Jessica Lange and director Billy Wilder, who used his own room as Fred MacMurray's in *Double Indemnity* (the hotel's rooftop was used for a scene in *The Doors*). The accommodations include sixty-three "keys"—hotel lingo for rooms—including luxury suites with sweeping views and more cozy poolside cottages, which run from $195 to $1,400 per night, the cost of the two-bedroom penthouse with its 1,250-square foot terrace. It was at the Marmont that comedian John Belushi died of a drug overdose in 1982. The hotel's newest feature is its adjacent **Bar Marmont**, a trendy spot presided over by an elegant (and bald) transvestite host/hostess; regulars reportedly include Drew Barrymore, Ethan Hawke, Courtney Love and more wannabes than there are stars in heaven.

The Argyle (8358 Sunset Blvd.). Formerly the St. James's Club and, before that, the Sunset Tower, this opulent, art deco masterpiece has been seen in many films, including the *noir* classic, *Murder, My Sweet*. Lore has it that John Wayne once kept a pet cow on the balcony of his twelfth floor penthouse suite. An exclusive restaurant is situated on the ground floor, while valets attend to arriving patrons out front.

Thunder Roadhouse (8371 Sunset Blvd.). This stylized biker bar, co-owned by actors Dennis Hopper and Peter Fonda and country singer Dwight Yoakam, was filled with motorcycle-themed collectibles and attracted a motorcycle-riding Hollywood crowd that lined up its fancy "hogs" out front while dining and drinking inside. The landmark watering hole was gutted by fire in the summer of 1997, but may be rebuilt.

The House of Blues (8430 Sunset Blvd.). This is the third House of Blues but the first in California. Designed to look like a bayou shack, it offers a wide range of blues-based music, along with southern cooking and expansive views of the city. It draws top acts as well as many celebrity patrons.

The Comedy Store (8433 Sunset Blvd.). Located on the former site of Ciro's, the Comedy Store is probably the single most important showcase for launching comedy careers in Los Angeles (its chief rival being the Improv, on Melrose Avenue in West Hollywood). The Comedy Store is owned by Mitzi Shore, wife of comic Sammy Shore (he used to open for Elvis) and mother of Pauly Shore (of MTV and schlock movie fame). Three rooms present performers ranging from top comedians to unknowns, testing their routines on open talent night.

Sunset Plaza (8589-8720 Sunset Blvd.). In *L.A. Access*, Richard Saul Wurman describes this oasislike stretch as "a cluster of exclusive stores and restaurants. Many of them have been restored to their original Colonial Revival, Neo-Classical, and Regency styles." Sunset Plaza is something of an aberration along the Strip, where elegance and "taste" suddenly interrupt the crasser commercialization that comes before and after.

Spago Hollywood (1114 Horn Ave., across from Tower Records, overlooking Sunset). This is the celebrity-packed restaurant owned by chef Wolfgang Puck, who has become a celebrity in his own right. Famous for its innovative pizzas and pastas, Spago is also known for seating favored customers at or near the front windows, while putting the less elite toward the back. Big-name stars show up regularly, although many have surely drifted down to Puck's newer and more elegant establishment, Spago in Beverly Hills.

Book Soup (8818 Sunset Blvd.). This venerable bookstore is crammed floor to ceiling with new books and is especially valued by the Hollywood crowd for its collections on art, cinema, screenwriting and related subject areas. It regularly attracts celebrities and big-name authors for book signings, and its customer service desk in the back (310/659-3110) is extremely helpful. Book Soup operates an adjacent international newsstand as well as the tasteful *Book Soup Bistro*.

The Viper Room (8852 Sunset Blvd.). Co-owned by actor Johnny Depp, this is the funkiest and most musically eclectic club on the Strip. It is painted drab black on the outside—the entrance is around the corner and down Larabee Street, with a beefy bouncer at the door—while the ambiance inside is that of a neighborhood dive. You can hear everything from punk rock to funkadelic to classic jazz torch singers, depending on the billing on a given night. Big-name rock groups sometimes drop in for impromptu jam sessions. Attire: fashionably unfashionable. This is the club where actor River Phoenix overdosed on a speedball, before stumbling out to the Strip to convulse and die on the sidewalk.

Whiskey A-Go-Go (8901 Sunset Blvd.). Opened in 1964, it specializes in live rock with a dance floor close to the stage, and remains one of the more popular clubs on the Strip. (Sometimes referred to as "the Whiskey," but not to be confused with *Whiskey*, a hip Hollywood hangout located just off the Strip in the posh *Sunset Marquis* hotel (1200 N. Alta Loma Rd.), a favorite of visiting rock stars.) The Whiskey A-Go-Go anchors the northwest corner of Sunset and San Vicente Boulevards and serves as the unofficial gateway to the final, crowded long block of the Strip that ends at Doheny Drive and serves as a veritable paradise for the rock 'n roll crowd. (Again, view *The Doors*.)

Duke's (8909 Sunset Blvd.). Often called the most popular coffee shop in West Hollywood, this venerable hangout was relocated to the Strip from its former location next to the Tropicana Motel (8585 Santa Monica Blvd.), a run-down but revered rock 'n roll haven that was torn down in 1988.

Rodeo Drive in Beverly Hills is perhaps the most famous luxury shopping district in the world. (Photo by John Morgan Wilson.)

As it edges up against the sudden palatial ambiance of Beverly Hills, this last stretch of the Strip also includes the *Roxy* (9009 Sunset Blvd., where Jack Nicholson used to hang out upstairs at *On the Rox*), the *Rainbow Bar & Grill* (9015 Sunset Blvd., where Joe DiMaggio first met and courted Marilyn Monroe, and long-haired rockers now arrive by limo to dine on pizza) and *Billboard Live* (9039 Sunset Blvd, the newest music venue here, located on the former site of the once-popular *Gazzarri's*).

"On weekend nights, this stretch of Sunset becomes an outrageous parade of cerulean-haired punks, tattooed bikers, and random voidoids," writes Gil Reavill, "one of the few verifiable pedestrian scenes in Los Angeles."

Beverly Hills

Like many adjoining communities, Beverly Hills was settled in the early 1800s by ranchers and farmers. The first settler was Maria Rita Valdez de la Villa, a woman of African descent who was granted a 4,500-acre rancho where her family tended horses and cattle. She sold her land in 1854 for $3,000 to two prominent

Tall, spindly palms grace the entrance to the Beverly Hills Hotel along Sunset Boulevard in Beverly Hills and can be seen in many neighborhoods throughout the area. (Photo by John Morgan Wilson.)

white residents, who subdivided much of it. In 1906, a real estate developer named Burton E. Green purchased part of the former rancho and founded a town he called Beverly (changed the next year to Beverly Hills). In 1912, with the movement of the film industry to the region, he opened the Beverly Hills Hotel (see the following sidebar, "The Pink Palace"). Thereafter, the surrounding bean and grain fields were gradually transformed into residential lots for movie stars and some of the most palatial homes in the world.

Today, "Bev Hills," as it is informally called, has a population of about thirty-two thousand, although the influx of workers and shoppers on weekdays swells that figure by five or six times. It is the quintessential city of taste and wealth in the Los Angeles area, more orderly and well-manicured than almost any other in the region and probably home to more stars and Hollywood power players than any other single city, as well as many top agencies and production companies. Star Maps, which pinpoint the current and former homes of celebrities, are hawked along the curbs of Sunset Boulevard, generally by young male Hispanics (a 1997 independent film, *Star Maps*, revolves around one such salesman).

Some other defining characteristics, as noted in *Los Angeles A to Z*:
- "Strict zoning, careful planning, and an absence of slums."
- "Curb parking, real estate sale signs, and billboards are closely regulated."
- "Utility poles are set back in alleys."
- "Curbside trees are planted and maintained by the city."
- The "distinctive Civic Center was elegantly reconstructed (1981-1982), at a cost of $110 million." The design blends Spanish cathedral and art deco.
- "The most palatial homes are on the hilly north side of town," while "less pretentious dwellings occupy the city's southern section."
- Shoppers spend nearly $700 million each year in Beverly Hills. The pricey boutiques and lavish window displays along fabled Rodeo Drive (a world unto itself in the heart of the city's "Golden Triangle" section) attracts visitors from all over the world.
- "More books are sold here per capita than in any other city in the world."
- Beverly Hills also has more doctors than any other city—550, or one for every 60 residents (comparing to the U.S. average of one for every 612 residents).
- "It also has 250 psychiatrists and 110 psychologists—one for every 90 or so inhabitants."

Beyond Beverly Hills

A number of communities beyond Beverly Hills bear strong Hollywood associations. They include:

Century City. Adjacent to Beverly Hills, this West Los Angeles business and shopping community occupies 176 acres that was once part of Twentieth Century Fox, which began carving up its valuable studio property and selling off

The Pink Palace

The Beverly Hills Hotel, long considered one of movieland's favorite gathering spots, is a sprawling pink complex of suites, ballrooms, bars, cafes and bungalows, designed in the Mission Revival style. Originally built for half a million dollars, it underwent a costly, two-year renovation before reopening in 1995.

In *Revision of Justice*, my mystery series character, Benjamin Justice, describes the hotel this way:

The Beverly Hills Hotel sat on twelve lushly landscaped acres along palm-fringed Sunset Boulevard.

The Pink Palace—as it was fondly known—looked swell for a resort built in 1912, which can happen after a two-year renovation that comes with a $140 million price tag. Even in Beverly Hills, that's an expensive facelift.

I arrived in the early afternoon, striding into a sanctuary that felt largely unchanged by time. Marilyn Monroe once sipped milk shakes here. Marlene Dietrich had been banished from the Polo Lounge for wearing pants. Elizabeth Taylor had cavorted with various husbands in a bungalow that now went for $2,000 a night, while the Presidential Suite inside the main building topped the rate chart at $3,000. Business had reportedly fallen off some since the hotel's reopening in 1995—something about the owner, the Sultan of Brunei, and his outspoken views on the Palestinian conflict—but the Pink Palace was still regarded by many as one of the prestige watering holes for the showbiz set, regardless of bloody territorial issues half a world away.

The valets out front were handling a string of mostly black or white vehicles, of which Rolls and Mercedes were the dominant brands . . .

Add a swimming pool surrounded by gorgeous starlets in bikinis hoping to be noticed (and a few male hunklets as well), tennis courts occupied by some of the world's most recognizable stars, lounges where multimillion dollar movie deals are worked out on cocktail napkins, lush lawns greener than new money, and vast gardens of azaleas, camellias, roses and magnolias bursting into thousands of pink and white blooms, and you have a pretty good idea why the Beverly Hills Hotel has managed to attract and fascinate so many for so long.

portions of it in the 1950s. Century City's angular and rather austere twin high-rise buildings, Century Plaza Towers and ABC Entertainment Center, dominate the surrounding landscape. A number of important agents, publicists, entertainment industry lawyers and producers are among the forty thousand people who work each day in Century City's ten million square feet of office space. Its futuristic look was put to use in *Conquest of the Planet of the Apes* (1972) and *The Turning Point* (1977), doubling for New York's Lincoln Center.

Westwood Village. "The Village," as the locals call it, is a largely commercial zone adjacent to the UCLA campus that has one of the highest concentrations of movie theaters to be found anywhere. A number of its theater buildings, replete with fanciful spires, domes, interior balconies and other architectural flourishes, date to the 1920s. As the west side developed in midcentury, the picturesque Village, with its grand theater marquees and attractive entrances, became a favorite place for the studios to premiere many of their movies. As more and more young people flocked into the village for entertainment in the 1960s and 1970s, however, older shoppers who supported the stores and upscale restaurants fled and the village began to suffer instability and economic decline. In 1988, its image was further marred when gang cross fire killed an innocent young woman in the heart of the Village, and took another blow in 1991 when street violence erupted after a screening of *New Jack City*. Rising crime and a parking shortage have added to the woes of this once-vibrant shopping and dining center, which is currently undergoing a surge of planning and redevelopment designed to bring back some of the lost glory.

Bel-Air. Fewer than eight thousand residents inhabit this haven in the Santa Monica Mountains west of Beverly Hills, but they are among the city's wealthiest and most socially elite, and their homes among the most palatial, with unparalleled views of the city and ocean. There is only one commercial enterprise within the boundaries of Bel-Air Estates: the lush and lavish Bel-Air Hotel, famous for its quiet seclusion, floating swans and world-class cuisine.

As in any other mountain and canyon community in the region, the slopes of Bel-Air are covered with many varieties of chaparral that become as dry as kindling during the summer, and vulnerable to the errant spark, carelessly tossed cigarette or sociopathic arsonist (the most common cause of wildfires in L.A.). In the fall of 1961, a major fire swept across the hills and canyons of Bel-Air, driven by relentless Santa Ana winds; the flames destroyed nearly $25 million worth of property, including the homes and memorabilia collections of several stars.

Santa Monica. The seaside town of Santa Monica began its significant development in 1887 with the opening of the Arcadia Hotel, an imposing, five-story structure that stood virtually alone on the isolated shoreline. Situated at the end of a rail line running from downtown Los Angeles that is now Santa Monica

Boulevard, the town grew as a seaside resort. By the 1920s, a number of movie stars were building homes along the beach, a stretch north of the Santa Monica pier that came to be known as the Gold Coast. Some of these beachfront mansions were later turned into clubs, hastening the city's expansion, and offshore gambling ships added to the attraction during Prohibition. With a balance of industry (inland), resort-style businesses near the wide, white sand beach and a growing population of renters, the city had grown to nearly ninety thousand by 1970. The more affluent built their fine homes in bucolic Santa Monica Canyon or on the ocean-view bluffs on the city's north side; Montana Avenue became the unofficial line of demarcation that supposedly separated wealth and snobbery from the rest of the middle-class city, and "north of Montana" became a common term. (A mystery novel, *North of Montana*, was published in 1995; the author, TV writer April Smith, makes her home north of Montana.)

In the 1970s, Santa Monica became a hotbed of political activism, led primarily by a sizable contingent of 1960s liberals who lived on the city's south side including actress Jane Fonda and then-husband Tom Hayden, later a U.S. Senator. This well-organized coalition, which spearheaded the renter's rights movement among other social causes, became so powerful that it was able to take over and control the city council for many years. To this day, despite more political balance, some political conservatives refer to the city as the People's Republic of Santa Monica. During the past decade, the city has undergone significant development (see sidebar, "Hollywood by the Sea," on page 194), including more upscale amusements on its vintage pier and the opening of the popular Third Street Promenade, a three-block outdoor pedestrian mall and entertainment zone, which has become the westside's trendiest dating and dining scene. The pier is a much-used shooting location, and its historic merry-go-round and roundhouse can be seen in *The Sting* (1973).

Pacific Palisades. This affluent residential community, situated north of Santa Monica on the steep bluffs overlooking the Pacific and stretching inland for not quite two miles, is famous for its ocean views and numerous examples of modernist architecture. "From the 1920s to the 1940s," according to *Los Angeles A to Z*, "Pacific Palisades was a popular area for artists, architects, writers, and theater people." Many stars, especially those with families, have sought the Palisades' quiet seclusion, a trend that continues today.

Malibu. Incorporated in 1990 as a city, Malibu is located twenty-six miles west of downtown Los Angeles on a twenty-five-mile stretch (including nearby Topanga Canyon) that encompasses beaches, palisades, canyons and mountains.

Once a rancho, it was purchased by Frederick Rindge in 1892, and his widow, May Rindge, waged a long and costly battle to preserve the land's isolation, even building her own private railway in 1906 to prevent a state coastal highway or Southern Pacific Railroad line from coming through. This enchanced Malibu's reputation as one of the country's most scenic and valuable privately owned areas. Mrs. Rindge eventually lost her legal battles with the state, which began construction in 1926 on the coastline road that is now known as the Pacific Coast Highway, or "PCH" to locals. In the 1930s, Mrs. Rindge began selling lots to movie people, and those lots along the beach came to be known collectively as the Malibu Movie Colony. Commonly referred to now as the Colony, one private stretch is now behind guarded gates with beachfront homes priced in the millions and tens of millions of dollars.

Stretches of Malibu along Pacific Coast Highway are now commercially glutted with restaurants, motels and other tourist attractions. The area has also been plagued over the years by devastating fires, flooding and earth slides. At times, PCH has been closed by rock and mud slides, and beachfront homes have been battered or even carried away by storm-driven waves. Nonetheless, Malibu remains the prestige location for celebrity homes away from the city, whether on the beach or the rising clifftops above.

Many movies have been shot here, from "beach blanket" pictures like *Malibu Beach* (1978), to more melodramatic fare like *The Sweet Ride* (1968).

The San Fernando Valley. This sprawling, triangular-shaped flatland northwest of downtown Los Angeles, known locally as just "the Valley," is the home of the so-called "valley girl" of the 1980s. It is also the location of NBC and several major studios (see studio list, chapter two), which built here decades ago when the land was plentiful and cheap. With the exception of Burbank and one or two smaller independent cities, the Valley is part of the city of Los Angeles, stretching twenty-four miles wide at its base with more than two million residents of its own. Isolated from more developed areas by various mountain ranges, the Valley was long considered a sort of dull, suburban "hicksville" by many Southland residents; comedian Johnny Carson, whose NBC "Tonight Show" broadcast weekdays from Burbank, was fond of making jokes at the city's expense.

Today, however, the densely populated San Fernando Valley, crisscrossed by five major freeways, is quickly developing into a modern metropolis, with all the amenities one finds elsewhere in the region. Many film and television industry people, including some stars, make their homes in more upscale Valley communities like Studio City and Encino, drawn by the quieter lifestyle, more reasonable real estate prices and secluded hillside homes that command fine views when the Valley's notoriously heavy air pollution allows. Although the Valley was long considered a largely white and politically conservative area, it now has a burgeoning population of working-class Hispanics. Over the years, efforts by disaffected Valley residents to secede from the city of Los Angeles or to form a separate school district have been vigorously but unsuccessfully waged.

Culver City. This fairly nondescript residential-industrial town is often the forgotten city when "Hollywood" is discussed, yet for more than fifty years it played a notable role in movie production as the home of the mightiest of the early studios, Metro-Goldwyn-Mayer. Situated eleven miles west of downtown Los Angeles on the less glamorous south side of the basin, Culver City had been a wild, lawless nightclub town during the Roaring Twenties, but became a "studio town" in the thirties and forties, with the arrival not just of MGM, but also Hal Roach Studios and Desilu Productions. The fabled MGM studio along Washington Boulevard was comprised of five separate backlots surrounded by fortresslike walls, one of which was used for the burning of Atlanta in *Gone With the Wind*. Its busy streets and walkways were named after its top stars, such as Clark Gable, the Barrymores, Greta Garbo, Katharine Hepburn, James Stewart, Elizabeth Taylor and Gene Kelly, all of whom worked, ate and shared adjacent bungalows inside the studio gates. (Lassie was another famous contract player.) In 1986, in financial straits, MGM sold the studio and its library to the Turner Broadcasting Co., who then sold the lot to Sony Pictures Entertainment, which occupies the acreage today. The city of Culver City, meanwhile, with a population of about forty thousand, has been undergoing significant redevelopment and historical preservation, and is beginning to shed its image as a faded, somewhat forlorn little town.

Dining and Hanging Out

It's always dangerous to catalog the "in" places catering to the Hollywood crowd, because "in" can be "out" by the time the ink dries. However, some establishments are so well-entrenched, they seem safe to mention, if only for historical purposes.

I'll lead off with two Hollywood "institutions"—Morton's and Hugo's, because they epitomize "power dining" in L.A.—then briefly mention a galaxy of other star favorites (in addition to several already noted above).

Morton's (8764 Melrose Ave.). This single-story restaurant at the corner of Melrose Avenue and Robertson Boulevard has long been the quintessential

Studio and Network Tours and Tickets

A number of the studios and networks offer guided tours and tickets to some shows, which can give the outsider at least a glimpse of how movies are shot and live TV shows are taped. Generally, there is a charge for the tours, but not for show tickets.

Be aware that because of so many no-shows, most show tapings are over-booked; seating is usually on a first-come basis, with ticketholders last in line sometimes turned away. Phone numbers are listed for questions regarding prices, reservation information and locations.

Paramount Pictures Two-hour guided tours are conducted 9 A.M. to 2 P.M. weekdays through sound stages, wardrobe, production, sets. Children must be older than ten. Information: (213) 956-1777. Television show tickets are available August through March. Information: (213) 956-5575.

Universal Studio Tours, Hollywood A tram tour of the Universal backlot is included with the theme park ticket package; runs daily, except Thanksgiving and Christmas, until 4:15 P.M. Information: (818) 777-3750.

Warner Bros. Studios (formerly *Burbank Studios*) Individual or group reservations may be made in advance for a two-hour tour of the costume, prop and construction departments; a Western street; and an actual film shoot (if schedules permit). Children must be ten or older. Information: (818) 972-TOUR.

KCET (PBS) Free one-hour tours are offered on Tuesdays and Thursdays at this studio, which is one of the oldest continually used lots in Hollywood. Once used primarily to shoot B movies, it has been occupied by KCET since 1971. Information: (213) 953-5346.

NBC Television Studio NBC in Burbank is the only major network in L.A. to offer a tour for the public. It is one-hour long and may include show tapings if desired. Information (for both tour and show tickets): (818) 840-3537.

CBS Television City Ticket information: (213) 852-2624. Tickets by mail: CBS Tickets, 7800 Beverly Blvd., Los Angeles, CA 90036 (specify name of show, date, size of party; include self-addressed, stamped envelope).

ABC-TV Ticket hotline: (310) 557-7777. Tickets by mail: ABC Guest Services, 4151 Prospect Ave., Los Angeles, CA 90027. E-mail information: kabc7@aol.com

In addition to the above sources, several outside services provide free tickets to shows:

Audiences Unlimited Information: (818) 753-3470. Ticket Line: (818) 506-0067. Walk-up window: Fox Television Center, 5746 Sunset Blvd. (at Van Ness Ave.); 8:30 A.M.–6 P.M. weekdays, 12 P.M.–5 P.M. weekends. *Note*: Tickets become available on Wednesdays for the following week's shows, but some same-day tickets are available. *By mail*: Audiences Unlimited, 100 Universal City Plaza,

Building 153, Universal City, CA 91608 (specify name of show, date, number in party; include SASE).
Audience Associates Provides reserved seats for TV tapings. Information: (213) 467-4697 or (213) 653-4105. E-mail information: tvtix@ecom.net
Preview House Needs audiences to preview TV pilots, commercials, etc. Information: 213/876-6600.

power-dining spot, though is has reportedly lost some of its luster in recent years. Mondays have been the traditional night when top stars and power brokers commandeered the best tables to dine expensively, make deals and schmooze. The unpretentious white building is heavily camouflaged by dense banana palms, and Rolls and Mercedes fill the small parking lot nightly. A tasteful, oak bar fronts the main room with the kitchen in the back, where the less elite are customarily seated. Reservations are recommended.

Hugo's. This is one of the industry's premiere power and networking breakfast spots, particularly for female agents and development executives on the way up and female stars doing their own producing. The scent of garlic and Italian cooking pervades the room and window tables are hard to come by. Most famous dishes: *Pasta alla mama* and pumpkin pancakes.

The Peninsula Beverly Hills (9882 Little Santa Monica Blvd. at Wilshire Blvd.). Opened in 1991, this two-hundred-room, French Renaissance-style hotel is situated next to Creative Artists Agency (CAA), Hollywood's most powerful agency. "The Peninsula" has quickly established itself as perhaps the number one watering hole of stars and power brokers, displacing the more venerable Beverly Hills Hotel. *Los Angeles Times* cultural reporter Jeanine Stein has written that "the rooftop pool is deal-making central," and that the Peninsula's Club Bar has "a rep as a see-and-be-seen scene. Go on a Friday night and you'll be competing for oxygen with local business types and entertainment execs. Be sure to note the number of patrons on cellular phones." The Belvedere is the main restaurant, with indoor and patio dining. Rooms currently start at $350 a night.

The Four Seasons Hotel (300 S. Doheny Dr., Beverly Hills). A premiere power breakfast spot, where according to *Buzz*, "New York media types playing with their cell phones mix with Hollywood publicists working theirs, where egg-white omelets and cantaloupe juice are de rigueur and cigar smokers politely wait till lunchtime to light up." The presidential suite rents for $4,000 a night, topped only by the nearby Regent Beverly Wilshire Hotel, whose top suite goes for $5,000.

The Ivy (113 N. Robertson Blvd., Beverly Hills). "A lunch favorite with industry types and ladies who lunch," as *L.A. Access* puts it. "It's Southwestern in feeling, with adobe walls, open hearths, antiques, and an ivy-strewn terrace." Valets out front. Famous for its luscious desserts.

The Polo Lounge. For decades the ultimate in tasteful power dining (breakfast, lunch and dinner), though that reputation has faded a bit. (See sidebar, "The Pink Palace" on page 203.)

Chasen's (246 N. Canon Dr., Beverly Hills). For decades the best-known restaurant in the region—lore has it that Elizabeth Taylor had Chasen's famous chili flown to her on distant film locations—this L.A. institution declined as its star clientele (the Reagans, Bob Hope, Jimmy Stewart, et al.) aged, dined out less frequently or died. When it could no longer support its large corner site at Beverly Boulevard and Doheny Drive, it moved to its current spot, the site of the former Bistro, taking its vaunted reputation with it.

Jimmy's (201 Moreno Dr., Beverly Hills). A pricey, intimate haunt of the rich and famous, reknowned for its veal chops and pleasant piano bar, it's tucked away on a discreet corner of Beverly Hills off Little Santa Monica Boulevard.

Palm (9001 Santa Monica Blvd., West Hollywood). Located just west of WeHo's gayest club section, this high-priced, New York-style restaurant serves what some consider the best steak in town. Caricatures of its more famous patrons adorn the walls, including one or two who have since become infamous, such as O.J. Simpson and convicted swindler Bruce McNall, former owner of the L.A. Kings hockey team. (This restaurant is not to be confused with *The Palms*, a popular, sometimes rowdy lesbian dance bar a few blocks east at 8572 Santa Monica Blvd.)

Locanda Veneta (8638 W. Third St.). In business since the late eighties, this is considered by many to be one of the more authentic and tasty trattorias around. It's located across from Cedar-Sinai Medical Center, the area's premiere hospital for the stars, in a neighborhood that includes the Steven Spielberg Research Pediatric Center and two streets with famous names: George Burns Road and Gracie Allen Drive.

Matteo's (2321 Westwood Blvd., West Los Angeles). Another favorite of Hollywood's older generation, which turns Sunday evenings into something of a movieland family gathering.

Dan Tana's (9071 Santa Monica Blvd., West Hollywood). A New York-style roadhouse and an old Hollywood favorite that is crowded, noisy and pricey. Don't expect friendly service, but you may spot a graying star or two dining or hanging out at the bar. (Two doors up at 9081 is the legendary ***Troubadour***, where such greats as Bruce Springsteen, Miles Davis, Elton John, Janis Joplin and Van Morrison have performed.)

El Coyote (7312 Beverly Blvd., Los Angeles). Established in the early 1930s, the El Coyote is a place better known for the potency and cheap price of its margaritas than the quality of its Mexican food or its decor, which is on the tacky and outlandish side (part of the fun). One of the funkier places the hip have helped make famous.

Formosa Cafe (7156 Santa Monica Blvd., West Hollywood). This venerable Chinese-style restaurant located next to the faded Warner-Hollywood Studios is a throwback to another era, much better known for its stiff drinks and Chandleresque ambiance than its food. The long bar near the entrance is backed by panels of glossy 8×10s of the famous who have come here to drink and mingle, from Sinatra to Elvis, a tradition that continues today among hip, younger stars and wannabes. Situated in a neighborhood where many of the strolling hookers appear to be female, but aren't.

Teru Sushi (11940 Ventura Blvd., Studio City). This colorful sushi palace, with its theatrical presentation of its Japanese seafood specialties, is credited by some with launching the sushi craze that swept Los Angeles in the 1980s. It is extremely popular with Hollywood folks working on Valley lots and locations.

Langer's (704 S. Alvarado St. at Seventh St., Los Angeles). This decades-old New York-style deli, noted for its pastrami sandwiches, among other items, almost closed as crime overtook this neighborhood just west of downtown, and was nearly finished by the riots of 1992. It has survived, in part by offering curbside take-out service to those who call ahead.

Canter's (419 N. Fairfax Ave., midtown Los Angeles). A spacious, bustling deli restaurant and bakery in the heart of the Jewish Fairfax district just north of Farmer's Market and CBS Television City. Physically unchanged after many decades, Canter's continues to be one of the most popular late-night and after-hours eateries for club-hopping celebs and musicians.

Hal's (1349 Abbot Kinney Blvd., Venice Beach). Located on a funky, culturally eclectic stretch in the artsy beach community of Venice, Hal's Bar & Grill has long been a favorite for its relaxed ambiance and pleasant jazz.

Chinois-on-Main (2709 Main St., Santa Monica). Considered by many to be Wolfgang Puck's finest restaurant for both its style and cuisine, with prices that measure up. Those at the top of the Hollywood ladder *never* get seated near the open kitchen.

A slew of other, newer establishments were trendy in the late 1990s, such as *Jones*, *Drai's*, *LeBoheme*, *Swingers*, *Pinot*, the *Buffalo Club* and on and on. But as fast as styles and tastes change in Hollywood, one can't be sure how long any will stay "hot." To keep current, consult *Buzz* and *Buzz Weekly*.

For More Information on Geographic Hollywood

A number of resources are available to help you get more detailed information on Hollywood and related areas, then and now. They include:

Organizations

Hollywood Chamber of Commerce (6255 Sunset Blvd., Suite 911, Hollywood, CA 90028; 213/469-8311)

Hollywood Arts Council (P.O. Box 931056, Hollywood, CA 90093; 213/462-2355)

Hollywood Visitor Information Center (Janes House, 6541 Hollywood Blvd., Hollywood, CA 90028; 213/689-8822)

Hollywood Heritage (1824 N. Curson Ave., Hollywood, CA 90046; 213/874-4005)

Los Angeles Convention and Visitors Bureau (633 W. Fifth St., Suite 600, Los Angeles, CA 90071; 213/624-7300)

West Hollywood Convention and Visitors Bureau (8687 Melrose Ave., M-26, West Hollywood, CA 90096; 310/289-2525)

Beverly Hills Visitors Bureau (239 S. Beverly Dr., Beverly Hills, CA 90212; 310/271-8174)

Guide and Reference Books

Curbside L.A., An Offbeat Guide to the City of Angels, Cecilia Rasmussen (*Los Angeles Times*)

Downtown Los Angeles: A Walking Guide, Rober D. Herman (City Vista Press)

Frommer's Los Angeles, Dan Levine (Macmillan)

Hollywood and the Best of Los Angeles, Gil Reavill (Compass American Guides)

Hollywood Handbook, Andre Balazs (Rizzoli)

Hollywood: The First Hundred Years, Bruce T. Torrence (New York Zoetrope)

LA Lost & Found: An Architectural History of Los Angeles, Sam Hall Kaplan (Crown)

Black Hollywood Hot Spots

As African-Americans have increasingly broken through to positions of influence before and behind the camera in recent years, they have become a more visible presence in the white-dominated Hollywood social and business scene. Yet many also have their own favorite places to meet, relax and satisfy their personal cultural tastes.

Here is a sampling of what *Movieline* magazine terms "Black Hollywood Hot Spots," organized by regions of the city (subject, of course, to change):

The Crenshaw district M & M's Soul Food (the biggest of five M & M's is located here), Gainesville (jazz).

Inglewood The Forum Club, where the stars and Lakers mix.

Southwest L.A. Joseph's (jazz upstairs, hip-hop downstairs).

Baldwin Hills Magic Johnson Theaters, Fifth St. Dick's Coffee Co. (jazz and java), Comedy Act Theatre, Boulevard Cafe, Harold & Belle's cafe, Dulan's (soul food), World Stage (jazz).

Pico-Wilshire area Jewel's Catch One Disco, Maurice's Snack 'n Chat, Mo' Better Burger.

Hollywood Roscoe's House of Chicken 'n Waffles, Martini Lounge (hip-hop on Sundays), Arena (gay and mixed disco).

Melrose Avenue and vicinity Georgia (power dining; co-owned by Denzel Washington and Eddie Murphy); Canio West, Elgin Charles, Winston's (all beauty salons); Spike's Joint West (Spike Lee merchandise).

West Hollywood Club Nice.

West L.A. Century Club (Sunday night slick R&B, hip-hop).

Santa Monica Kingston 21 (live reggae).

Marina del Rey Aunt Kizzy's Back Porch (the ultimate commercial success with soul food).

The Valley B.B. King's Blues Club at Universal City Walk. It should be noted that the Valley is also the setting for a large concentration of black-owned entertainment companies, including Black Entertainment Television, the offices of Quincy Jones and David Saltzman, New Breed Records, The Syndicate (Ice T's company), Aftermath Entertainment (Dr. Dre's label) and Death Row Records (Snoop Doggy Dog, etc.). Two L.A. area radio stations with significant African-American audiences are KKBT/The Beat (92.3 FM—contemporary music) and KLON-FM (88.1—"straight-ahead" jazz).

L.A. Access, Richard Saul Wurman (HarperPerennial)

Los Angeles: An Architectural Guide, David Gebhard and Robert Winter (Gibbs-Smith)

Los Angeles A to Z, Leonard Pitt and Dale Pitt (University of California Press)
The L.A. Musical History Tour, Art Fein (Faber and Faber)
The Movie Lover's Guide to Hollywood, Richard Alleman (HarperCollins)
The Thomas Guide, Los Angeles Street Guide and Directory (Thomas Bros. Maps)
Translating L.A.: A Tour of the Rainbow City, Paul Theroux (Norton)
The Ultimate Hollywood Tour Book, William H. Gordon (North Ridge Books)

Publications
Discover Hollywood is a quarterly magazine with features, listings and photos covering Hollywood cultural events (published by the Hollywood Arts Council, listed above). Other publications that frequently run features on Hollywood, both current and past: *Los Angeles Times*, *L.A. Weekly*, *Los Angeles Magazine*, *Buzz*, *Movieline*.

Feature Films Shot on Location in Southern California
The following pictures show Los Angeles at various points in its history. As films, their quality varies greatly; most are listed with capsule reviews and descriptions in *Leonard Maltin's Video Guide*. The comedies of Charlie Chaplin, Buster Keaton, Harold Lloyd, Laurel and Hardy, Charlie Chase, and the Keystone Kops also provide valuable glimpses of the city early in the century. For those titles, consult *Leslie Halliwell's Filmgoer's Companion*, which is arranged by star names, followed by their credits. For a select list of "Feature Films" about Hollywood, see chapter one.

The Mark of Zorro (1920, 1940)	*In a Lonely Place* (1950)
It's a Gift (1934)	*The Ring* (1952)
Ramona (1936)	*Dragnet* (1954)
The Saint in Palm Springs (1941)	*Kiss Me Deadly* (1955)
Double Indemnity (1944)	*Rebel Without a Cause* (1955)
Murder, My Sweet (1944)	*The Lineup* (1958)
Mildred Pierce (1945)	*Beach Party* (1963)
The Postman Always Rings Twice (1946)	*Bikini Beach* (1964)
	Muscle Beach Party (1964)
The Big Sleep (1946)	*Pajama Party* (1964)
He Walked by Night (1948)	*Beach Party Bingo* (1965)
DOA (1949)	*How to Stuff a Wild Bikini* (1965)

The Loved One (1965)
Riot on Sunset Strip (1967)
Planet of the Apes (1968)
The Sweet Ride (1968)
They Shoot Horses, Don't They?
   (1969)
The Long Goodbye (1973)
Chinatown (1974)
Shampoo (1975)
The Pom-Pom Girls (1976)
Annie Hall (1977)
Big Wednesday (1978)
California Suite (1978)
Malibu Beach (1978)
Boulevard Nights (1979)
California Dreaming (1979)
Walk Proud (1979)
Fade to Black (1980)
True Confessions (1981)
Zoot Suit (1981)
Bladerunner (1982)
Fast Times at Ridgemont High (1982)
Valley Girl (1983)
Against All Odds (1984)
Beverly Hills Cop (1984)
Brother From Another Planet (1986)
Down and Out in Beverly Hills (1986)
Echo Park (1986)
Born in East L.A. (1987)
Dragnet (1987)
Less Than Zero (1987)
Stand and Deliver (1987)

La Bamba (1987)
Colors (1988)
Tequila Sunrise (1988)
Who Framed Roger Rabbit? (1988)
Miracle Mile (1989)
Scenes From the Class Struggle in
   Beverly Hills (1989)
Side Out (1990)
To Sleep With Anger (1990)
The Two Jakes (1990)
Boyz 'n the Hood (1991)
Bugsy (1991)
Dead Again (1991)
Defending Your Life (1991)
Grand Canyon (1991)
L.A. Story (1991)
Life Stinks (1991)
Scenes From a Mall (1991)
The Doors (1991)
The Taking of Beverly Hills (1991)
American Me (1992)
Venice/Venice (1992)
The Beverly Hillbillies (1993)
Falling Down (1993)
Escape From L.A. (1994)
The Brady Bunch (1995)
Mi Familia (My Family) (1995)
Swingers (1996)
Mulholland Falls (1996)
Star Maps (1997)
L.A. Confidential (1997)

CHAPTER EIGHT

The Hollywood "Lifestyle"

I t's been written many times that Hollywood is a place of business built on fantasy and illusion. To be sure, the business is very much about make-believe, from the first conception of a movie through the script, the casting (both imagined and real), the budget (both imagined and real), certainly the acting and the shooting and, finally, the projection of the completed film in darkened theaters to audiences willing to be fooled. Great value is placed on the ability to feign credibility, manipulate emotions, deliberately deceive.

Many observers of Hollywood have also noted that this sense of illusion seems to permeate other aspects and activities of the industry, consciously or otherwise. Publicity, promotion, deal-making, socializing, even the utterance of such simple phrases as "Let's do lunch!" or "I love this guy!" seem tinged with ambiguity, if not blatant insincerity.

In *Revision of Justice*, one of my "industry" characters says frankly, "In my business, a friend is someone who stabs you in the *front*. If you can't tell the right lies to the right people at the right time, you're considered an amateur." It's a highly competitive, often cutthroat business in which the stakes are extremely high, where "situational ethics" are justified as just "playing the Hollywood game" and insincerity, even outright dishonesty, are taken for granted by many.

A few examples from everyday life in Hollywood:

- Studio chiefs make promises to directors about "final cuts" they don't intend to honor.
- Agents promise to give scripts a quick reading or return phone calls,

knowing they won't.

- During negotiations, agents fabricate or exaggerate other financial offers on a project to inflate the bidding price.
- Producers lie to potential investors about how much money they have already raised for a project or what stars have committed to it.
- Casting directors lead on starry-eyed, young actors with promises of a future part and a SAG card, so they can use them sexually.
- Stars allow their names to appear on charity executive rosters when they know little or nothing about the organization and perform no official work.
- The studios know they will be cheated by foreign distributors, who will underreport box-office figures overseas, skimming revenues; in turn, the studios inflate domestic box-office figures to the press.
- Stars and other percentage players assume the studios will try to cheat them out of their profits on a picture.
- Executives take their spouses and lovers to pricey restaurants, charging it off on their expense reports, and sometimes exchange their first-class air tickets for tourist class, pocketing the difference.
- Directors expect actors to lie about their credits, experience and, especially, their ages. (In Hollywood, just about *everyone* lies about their age.)
- Directors tell actors their readings were "terrific" or "very interesting," even if they were awful.
- Reporters assume publicists will lie to them from time to time instead of offering an honest "no comment."
- Publicists know that savvy reporters will deceive them about the angle they are pursuing, especially if they intend to write a hatchet job.
- Critics fall asleep during screenings, then review the film as if they'd seen the whole thing.
- Critics write up raves for films they don't particularly like, hoping to curry favor with an actor, director or producer they'd like to work for.
- Producers squeeze "free" options from writers by claiming there isn't enough money to pay the writers a fair price, even as they smoke $50 cigars, sit on $10,000 custom-made sofas and drive $180,000 automobiles.
- Producers shop around scripts to test the marketplace without first acquiring the rights, which would be the fair and ethical approach.
- Gossip columnists, reporters and editors exploit the private lives of others, while carefully concealing their own secrets.
- Producers tell writers they have "a done deal," when they don't.

217

- Writers (or their agents) tell producers they are getting "first look" on a hot, new screenplay when it's not true, or lie about how much they made for their last rewrite to jack up their fee on the next one.
- Reporters make up quotes from fictitious sources, use real quotes out of context or doctor them without permission to enhance their articles.
- Those with Hollywood ambitions slip their scripts to directors and producers during interviews, then write fawning articles about them, hoping to gain their favor.
- They pad their expense reports, along with just about everyone else.
- The studios send promotional trailers to exhibitors that include scenes that will not appear in the released film, or sequences edited for pace and brevity to suggest more compelling action than audiences will actually see.
- Theater owners willingly engage in this time-honored form of false advertising.
- Prop masters and set designers sell valuable props on the side and pocket the cash, knowing the theft will be overlooked in the chaos of production.
- Receptionists tell callers that their bosses are in a meeting or out of the office when they aren't.
- Everyone tells everyone else they loved their last movie, even if they didn't.

And on and on.

Is every person who works in Hollywood a liar, cheat and scoundrel? Certainly not. From time to time, one bumps into a man or woman whose integrity is surprisingly intact. Yet it can be safely said that unabashed deception is practiced routinely by many, if not most, from the bottom to the top, from the wannabes to the most successful, who have learned that dishonesty is just part of the process of doing business in Tinseltown. In the *Los Angeles Times*, veteran entertainment journalist Patrick Goldstein summed up the situation: "Here's the awful truth: In Hollywood, the truth doesn't count for very much."

So how does one get to the "truth" of Hollywood? In previous chapters, we've attempted to explain how Hollywood "works" in a practical, concrete manner, focusing on the work and the jobs. In this chapter, we'll attempt to get at the more illusive nature of Tinseltown by exploring how many of its denizens live, play, think, spend their money and treat others. In the process we'll explore relatively frivolous subjects, status symbols like cigars and power cars, and more serious issues like sexism, racism and "graylisting."

> **"**A place where you spend more than you make on things you don't need to impress people you don't like.**"**
> —COMEDIAN KEN MURRAY ON BEVERLY HILLS' RODEO DRIVE

Status Symbols

During the 1980s, when John Travolta's career was in a slump between *Urban Cowboy* (1980) and *Look Who's Talking* (1989), he was still seen tooling about town in a fine-looking Rolls Royce (maybe it was a Bentley—doesn't matter) and flying hither and yon in his own private jet. Hollywood insiders marveled that after a string of flops—several of his movies during that period went straight to video—he could still live in such style and luxury. Later, after his comeback was complete with *Pulp Fiction* (1994), he revealed his secret during an interview: He had driven a *vintage* Rolls (or Bentley—doesn't matter), and flown a rather *old* jet, both classic models he had picked up at relatively bargain prices and polished up to look like new.

Because both items were venerable Hollywood status symbols, they allowed Travolta to keep up the appearance that he was still on top, which is such a vital part of the star *mystique*. In Tinseltown, a great many career climbers are more than willing to pay big bucks for objects that carry the perception of success and prestige, if not the actual substance. These status symbols change with time, trends and styles, but a few have held fairly steady through the years.

The Corporate Jet

"If there's one thing the entertainment industry has grown to love, it's the private jet, that sexy, $30-million-plus symbol of corporate success and, some would say, excess," freelance writer Scott Collins reported in the *Los Angeles Times Magazine*. "Moguls such as David Geffen and Barry Diller have them; so do stars such as Arnold Schwarzenegger, Tom Cruise and John Travolta, who pilots the Lear and Gulfstream II jets that he owns, and even named his son Jett." With annual fuel and maintenance costs running close to $1 million, it's the ultimate power perk—and, of course, tax deductible. The most popular brand name among the Hollywood elite in the 1990s: Gulfstream (models I, II or III).

Power Cars

Rolls and Benz, of course, remain two of the most durable brand names in terms of prestige, though one of the more recent status symbols has been the

"Budget" 90210

Rather than offering the usual Fords and Toyotas one finds at most Budget Car and Truck Rental offices, the Beverly Hills branch specializes in renting dream cars for L.A. social climbers. The lot near the apex of Wilshire and Santa Monica Boulevards is filled with such powermobiles as the Mercedes-Benz SL500 roadster, Mercedes SLK, Jaguar XK8 convertible, Porsche Boxster, Dodge Viper and BMW Z3 convertibles (just like James Bond drove in *Goldeneye*). General rates: $200 to $600 per day, plus mileage.

In the Land of the Limo

Mercedes Limousine Service, based at the Beverly Hills Hotel, charges $60 per hour plus 20 percent for the driver, for a basic Lincoln Continental stretch limo. The more majestic S600 Mercedes limo rents for $110 per hour plus 20 percent for the driver. An extra fee is reportedly charged if the customer throws up in the back of the car.

ubiquitous sports utility vehicle, which one sees increasingly in the gated driveways of Bev Hills and Bel-Air. That's partly due to the danger that comes with driving a luxury car in L.A. (carjacking), and partly because it's a kind of cool, reverse snobbery—a way to let people know that you're so successful, you don't *need* to be seen behind the wheel of a $150,000 automobile. (The equivalent in dress would be wearing a pair of carefully faded jeans and scuffed cowboy boots with a $600 Armani sport coat, or a pair of $400 Italian loafers without socks).

Oscar Parties

These are traditionally "viewing" and "post" parties, held in posh locales around town, in which hundreds gather to watch the televised Academy Awards shown on big screens, after which many of the nominees and winners show up. Until his death in 1993 the most exclusive Oscar party was thrown by superagent Irving "Swifty" Lazar and his wife Mary. It was the ultimate "A list" party—to be invited put you on the top rung of Hollywood's social ladder; to be left off was to be told you didn't quite measure up or really matter.

Body Sculpting

According to data compiled by the American Society of Plastic and Reconstructive Surgeons, more plastic surgery operations take place in the Pacific Coast region of the United States than any other. Liposuction, the process of inserting a needle into fatty pockets of the body and sucking out unwanted cellulite, was the most common procedure, followed by eyelid surgery, breast augmentation and rhinoplasty ("nose job"). The Pacific region led all others in the number of chin augmentations performed.

In recent years, with Hollywood growing more socially and politically conscious, the more prominent Oscar night parties or balls tend to benefit charities or other nonprofit organizations, including the AIDS Healthcare Foundation, People for Children and Animals, the Sorvino Asthma Foundation and the Foundation for the Performing Arts. In the late 1990s, the hottest ticket—and highest-priced at $1,000—has been the Elton John AIDS Foundation Academy Awards Party, held at the elegant Maple Drive Restaurant in Beverly Hills, which is always sold out well in advance. Typically, major stars lend their names to their favorite charity events and often show up to mingle. On Oscar night, the city's streets are clogged with rented limousines as Hollywood's most famous make their way from party to party.

Oscar Night Gowns

What Hollywood's most famous women wear to the Academy Award ceremonies becomes the focus of enormous attention by the fashion press, with male apparel also starting to get some notice in recent years. Status points are earned by showing up in an outfit personally designed by one of the world's top designers, with such names as Oscar de la Renta, Prada, Gucci, Gianni Versace, Donna Karen and Armani topping the list in the 1990s. Further status is gained if the reviews are good, although the smarter actors, who sometimes show up in offbeat, idiosyncratic outfits, know that it's being noticed and photographed, not critiqued, that really counts.

Personal Trainers

Having one's own personal trainer (ideally with one's own at-home gym) has been around since at least the early 1980s, when a bodybuilder and likable lug named

---

One for the Road

In 1997, actor Woody Harrelson announced plans to open an "oxygen bar" in West Hollywood, where patrons could insert plastic tubes in their nose and get high on fresh air.

Jake Steinfeld became known as "the bodybuilder to the stars" and the progenitor of countless clones. So successful was Steinfeld and his "Body by Jake" approach that it spawned books, videocassettes and his own television show, as well as numerous movie credits as the star's personal trainer. These muscle-bound motivators are now as common as tummy tucks in fitness-crazed Hollywood. Personal trainers generally charge from $50 to $150 per hour, make house calls and sometimes travel with their star clients when they are filming on location. Most are male, with women showing up more often in the aerobics area.

In the mid-1990s, the word "abs" dominated Hollywood fitness conversation as the market became glutted with trainers, devices and techniques specializing in creating tight, rippled abdominal muscles (a.k.a. "killer abs"). "Facade training"—the intense working out of a particular anatomical area—was hot in the late 1990s, especially for actors preparing for roles that called for specific body part exposure. (For an example, see Johnny Depp's chiseled chest in *Don Juan DeMarco*.) The fat farms of choice are the Golden Door and La Costa, where Jack Nicholson, among many stars, reportedly goes to shape up before starting a new movie. Both are hidden well away from L.A. in the San Diego area.

Golf

According to the authoritative *Los Angeles A to Z*, "Country clubs were established [in Los Angeles] in the late nineteenth century by wealthy white Protestants to preserve the privileges of class. Golf was a major attraction. The largest club, organized in 1897 by banker Joseph F. Sartori and others as the Los Angeles Golf Club, changed its name a year later to Los Angeles Country Club [now located on Wilshire Boulevard, just west of Beverly Hills]. In addition to nonwhites, the club excluded movie people and Jews." The most fashionable club in the first half of the century was the Midwick Country Club, a hillside course in Pasadena, which fielded a championship polo team and attracted personalities ranging from General George Patton Jr. to Will Rogers, David Niven, Spencer Tracy and Walt Disney. (It was later subdivided into a residential community whose streets still bear many famous names from its country club days.)

Today, with about twenty country clubs in the Los Angeles region, the most popular among Hollywood's golfing elite are the Bel-Air Country Club, the Riviera Country Club and the Hillcrest Country Club, which was founded by prominent Jews in the entertainment industry who had been excluded elsewhere and became one of the prestige country clubs on the city's west side. The Los Angeles Country Club remains the city's most elite private course and reportedly continues to be "very selective" in its membership restrictions. It costs tens of thousands of dollars to join the better clubs—into the six figures for a few elite courses—with monthly dues running several hundred.

Wristwatches

Many climbers in the so-called New Hollywood of the eighties and nineties spurn more ostentatious status symbols, particularly jewelry. One of the notable exceptions was a high profile studio marketing exec, who for years draped gaudy gold chains around his neck, displaying them with an open collar that also showed off his hairy chest. For those who still favor jewelry but exhibit more taste, Rolex for the men and Cartier for the women are still at the top of the status lists. Since an authentic Rolex or Cartier can cost tens of thousands of dollars, wearing one can be dangerous in a city like L.A. One local robber, dubbed "the Rolex bandit," specialized in holding up Rolex-wearing executives right in their offices in broad daylight, and even murdered one victim.

Cigars

This craze gained momentum in the mid-1990s as smoking was banned in bars and restaurants in many Southland cities, and the dangers of habitual cigarette smoking and secondary smoke became ever more apparent and unfashionable. Private cigar clubs opened in Beverly Hills, West Hollywood, Studio City and elsewhere, offering as many as two hundred elite brands of cigars. One of the more elegant was Hamilton's (9713 Little Santa Monica Blvd., Beverly Hills; 310/278-0347), co-owned by actor George Hamilton, where the price of cigars

---

Bruce Willis and Demi Moore have leased their Malibu house at $50,000-plus per month for the summer, sources say.

—ITEM IN THE *LOS ANGELES TIMES*'S "HOT PROPERTY" COLUMN

Go to Jail, Call Your Insurance Agent

Robert Downey, Jr. was involved in so many incidents involving heroin and cocaine possession at the peak of his career, according to press reports, that he became virtually uninsurable for casting and filming. In 1997, this led to a new kind of insurance policy that was created especially for him: incarceration coverage. To secure Downey's services for *U.S. Marshals*, Warner Bros. paid a premium reportedly in the half-million-dollar range for a policy that would cover losses if Downey was arrested and the production was shut down or delayed. According to one report, Downey lost another role because he was unwilling to personally cover the $700,000 needed to insure him. Steady work only seemed to exacerbate his drug dependency, and in late 1997, he was sentenced to a six-month jail term.

---

ranged from $4.25 to $60 and a glass of fine single malt went as high as $37. The status symbol cigar brands include Davidoffs, Paul Garmirians, Avos and Partagas. The Cuban Montecristo No. 2, shaped like a torpedo, is also quite popular. Also part of the trend: cigar books, cigar magazines, cigar seminars and private humidors costing several hundred dollars.

Motorcycles

Ever since a leather-jacketed Marlon Brando rode a chopper into a small town in the *Wild One* (1954)—*the* biker flick prototype—Hollywood has had a fascination with motorcycles. "Hogs" rose to new Tinseltown popularity in the 1990s, so trendy that a posh bar and restaurant opened on the Sunset Strip catering especially to celebrity bikers (see "Thunder Roadhouse," in chapter seven). Harley-Davidson was the brand name of choice, with the Softail the most popular model among celebs, according to sales reps in the know. Price range: $16,000 to $50,000, depending on accessories.

Drugs

Drug use and addiction among Hollywood's elite is now so common that stars readily confess their addictions to the tabloids, and announcements about rehab center visits are announced in publicity press releases, put out by the celebrity addicts' own publicists. While cocaine continues to be the drug of choice in Hollywood circles, amphetamines ("crystal" or "crystal meth") and Ecstasy became popular with the Hollywood crowd in the early 1990s, and heroin made a big comeback toward the end of the decade as a "cool" drug for the ultra-hip, a high grade of brown heroin in particular.

While the stars travel far and wide for detox treatment, from the Exodus Recovery Center in Venice Beach (where rock star Kurt Cobain spent two days before escaping and committing suicide in 1994) to the Hazelden Foundation clinic in Minnesota (where "Friends" TV star Matthew Perry underwent treatment for his addiction to "prescription painkillers" in 1997), the rehab center of choice for most well-heeled Hollywood addicts continues to be the comfortable Betty Ford Clinic in the desert resort community of Palm Springs. It was here that actress Elizabeth Taylor met the construction worker who became her seventh husband (eighth if you count her repeat marriage to Richard Burton).

Hollywood Philanthropy

While Hollywood may stand as a towering symbol of vanity, greed, wealth, privilege, hedonism and waste—and there is surely plenty of that—it can also be a place of great generosity and giving. Each year, tens of millions of dollars are raised for charitable causes through entertainment industry sources or connections, a tradition that goes back to the earliest years of the movie business.

Today, for example, one finds the name of David Geffen on the side of the AIDS Project Los Angeles (APLA) building, a one-time television studio located at Fountain Avenue and Vine Street in Hollywood, which was purchased and renovated partly with millions of dollars provided by the film and music mogul. For many years, actor Edward James Olmos lent his name and active support to the AIDS Healthcare Foundation and the Minority AIDS Project when they were fledgling organizations serving primarily minority and poor clients, while most of Hollywood's money went to the more-publicized APLA, which served a largely west-side clientele. In West Hollywood, as one turns off San Vicente Boulevard into the massive Cedars-Sinai Medical Center complex, he or she drives along Gracie Allen Drive, passes under the Max Factor Family Tower and reaches George Burns Road facing the Steven Spielberg Pediatric Research Center—names representing millions of dollars in donations. Paul Newman has generated millions for needy causes through his nonprofit line of Newman's Own salad dressings, pasta sauces and popcorn. The Permanent Charities of the Entertainment Industries, a venerable coalition of Hollywood foundations and donor organizations, has raised tens of millions for a wide range of charitable groups. And in 1997, media mogul Ted Turner, married to retired actress-producer Jane Fonda, announced a $1 billion gift over ten years to various humanitarian programs run by the United Nations, said to be the largest personal charitable donation in world history.

These are but a few examples of the kind of philanthropy and fund-raising that goes on regularly in Hollywood. True, some fund-raising events are staged with a degree of pomp and lavishness that appears costly and unnecessary, most of the giving is tax-deductible and cynics frequently question the sincerity behind these acts of altruism, particularly when they are well-publicized. Nonetheless, year in and year out, there is probably more charitable fund-raising achieved by Hollywood's creative and business community than any other industry of comparable size anywhere in the world.

The following is a select list of nonprofit organizations that benefit from strong Hollywood support:

AIDS Healthcare Foundation
   (AHF)
AIDS Project, Los Angeles (APLA)
Alzheimer's Association
American Equine Rescue
   Organization
American Humane Association
American Oceans Campaign
American Paralysis Association
Artists in Support of Cancer
   Research (The Jonsson
   Comprehensive Cancer Center
   Foundation at UCLA)
Barbara Davis Center for
   Childhood Diabetes
Barbara Sinatra's Children Center
   at Eisenhower Medical Center
   and Desert Hospital
Best Friends Animal Sanctuary
Camp Pacific Heartland
Celebrity Outreach Foundation
Childhelp USA
Children of the Night
Childrens Hospital

Children's Institute International
Christopher Reeve Foundation
City Hearts
Clooney (Betty) Foundation
Earth Communications Office
Education 1st
Elton John AIDS Foundation
ERAS Center for At Risk Children
Friends Outside
Fulfillment Fund
Fund for Animals
Give the Gift of Sight
Greater Los Angeles Zoo
   Foundation
Heal the Bay
House Ear Institute
Jimmy Stewart Relay Marathon
John Wayne Cancer Institute
Los Angeles Free Clinic
Los Angeles Mission
Los Angeles Police and Celebrity
   Golf Tournament
March of Dimes
Memorial Sloan-Kettering Cancer

Center—Home Care Program
Mr. Holland's Opus Foundation
Nahapetov Friendship Foundation
Newman (Scott) Foundation
Nexus
Pediatrics AIDS Foundation
People for Children and Animals
People for the Ethical Treatment of
Animals (PETA)
Pet Pride/ASPCA
Pets Are Wonderful Support
(PAWS)
Rainforest Foundation
Rape Treatment Center of the
Santa Monica-UCLA Medical
Center
Revlon Run/Walk for Women, The
(Revlon/UCLA Women's
Cancer Research Program)

Rhonda Fleming Mann Resource
Center for Women With Cancer
at UCLA
Rogers (Will) Hospital
Sorvino Asthma Foundation (actor
Paul Sorvino)
St. Judes Children's Research
Hospital
Starlight Foundation
Stroke Association of Southern
California
UNICEF
United Negro College Fund
Variety Club—The Children's
Charity
Wildlife Preservation Trust
International
Women's Guild of Cedars-Sinai
Medical Center

The Jewish Influence

The strong presence of Jews in Hollywood is obvious and undeniable. One sees
it in the proliferation of Jewish names on both the creative and business sides
of the community reflecting to some extent the scholarly traditions of Judaism,
which yields so many successful men and women in the professions and the arts.
One finds it in the social activism and political liberalism that has been a visible
part of Hollywood for so long and reflects similar sentiments in much of the
general Jewish community. Certainly, it can be seen in many Hollywood films,
going back to *The Jazz Singer* and beyond, in which Jewish customs, culture and
family life were treated with a special warmth and sensibility (although anti-
Semitism was largely unexplored as a theme in Hollywood movies until after
World War II, as were a number of extremely sensitive and controversial issues).
This deep and continuing Jewish influence in Hollywood is hardly surprising,
given the industry's beginnings.

"The founders of the great Hollywood studios all came from similar backgrounds," notes David Shipman in *The Story of Cinema*, identifying that heritage
as largely German-Jewish (not quite true, but almost). One reason, explains

Linda Buzzell, in *How to Make It in Hollywood*, was the virulent anti-Semitism that pervaded big business at the turn of the century, when the movies began to show commercial promise: "Among the founders of the movie industry were a number of Eastern European Jewish immigrants who discovered this new field open to them, as corporate America was not."

So strong is the Jewish presence in Hollywood that, at this writing, at least four local Jewish congregations cater to the arts and entertainment industry. These include the Synagogue for the Performing Arts, the Creative Arts Temple, Temple Shalom for the Arts, and Shofar, one of the major Jewish congregations on the city's west side, which was open to Jews from all walks of life but had a sizable entertainment industry following.

Linda Buzzell also notes that "a rich fund of delightful Yiddish expressions are commonly used around town" (though less so than in earlier decades when so many Jews came to Hollywood from New York, bringing with them the expressions of their immigrant parents and grandparents). A few common Yiddish terms, such as "shmoozing" and "chutzpah," are now used widely by Jews and gentiles alike. Terms less familiar to many gentiles, as singled out by Buzzell, include "bubkos" or "bopkes" (meaning trivial or worthless); "cockamamie" (ridiculous, silly); "dreck" (garbage, crap); "hondel" (to bargain); "kvell" (to burst with pride over something); "kvetch" (to complain); "macher" (a big shot, operator); "mench" or "mensch" (person of integrity, upright guy); "meshugge" (crazy, over the top); "shlep" (as a verb, to drag; as a noun, a fair distance); "schnook" and "schlemiel" (unflattering terms for "ineffective people"); "shtik" or "shtick" (piece of actorish business, bit of clever deviousness); "yenta" (a person, frequently female, good at matchmaking or getting people together, whether for a party or a business deal). (For more on "Yinglish," Buzzell recommends Leo Rosten's *The Joys of Yiddish*.)

The presence of so many Jews in Tinseltown adds a special flavor to the offices of certain agents and producers, as noted in a *Premiere* article on Jon Peters, who rose from hairdresser, and boyfriend, of Barbra Streisand to become a high-profile movie mogul: "Peters does his street-schmooze shtick: 'Aaayyy, sweetie!' he'll yell into the phone. 'How ya doin'?' "

That said, there are at least as many Jews in Hollywood, if not more, who operate with considerably less "shtick" and "schmooze," undermining certain stereotypes that have unfairly derived from the most colorful or extreme examples. (There is some irony in the fact that many of Hollywood's greatest stars changed their Jewish surnames to ones that sounded more gentile, ostensibly to broaden their appeal to a mass audience; they gained their wealth and fame in an industry dominated at the top by Jews, in part by masking their own Jewishness for a larger world where anti-Semitism still flourished.)

Despite so many successful Jews in Hollywood, the media sometimes exaggerates the situation or simply gets the facts wrong. In 1997, E! Online, the World Wide Web site of E! Entertainment (http://www.eonline.com), offered an item titled "Do Jews run Hollywood? You bet they do—and what of it?" The piece was well-meaning, intending to confront the Jewish question head-on in a positive way, and mentioned a dozen or so prominent figures of Jewish ancestry, including Darryl Zanuck, a cofounder (with Joseph Schenck) of Twentieth Century, which later became Twentieth Century Fox.

Unfortunately, as *Los Angeles* magazine later pointed out, Zanuck was "a nice Christian boy from Wahoo, Nebraska." Which serves as a useful reminder for all of us about the influence, conscious or unconscious, of stereotypes and generalizations.

Hollywood Politics

"From the days of the studio moguls, show business and presidential politics have been inextricably linked," Robert W. Welkos reported in the *Los Angeles Times*. "Al Jolson drummed up support for Warren G. Harding and Calvin Coolidge. MGM's Louis B. Mayer cultivated Herbert Hoover's friendship. Movie barons Jack and Harry Warner organized a star-studded campaign pageant for Franklin D. Roosevelt. And Frank Sinatra became a fixture of John F. Kennedy's Camelot."

A strong liberal contingent has always been apparent in Tinseltown, though being a liberal became something of an occupational hazard during the Red-baiting era of Joseph McCarthy in the late 1940s and early 1950s, when John Wayne and some fellow right-wing cronies, fired by patriotism and outraged by Stalinism, led a movement to cleanse Hollywood of "commie sympathizers." In more recent decades, following the eras of President John F. Kennedy and the Vietnam War, liberals held sway. With major stars and power players like Warren Beatty, Jane Fonda, Barbra Streisand, David Geffen and Michael Douglas—to name but a few of the most prominent—campaigning for liberal Democrats, being to the left of center became both fashionable and comfortable for Hollywood's liberal elite. Industry groups such as the Hollywood Women's Political Committee, the Show Coalition, the Environmental Media Association, and the Caucus for Producers, Directors and Writers, able to tap star power for

> **"**Los Angeles is the source and home of more political, economic, and religious idiocy than all the rest of the country together.**"**
>
> —WESTBROOK PEGLER

fund-raising events and dig into Hollywood's deep pockets, became influential organizations. Hollywood was a crucial fund-raising center for such Democrat candidates as George McGovern, Gary Hart and Bill Clinton. David Geffen, for example, reportedly raised $10 million for Democratic Party candidates during the 1996 election through his entertainment contacts, pulling in $1.7 million for a single social gathering in Malibu at which President Clinton appeared.

Throughout the 1970s and much of the 1980s, being openly and adamantly conservative was considered a potential career handicap; veteran film star Charleton Heston and producer Lionel Chetwynd were among a very few who dared to make their right-leaning political views known. (Heston went so far as to openly support the National Rifle Association, one of the most unpopular lobbying groups with Hollywood's liberal wing.) In the 1980s, with the White House occupied by Republican Ronald Reagan and a new conservative mood sweeping the nation, more and more of Hollywood's elite began to come out of the conservative closet. By the mid-1990s, such prominent figures as Arnold Schwarzenegger, Kevin Costner, Clint Eastwood and Tom Selleck were visibly and vocally supporting Republican candidates.

Many liberals, meanwhile, were keeping a low profile, part of a growing cynicism with Washington politics in general, and disappointment with President Clinton in particular, following his waffling or capitulation on such issues as welfare reform and gays in the military. "Politics is not a sport," Warren Beatty told the *Los Angeles Times*. "Winning isn't everything. Leading is. I have no interest in a Democratic Party that seeks to become a liberal Republican party just to win." After the fund-raising scandal that engulfed the Democrats following the 1996 election—a story broken by the *Times*—the powerful Hollywood Women's Political Committee, which had raised millions for liberal candidates and causes since its founding in 1984, announced that it was folding up. In an official statement, its 275 members said, "We will no longer collaborate with a system that promotes the buying and selling of political candidates."

In Hollywood political circles, at least, it was a bombshell, and may have signaled the end of an era when liberal candidates could automatically count

Tinseltown as an easy place to fill their campaign coffers. Yet the Hollywood-Washington connection was unlikely to be permanently severed. As political reporter Ronald Brownstein notes in *The Power and the Glitter*, his history of politics in Hollywood, "Celebrities looked to politicians to validate them as part of the company of serious men and women; politicians looked to celebrities to validate them as part of the company of the famous."

Sexism

With the exception of publicity and, to some extent, television production and casting, the entertainment industry is dominated by men, particularly in the area of feature films. No matter how you look at the issue, no matter what the source—research by the Ford Foundation, statistics from the Screen Actors Guild and the Director's Guild, reports in the *Los Angeles Times* and other publications—the conclusion is the same: Over the decades, women (and ethnic minorities) have had to wage a constant struggle to break through the barriers of the "old boy's club," and find their rightful place before and behind the camera, a situation that has slowly been improving in recent years.

Even then, throughout the 1990s, women actors appeared in less than a third of all roles in feature films, earned less than half of what male actors made per job, and roughly a third of the total income. In the late 1990s, women comprised about 20 percent of the 10,300-member Directors Guild (these figures are approximate); though the number of women directors is rising, as recently as 1995, only 10 percent of all American films released were directed by females, a figure that actually declined slightly the following year. By comparison, roughly 20 percent of all television situation comedies are directed by women, and female writers contribute more than a third of the scripts. In the screenwriting field, women represent nearly a quarter of the screenplay credits, as well as the membership of the Writers Guild of America, west, whose statistics indicate that females writers are consistently paid less than their male counterparts for essentially the same work. On *Premiere* magazine's 1997 list of Hollywood's hundred "most powerful" people, only one woman, Paramount CEO Sherry Lansing, was listed among the top fifty; only fourteen women were included overall (most of them actresses), and a number of the female producers were coupled with male partners. While nearly half of Paramount's executives in 1997 were women, that number was able to pull up the overall studio figure to only 30 percent.

This dominance by white males not only impacts employment and earning opportunities of others, but greatly affects the images that end up on screen,

> ❝ ❝ Being an actress is such a humiliating business anyway, and as you get older, it becomes more humiliating because you've got less to sell. ❞ ❞
>
> —KATHARINE HEPBURN (1955)

> ❝ ❝ There are only three ages for women in Hollywood—babe, district attorney and *Driving Miss Daisy.* ❞ ❞
>
> —GOLDIE HAWN IN *THE FIRST WIVES CLUB*

where violence, male sexual fantasies and the sexual objectification of women have been staples for so long. Nowhere are women more visibly discriminated against in Hollywood than in the area of age. While actors like Clint Eastwood, Sean Connery, Jack Nicholson and Harrison Ford continue to work regularly as film stars with graying or thinning hair and often with a much younger woman as their romantic interest, most leading ladies over forty find fewer and fewer roles as they age and are increasingly offered "character parts." The women who retain their glamour as they grow older, for example, Anne Bancroft, Lauren Bacall, Rita Moreno, Lena Horne and Dyan Cannon, are generally given smaller roles or turn up in smaller films, working for a fraction of the money accorded mature male stars, if they work at all. (See "Ageism and 'the Graylist' " on page 237.)

This blatant form of discrimination has led more and more Hollywood actresses to go into producing to create projects for themselves, often with female partners; nearly a quarter of all feature films are now produced or coproduced by women. Women in the industry are also known to engage in an almost fierce bonding and networking system that simply does not exist among the men, who are more likely to gather for weekly poker parties than engage in serious discussions about problems of discrimination and inclusion in the industry they run. Examples of female networking range from the more casual, such as director Martha Coolidge's weekend horseback riding group of industry women, to Cinewomen and Women in Film, well-organized groups that honor and support women in the industry and lobby against sexism. (See "Hollywood Minority Organizations and Support Groups" on page 242.)

These issues are addressed in a number of excellent books, including *When Women Call the Shots: The Developing Power and Influence of Women in Television and*

> ❝ I spent my life searching for a man I could look up to without lying down. ❞
> —SCREENWRITER FRANCES MARION

Film, by Dr. Linda Seger; *Hello, He Lied—and Other Truths From the Hollywood Trenches*, by Linda Obst, a prominent Hollywood producer; and *Without Lying Down: Frances Marion and the Powerful Women of Hollywood*, by Cari Beauchamp. A good resource web site is ShowBizWomen: Opening the Doors to Hollywood (http://www.showbizwomen.com).

Racism and Ethnic Stereotyping

Although Hollywood is often portrayed as a bastion of political liberalism and many of its top executives like to wear their liberal conscience on their sleeves, the reality behind the rhetoric is often quite different. "Nobody is thinking about diversity," admitted prominent producer and former studio chief Mike Medavoy during a 1997 industry forum on racism and other forms of discrimination. "They don't understand it."

Only about 5 percent of the total directing force in Hollywood is comprised of minority men and women, with blacks comprising barely more than 2 percent. The figure for ethnic minorities is slightly lower for membership in the Writer's Guild of America, west, where African-Americans account for less than 3 percent of the total. A WGA study found that, even when employed, writers of color are consistently paid less than their white male counterparts. As regrettable as these findings are, the situation was even more bleak in the 1980s; only 2 percent of all employed film and TV writers during the decade were nonwhite. A Ford Foundation study concluded at the end of the 1980s that "a core of overwhelmingly white producers and writers are 'creating characters in their own images,' producing artificial portrayals of blacks and other minorities on TV."

Although the number of minority faces increased dramatically in the 1990s in both TV and feature films, most leading black actors on TV were seen in comic rather than dramatic roles. Asian-Americans continue to be one of the most underrepresented groups in both mediums, usually relegated to stereotypical, secondary roles and rarely seen as romantic or principal characters; they suffer from a similar "invisibility" in most other creative and business segments of the industry. With one or two notable exceptions, Native American actors are rarely seen except in sporadic "Indian" projects, such as *Dances With Wolves*.

The Casting Couch: Myth or Reality?

Hollywood is a place filled with attractive people, and sexual harassment and exploitation by people in positions of power and authority are facts of life.

"A producer we know brags that he sometimes beds three actresses a day while he is casting a new project," write Gail Resnik and Scott Trost in *All You Need to Know About the Movie and TV Business,* who add: "Anyone who tells you the casting couch is a thing of the past is a liar or a fool."

One of the most common ploys by producers and directors goes something like this: "You seem perfect for the role, but it does call for a passionate sex scene. We'll need to rehearse that part of the script to be sure you can handle it." Or: "You realize that some nudity may be required. Could you please remove your clothes?" Or: "Your body looks fine for the nude scenes, but we'll need to take some Polaroids in case we want to call you back."

The casting couch is not exclusively heterosexual, of course. For years, a male casting director for a popular daytime soap opera seduced aspiring actors, both straight and gay, while promising them "walk-ons" (one- or two-line parts) that could help them earn their SAG cards. It began with drinks, then dinners, then "sleep-overs" on the casting director's couch that eventually moved into the bedroom, abetted by alcohol and drugs. One handsome actor I met who earned his SAG card this way on this particular soap never recovered from his loss of self-respect and eventually quit the business. Hollywood is littered with used-up men and women like that.

Most women and men who face similar situations no doubt have enough self-respect and confidence to resist such pressure. Some even have the courage to file lawsuits or grievances with the Screen Actor's Guild. In truth, however, most cases probably go unreported because the victims fear career repercussions.

One could surely document cases of men and women sleeping their way upward in the industry, yet using the casting couch as a stepping-stone can also be a serious career drawback. Years ago, when I wrote a piece for *Los Angeles* magazine on the subject, an attractive (and now very successful) actress told me, "The last person a producer wants on the set is some bimbo who gave him a one night stand, especially when his wife or girlfriend shows up."

The beginning of the 1990s saw an explosion of new African-American filmmakers in Hollywood following the lead of director Spike Lee in the 1980s, but of nearly two dozen black directors who made their feature film debuts, relatively few survived with stable careers. It seemed to some observers that minority filmmakers were not given as many chances at success as their white counterparts, who customarily were allowed a string of several box-office failures before they were written off by the mainstream movie industry.

One sign of progress in the 1980s and 1990s was seen in the principal casting of feature films. With the rise of African-American stars such as Eddie Murphy, Whoopi Goldberg, Denzel Washington, Whitney Houston, Morgan Freeman, Wesley Snipes, Laurence Fishburn, Angela Bassett and Cuba Gooding, Jr., African-American actors were achieving unprecedented visibility on the big screen, in roles of more prominence, dignity and complexity. However, this handful of high-profile examples tended to mask a deeper and continuing problem: the pervasive inequity ingrained in the Hollywood system, where minorities were noticeably excluded from most positions of influence and power. A particularly glaring example has been the Academy of Motion Picture Arts and Sciences, the venerable organization that hands out the Oscars and claims to stand for what is best about the film industry: In 1996, the Academy's nominating and voting membership of 5,043 included fewer than two hundred African-Americans. The situation came into sharp focus that year, when only one Oscar nominee out of 166 was black. In a hard-hitting cover story (March 18, 1996), *People* magazine dubbed it the "Hollywood Blackout," calling the industry's "continued exclusion of African-Americans [a] national disgrace."

Young African-American actresses were special victims of this "cultural apartheid," as roles for teen- and college-aged black females were almost nonexistent. "Unless white people in Hollywood write us into the script as hookers," says one young African-American actress, "it's as if we don't exist to them." Prominent actor Esai Morales (*La Bamba*, *The Disappearance of Garcia Lorca*) voiced a similar complaint regarding Latinos in film when he spoke to the congressional Hispanic Caucus in 1997: "We can't break into mainstream films as mainstream characters because scriptwriters and directors don't visualize us as mainstream individuals." I have covered this issue as a reporter for more than two decades, and in interview after interview, minority actors and filmmakers agree: Until there are significant numbers of minority persons in "power" positions, the slights, insults, stereotypes and exclusion will continue.

In addition to Hollywood's long history of ethnic stereotyping, another convenient and caricatured villain was seen with increasing frequency in the 1990s in both television and feature films: the evil Arab or Muslim, often written into scripts as a psychopathic terrorist but seldom as anything else (despite the fact that most of the world's 1.5 billion Muslims live *outside* the mideast). Off-camera, a growing number of organizations worked to counter this overt and covert

Oversight or Racism?

I n 1996, Twentieth Century Fox sent out 5,043 videocassette copies of *A Walk in the Clouds*, a low-profile film starring Keanu Reeves, to Oscar-nominating members of the Academy of Motion Picture Arts and Sciences. According to *People*, the studio did not send out any such promo cassettes of *Waiting to Exhale*, a box-office hit released the same year that featured an African-American cast, director and story line.

racism, and the Reverend Jesse Jackson and other prominent figures lobbied and spoke out against it.

Books in this subject area: *Black Film/White Money*, by Jesse Rhines; *From Sambo to Superspade: The Black Experience in Motion Pictures*, by Daniel J. Leab; and *Black Hollywood: The Black Performer in Motion Pictures*, by Gary Null.

Discrimination Below-the-Line

Several decades back, the Hollywood crafts unions were almost all white and mostly male, a situation that has gradually been changing under pressure from civil rights activists and organizations. By 1995, one of the largest labor guilds, Local 44 (set decorators and prop masters), counted roughly one-third of its four thousand members as female or minority, although blacks accounted for less than 2 percent of the total.

Whatever the progress in certain quarters, the employment of minorities on film and TV crews was far below the proportion of nonwhite residents within the general population of Southern California (see chapter seven). The studios blamed the problem on the union roster system and the lack of minorities with sufficient screen credits, while the unions blamed studio hiring practices. The essential problem, as almost everyone knew, was that most of the supervisory (hiring) positions were occupied by white males, who tended to hire those they had previously worked with, socialized with or knew through the references of friends or family. Because of this time-honored system of nepotism and crony-ism, minority hiring was often done on a token basis rather than as a consistent practice. It is not uncommon, for example, when a prominent African-American is hired to host a one-shot television special, to appear in a pilot or to star in a movie, for the production company to suddenly put out a special call for black crew members to avoid offending the black star with the usual lily-white crew.

> **"**Gray hair is the kiss of death in this town.**"**
> —VETERAN SCREENWRITER, FIFTY-THREE (UNABLE TO GET WORK)

(As recently as 1995, I worked as a writer on two TV productions where crews were temporarily "peppered" in this manner, before returning to the standard caucasian crew.)

With legislation enacted in California in 1997 that ended affirmative action hiring in the state, Hollywood's shameful racial imbalance was likely to get worse. Acknowledging the problem, Directors Guild president Jack Shea placed the responsibility directly on those who do the hiring: "Producers must find more effective ways to bring talented females and individuals with a diversity of ethnic backgrounds into our business."

Ageism and the "Graylist"

Age discrimination is obviously a serious issue throughout society and many areas of employment, but it's especially prevalent and destructive to careers in Hollywood, not just in the case of actresses (as previously discussed), but in other above-the-line fields, such as writing, producing and directing.

Some years back, at the behest of the Caucus for Producers, Writers and Directors, the International Documentary Association produced a documentary called *Power and Fear: The Hollywood Graylist*, which revealed how serious the situation had become as even the most acclaimed creative people became less and less employed in an industry that puts such a high premium on youth and reaching the youthful audience. As Linda Buzzell writes in *How to Make It in Hollywood*: "Hollywood conventional wisdom says that the industry is a young person's game, and if you haven't made it big by forty, you never will."

Scriptwriters, in particular, are subject to severe age discrimination; one hears constantly of successful TV and film writers whose careers go inexplicably into decline as they approach or pass the threshold of fifty. A writer for *Buzz* summed it up like this: "Old screenwriters never die, they just *fade out*."

No one has studied the problem more thoroughly than the Writers Guild of America, whose Age Awareness Committee has concluded that many, if not most, top agents will not sign a new screenwriting client over forty unless the writer has an extremely strong track record of hit TV shows or movies, and is "easier to sell." A WGA study in 1994 showed that the bulk of Guild writers who earned credits that year fell between the ages of thirty and fifty-five, with the average age forty-two; only seventeen credited writers were over sixty, and only eight were over seventy (out of several thousand). While a 1997 analysis found that 56 percent of the Guild membership—roughly 4,500 members—was over forty, studies also indicate that income generally declines for members as they move into middle age, which is quite the reverse of most trades and professions, where one's mature years are also the highest years of earning power.

Why are seasoned writers as well as other above-the-line talent cast off so early in life? In 1993, in one of my *Writer's Digest* columns, I listed some of the oft-heard explanations: "It's a competitive, high-energy business run by young executives raised on television, rather than novels or classic films—men and women who don't understand the language, concepts or themes of seasoned writers; these semiliterate tyros feel inadequate and even threatened when they have to deal with mature writers; they feel that 'old guys' can't write the kind of youth-oriented movies that appeal to the younger audience that buys most of the tickets; young executives and agents tend to hang out with their peers, and screenwriting is a social business, fueled to a great extent by personal relationships." Long hours, mental and physical stress and a grinding schedule are other reasons one often hears, especially when discussing the age issue in hiring below-the-line trade technicians and crew members. One Hollywood veteran holds this view: "I think that when these young executives have a meeting with someone over fifty, they see their parents walking in the door, and they simply can't deal with it."

Ironically, as psychologist Linda Buzzell notes, those who often have the hardest time coping with Hollywood's age discrimination are white males over forty-five. Unlike women and minorities, who are more accustomed to being shut out, these white males are suddenly faced with being part of the "out crowd" instead of the "in crowd," and may be experiencing discrimination firsthand for the first time.

The Gay Factor

According to gay historians, there was a visible, sophisticated and very socially active homosexual subculture in Hollywood's creative community as early as the 1920s, which included some of the silver screen's biggest stars, both male and female.

"This was an era in which the press didn't pry into private lives, and studio chieftains were blasé when it came to their stars' homosexuality," wrote William J. Mann in the gay Los Angeles newsmagazine, *Frontiers*. That subculture, which attracted many heterosexual celebrities on a social basis, continued to flourish but was gradually forced underground in the 1930s by a general moral backlash and, in particular, the much-feared Hays Office (see "Censorship and the Production Code" in chapter one). According to Mann and other writers, a number of major stars who had engaged in fairly open same-sex relationships in the 1920s entered marriages of convenience in the 1930s and 1940s, some arranged by the studios to which they were under contract, and frequently with spouses who were themselves homosexual.

Outsiders may be shocked by some of the names that turn up in various gay Hollywood histories, among them Gary Cooper, Claudette Colbert, Tyrone Power, Marlene Dietrich, Cary Grant, Robert Taylor, Ramon Novarro, Gilbert Roland, Greta Garbo, Janet Gaynor, Cesar Romero, Randolph Scott, Tallulah Bankhead, Montgomery Clift, James Dean, Sal Mineo and Anthony Perkins. Some of these names may or may not rightfully belong in such histories, yet there's considerable evidence that many were secretly gay or actively bi-sexual. To more worldly gays and lesbians in contemporary Hollywood, it's largely a moot point, since they know how common homosexuality has always been in Tinseltown and see no particular shame in it.

That was not always the case, of course: When researching and writing about the closeted stars of decades past, historians frequently uncover lives of private anguish, and talents stunted or careers cut short by the debilitating effects of self-repression and denial. Montgomery Clift is said to be one such person, an actor of great promise filled with self-doubt and self-loathing who drank himself to an early death. The late Rock Hudson, of course, remains the epitome of the tormented closeted Hollywood actor. Another heavy drinker, he was part of a very active gay social circle in Hollywood, but in public and with the media, he was always on guard against being "found out." In the process, he developed a glib, masked personality and, despite enormous commercial success, consistently avoided risky creative choices as he "played it safe."

The late gay activist and film historian Vito Russo, author of *The Celluloid Closet: A History of Homosexuality in the Movies*, once suggested to me that this "blunting" of one's persona was the greatest price many gay actors pay for having to lead a double life—the loss of uniqueness and boldness that is the performer's greatest gift.

At the same time, one can't overlook Hudson's enviable career, and the fact that there are surely as many tormented, alcoholic straight actors, if not more.

The Second Career of Billy Haines

William "Billy" Haines, a leading man of the silent era and early talkies (*Tell It to the Marines, Navy Blues, The Fast Life*), was one of the most prominent members of Hollywood's gay social circle of the time who refused to "play straight" during the repressive Hays era of the 1930s. "Hounded out of an MGM contract because of his open homosexuality," writes Gil Reavill in *Hollywood and the Best of Los Angeles*, "Haines had a second career as the decorator of choice for star homes and studio offices—some of the same offices from which he had been banished as an actor." It's been said that it was primarily Hollywood leading ladies and socialite wives, sympathetic to the plight of many gay male friends, who were responsible for Haines' second career. His West Hollywood showroom was located at 8720 Sunset Boulevard, now the site of Le Dome restaurant.

The Impact of AIDS

Although the general public was aware that closeted gay actors worked in Hollywood, particularly through the scandal magazines of the 1950s, which exposed a handful of minor celebrities and ruined a few careers, it remained a fairly well-kept secret into the early 1980s. The mainstream press simply did not mention the sexual preference of actors known to be gay, TV talk show hosts carefully avoided asking them questions about their private lives, and heterosexual fans were happy to go to the movies with blinders on and their fantasies about their favorite stars intact.

Much of that changed in 1985 with Rock Hudson's passing from AIDS. As the story of Hudson's drawn-out death and the AIDS epidemic in general was splashed across front pages and nightly news shows, the public's ignorance of homosexuality and illusions about Hollywood's gods and goddesses were forever altered. As the modern-day plague spread and the death toll in Hollywood's creative community became particularly high, more and more prominent Hollywood men and women came forward to help with the cause, heterosexuals and homosexuals alike. In time, at least for nonactors, homosexuality began to lose much of its stigma in the face of the mounting horror of the disease. As one gay studio executive put it, "Hiding in the closet and worrying about my career just didn't seem all that important anymore. I felt we all needed to stand up and be counted."

Hollywood's "Velvet Mafia"

Throughout the 1970s and 1980s, hundreds of gay people built successful careers while working within the Hollywood studio system. Many were closeted to protect their careers but maintained a close, private alliance that included a few extremely powerful executives. Because of the clubbiness and growing clout of this mostly male group, it came to be known in some circles as "the gay mafia" or "the velvet mafia."

Increasingly, members of the so-called velvet mafia came out publicly in the late 1980s and throughout the 1990s, particularly as AIDS causes expressed a need for prominent spokespersons and role models, or under the pressure of being outed by the militant gay press or the tabloids. Today, with so many successful lesbians and gay men working so openly in Hollywood, the velvet mafia has lost much of its underground mystique. In fact, more than two hundred writers, producers, publicity agents and lawyers who are openly gay have formed an official organization, Out There, that provides networking and media advice on gay issues within the industry.

When the public outing of celebrities took hold in segments of the gay and tabloid press at the end of the decade (see "The Outing Trend" in chapter six), the Hollywood closet was further shaken. Today, literally hundreds of Hollywood writers, producers, directors, studio executives, publicists and agents, along with a handful of courageous actors, are openly living as gay men and women, either by publicly acknowledging their sexual orientation if and when it becomes an issue or visibly aligning themselves with gay causes. With the much-publicized and controversial coming out of television star Ellen DeGeneres and her lover, film actress Anne Heche, in 1997, honesty and openness on the part of Hollywood's lesbian and gay community reached a new milestone—criticized and condemned in some quarters, welcomed as long overdue in others. Another threshold was crossed that same year when prominent television actor Michael Jeter ("Evening Shade") publicly acknowledged that he was not only gay, but HIV-positive and continued to work.

At the same time, Hollywood's portrayal of homosexuals in feature films, which had been almost exclusively negative or stereotyped until the 1980s, continued to become more balanced as well as more common. *Philadelphia* (1993), with its sensitive story about an AIDS-afflicted gay man, was considered a landmark project among big studio pictures, and the even greater box-office

Hollywood Minority Organizations and Support Groups

American-Arab Anti-Discrimination Committee (In Washington, 202/244-2990; western region, 714/636-1232)

American Indians in Film (65 N. Allen, Suite #105, Pasadena, CA 91106; 626/578-0344)

American Indian Registry for the Performing Arts (see Media Image Coalition)

American Jewish Congress (213/651-4601)

Association of Asian Pacific American Artists (see Media Image Coalition)

Black American Cinema Society (3617 Mont Clair St., Los Angeles, CA 90018; 213/737-3292)

Black Filmmaker Foundation, West Coast (2049 Century Park E., 42nd Floor, Los Angeles, CA 90067; 310/201-9579)

Catholics in Media (818/907-2734)

Cinewomen (9903 Santa Monica Blvd., Suite 461, Beverly Hills, CA 90212; 310/855-8720)

Coalition to Protect Animals in Entertainment (P.O. Box 2448, Riverside, CA 92516-2448; Animal Safety Hotline 909/682-7872; fax: 909/784-4262)

Deaf Entertainment Foundation (E-mail: DEAFENT@AOL.com; 213/782-1344)

Disabled People Against Defamation (see Media Image Coalition)

Gay and Lesbian Alliance Against Defamation (GLAAD) (8455 Beverly Blvd., Suite 305, Los Angeles, CA 90048; 213/658-6775; fax 213/658-6776)

Greek Americans in the Arts and Entertainment (1515 Midvale Ave., Los Angeles, CA 90024; 310/477-7188)

Hollywood Supports (AIDS and HIV antidiscrimination group) (213/655-7705)

Media Access Office (P.O. Box 3778, Hollywood, CA 90078; 818/752-1196)

Media Action Network for Asian Americans (213/486-4433)

Media Image Coalition (a coalition of organizations aligned with the L.A. County Human Relations Commission involved in the inclusion, access and images of minorities in the media) (213/974-7621)

Multi-Cultural Motion Picture Association/Diversity Awards (9244 Wilshire Blvd., Suite 201, Beverly Hills, CA 90212; 310/285-9743)

Multi-Racial Americans of Southern California (310/836-1535)

Muslim Public Affairs Council (213/383-3443)

National Association for the Advancement of Colored People (NAACP), Beverley Hills/Hollywood Chapter (7000 Hollywood Blvd., Hollywood, CA 90028; (213/464-7616).

National Conference (Multi-cultural human relations organization)(1055 Wilshire Blvd., Suite 1615, Los Angeles, CA 90017; 213/250-8787)

National Hispanic Academy of Media Arts and Sciences (see Media Image Coalition)

The National Hispanic Foundation for the Arts (1101 30th St. NW, Suite 500, Washington, DC 20007; 202/625-8330)
National Hispanic Media Coalition (3550 Wilshire Blvd., Suite 670, Los Angeles, CA 90010; 213/385-8573)
National Italian-American Foundation (202/387-0600)
National Stuttering Project (714/661-2215)
Nosotros ("Us") (1314 N. Wilton Pl., Hollywood, CA 90028; 213/465-4167)
Polish-American Public Relations Committee (310/829-1527)
UCLA Chicano/Latino Film and Television Association (310/659-5872)
Women @ Work (support and networking group for professional actresses over 35, 2115 Devonshire St., Chatsworth, CA 91311; 818/299-8700)
Women in Film (6464 Sunset Blvd., Suite 550, Hollywood, CA 90028; 213/463-6040; fax: 213/463-0963)

For a more complete list of similar organizations by category, particularly at the national level, consult the *Encyclopedia of Associations*, available in many public libraries.

---

success of *The Birdcage* (1996), a comedy revolving around an older gay male couple, further encouraged the studios to develop scripts with gay story lines. Toward the end of the decade, a number of high-profile films were slated for production or being released that featured prominent gay characters, including *My Best Friend's Wedding* (costarring an openly gay actor, Rupert Everett), *In and Out* (featuring a much-publicized kiss between actors Kevin Kline and Tom Selleck) and *Midnight in the Garden of Good and Evil*, directed by one of Hollywood's more macho politically conservative actors, Clint Eastwood.

Meanwhile, that most family-oriented of all the studios, Disney, was under fire from certain religious groups after according full benefits to the domestic partners of its lesbian and gay male employees, and other Hollywood companies were doing likewise.

Beyond Hollywood, in the American heartland, homosexuals continued to face severe opposition, discrimination and sometimes violent recrimination; much of America clearly objected to same-sex affection on moral, religious or simply personal grounds. But in Tinseltown, at least, lesbians and gay men were making some small but hard-won gains, and even beginning to sense a safety net beneath them.

Useful books on this subject include: *Wisecracker: The Gay Hollywood of William Haines*, by William J. Mann; *Nazimova: A Biography*, by Gavin Lambert;

George Cukor: A Double Life, by Patrick McGilligan; *George Cukor, Master of Elegance: Hollywood's Legendary Director and His Stars*, by Emanuel Levy; *Greta Garbo: A Life Apart*, by Karen Swenson; *Directed by Dorothy Arzner*, by Judith Mayne; *The Secret Life of Tyrone Power*, by Hector Arce; *Montgomery Clift*, by Patricia Bosworth; *The Life and Legend of James Dean*, by Donald Spoto; *Rock Hudson: His Story*, by Sara Davidson; *Split Image: The Life of Anthony Perkins*, by Charles Winicoff; *The Rise and Fall and Rise of David Geffen*, by Stephen Singular; *Laid Bare: A Memoir of Wrecked Lives and the Hollywood Death Trip*, by John Gilmore; and *Father of Frankenstein*, by Christopher Bram, a gay-themed novel that revolves around the real-life director James Whale. Also, the aforementioned *The Celluloid Closet: A History of Homosexuality in the Movies*, by Vito Russo, a landmark book that served as the basis of an excellent documentary of the same title. (I have omitted several titles on gay Hollywood written by one author in particular because I seriously question his journalistic ethics and credentials. For readers who might seek those books out, *caveat emptor*.)

Another source for research, by appointment only, is the One Institute/ International Gay and Lesbian Archives (213/666-4166), which is housed at USC.

Hollywood Scandals Through the Decades

Some Hollywood historians date Tinseltown scandals from 1920, the year a young American actress named Olive Thomas was found dead in a Paris hotel room from a barbiturate overdose. But it was the case of Roscoe "Fatty" Arbuckle that same year, and the lurid headlines and stories it generated, that shocked and titillated the nation and rocked the film industry.

One of the most popular comedians in the movies, Arbuckle was charged with manslaughter when a young actress named Virginia Rappe died of peritonitis due to a ruptured bladder after a wild party thrown by Arbuckle in San Francisco's St. Francis Hotel. Although he was acquitted after two mistrials, rumors of sex orgies circulated widely and Arbuckle's pictures were withdrawn from circulation, forcing him to go behind the camera, where he worked as a director under the name William Goodrich until he died in 1933.

Through the 1940s, overdoses, paternity suits, pregnancies outside of wedlock and even divorces were enough to make headlines, but as social mores changed after World War II and the public grew more worldly, it took more disturbing events to warrant much more than passing attention.

Some historians note that the stars ruined by scandal tend to be those whose screen images are most at odds with the sordid revelations that engulf them, while those who survive professionally have less innocent public images to begin with. Many have salvaged their careers by seeking public forgiveness through frank confessions and apologies, and shrewd public relations campaigns to restore their images.

Among the other more prominent Hollywood scandals through the years:

1922: Director William Desmond Taylor is found dead in his Hoover Street apartment. Screen ingenue Mary Miles Minter, said to be having an affair with Taylor, is among the suspects named by the media, although the case is never solved. Actress Mabel Normand's career is ruined simply because she was among the last to see Taylor alive.

1923: Silent film star Wallace Reid, Hollywood's embodiment of the ideal young leading man, dies of drug addiction at age thirty-two.

1927: Actor Paul Kelly, involved in an affair with actress Dorothy Mackaye, kills her husband, actor Ray Raymond, during an argument in Raymond's Hollywood Hills home. After a botched cover-up, Kelly serves a prison term for murder, Mackaye for conspiracy.

1932: The naked body of MGM executive Paul Bern is found in the home he shares with Hollywood's original blonde bombshell, Jean Harlow, only weeks after they marry. Harlow's career is untouched by her husband's strange death, which is ruled a suicide.

1935: Upon turning twenty-one, Jackie Coogan, the most popular child star of the silent era, is denied access to his millions by his mother, who keeps the money for herself. (California law was later revised to protect the earnings of child performers.) . . . Screen comedienne Thelma Todd is found dead of carbon monoxide poisoning in her Pacific Palisades garage. Foul play is suspected, but there are no arrests, and the case remains one of Hollywood's most famous unsolved mysteries.

1936: The diary of actress Mary Astor, which details her sexy extramarital affairs, is introduced as evidence during a courtroom child custody battle with her ex-husband.

1939: The popular fan magazine *Photoplay* runs a feature, "Hollywood's Unmarried Husbands and Wives," examining the private lives of some of Hollywood's most famous couples, including Clark Gable and Carole Lombard, and Robert Taylor and Barbara Stanwyck, who quickly marry to counter the adverse publicity.

> 66 In Hollywood, a girl's virtue is much less important than her hairdo. 99
> —MARILYN MONROE

1940: Errol Flynn, a rakish screen idol of the day, is tried and acquitted for the statutory rape of two teenage girls, without serious harm to his career.

1941: Larry Edmunds, owner of the legendary Hollywood bookstore bearing his name, commits suicide at thirty-five by sticking his head in his gas oven. Among his effects: souvenirs of his sexual encounters with famous movieland women (their diaphragms) and love notes to Edmunds from author Thomas Wolfe, scribbled in one of his novels.

1943: Screen icon and filmmaking genius Charlie Chaplin is embroiled in a paternity suit.

1946: Bill Tilden, for years the top-ranked professional tennis player and a darling of the Hollywood crowd, is sentenced to jail for fondling a fourteen-year-old boy. Both his career and social standing are forever destroyed.

1948: Rugged (and married) leading man Robert Mitchum is caught smoking marijuana with a young actress who is not his wife. Mitchum serves a two-month jail term, but his record is later expunged and his film career is not adversely affected.

1949: The saintly image and lofty career of Ingrid Bergman is shaken when she becomes pregnant by Italian director Roberto Rossellini during their secret extramarital affair.

1952: Revelations that actress/sex symbol Marilyn Monroe once posed nude for calendar photos pushes her movie career to even greater heights.

1957: The scandal sheet *Confidential* prints a story about the kidnapping of B-actress Marie "The Body" MacDonald, which turns out to be a publicity hoax.

1958: Cheryl Crane, teenage daughter of actress Lana Turner, stabs her mother's violent gangland boyfriend, Johnny Stompanato, to death. It is later ruled justifiable homicide, though rumors persist that Crane took the rap to save her guilty mother. . . . An investigation from the New York City D.A.'s office to a House Subcommittee in Washington uncovers widespread question-rigging among contestants on top-rated network quiz shows. The big-money quiz shows are taken off the air.

1962: Marilyn Monroe dies under mysterious circumstances that are ruled a drug overdose suicide.

1963: Screen star Elizabeth Taylor leaves husband Eddie Fisher, whom she had previously lured away from entertainer Debbie Reynolds, during an affair with British actor Richard Burton while filming *Cleopatra*. Burton then leaves his wife Sybil to marry Taylor. Taylor and Burton later divorce, remarry and divorce again.

1965: B-movie actor Tom Neal, best known for the film *noir* classic *Detour* (1945), gets six years in jail for involuntary manslaughter in the shooting death of his third wife, Gail Evatt.

1968: Former silent screen star Ramon Novarro, sixty-nine, is found beaten to death on Halloween with an art deco phallus—a gift from Rudolph Valentino forty-five years earlier—thrust down his throat. Two hustler-brothers are convicted of the robbery-murder. . . . Bobby Driscoll, one of the great child stars of the 1940s, is found dead of a drug overdose on a New York slum street and, unrecognized at thirty-one, is buried in a pauper's grave. . . . A year after his teenage son commits suicide, veteran character actor Albert Dekker hangs himself in his Hollywood apartment, clad in women's lacy silk lingerie with obscene comments about himself printed on his body in red lipstick.

1969: Diane Linkletter, daughter of television star Art Linkletter, jumps to her death from her sixth floor West Hollywood apartment while experiencing a bad LSD trip.

1970: Rock singer Janis Joplin dies of a morphine-heroin overdose at age twenty-seven in Hollywood's Landmark Hotel, one of several rock star drug deaths during the decade.

1977: Director Roman Polanski, whose wife, actress Sharon Tate, was killed during the Manson Family murders in 1969, flees the country rather than face trial for allegedly having sex with a thirteen-year-old girl while visiting the home of actor Jack Nicholson. . . . Elvis Presley is found dead of a heart attack at age forty-two in the bathroom of his Memphis home, just as a book is being published that reveals Presley's heavy drug dependency and other sordid details that his family and publicists have kept quiet. . . . Comedian and TV star Freddie Prinze, despondent over a separation from his wife, dies of a self-inflicted gunshot wound to the head, which is ruled "accidental." . . . Columbia Pictures production chief David Begelman is caught in a forgery and embezzlement scandal that engulfs the studio, with Begelman ousted. (After struggling for years to rebuild his career, he commits suicide in 1995.)

1978: In New York, Oscar-winning actor Gig Young, a tormented alcoholic, murders his bride of three weeks, German actress Kim Schmidt, then takes his own life. . . . Film icon Joan Crawford's daughter, Christina, publishes *Mommie Dearest*, detailing her late mother's alcoholism, paranoid behavior and sadistic child abuse.

1980: Playboy centerfold and budding actress Dorothy Stratten is murdered by her estranged and jealous husband, Paul Snider, while she is involved romantically with film director Peter Bogdanovich.

1981: Film star Natalie Wood drowns mysteriously in a Catalina Island harbor after a night of drinking aboard her yacht with her husband, Robert Wagner, and Christopher Walken, both prominent actors. . . . Leading porn star John Holmes is tried and acquitted in the drug-related massacre of five people in a Laurel Canyon home. Holmes later dies of AIDS complications.

1982: Film and TV comedian John Belushi dies from a speedball (cocaine-heroin) overdose in his room at West Hollywood's legendary Chateau Marmont Hotel.

1983: Actor Vic Morrow and two child extras are killed in a gory helicopter accident during the filming of *The Twilight Zone* movie. Director John Landis and others are charged with negligence, but later acquitted.

1984: Flamboyant but closeted piano entertainer Liberace is embroiled in a "palimony" lawsuit brought by a former boy-toy lover, who loses his case. Liberace, who dies of AIDS complications in 1987, goes to his grave denying he is gay or has AIDS.

1985: Screen icon Rock Hudson dies from AIDS after Hudson and his publicist deny and cover up his illness for months. A Hudson paramour later wins monetary damages from the late star's estate, charging that Hudson knowingly exposed him to the HIV virus.

1987: Popular TV evangelist Jim Bakker is ruined by headlined revelations of his extramarital affair with Jessica Hahn, followed by a forty-five-year prison sentence for misappropriating $158 million of his followers' contributions.

1988: A videotape circulates widely (including on TV) showing pretty-boy actor Rob Lowe having sex with a sixteen-year-old girl during the 1988 Democratic convention in Atlanta. . . . Bible-thumping televangelist Jimmy Swaggert, cousin of rock legend Jerry Lee Lewis, falls from grace when he is exposed for having sexual relations with a prostitute but reportedly continues to live a lavish lifestyle from his $100 million fortune.

1989: Millionaire video executive Jose Menendez and wife Kitty are brutally murdered in their Beverly Hills home by their two sons, Eric and Lyle. . . . Erstwhile celebrity Zsa Zsa Gabor is handcuffed and arrested after slapping a

Beverly Hills cop during a traffic stop, briefly returning her to the limelight. . . . Saddled with a drug conviction, producer Robert Evans (*Love Story*, *Godfather*) is linked, though never charged with a crime, to the victim and his convicted murderers in the so-called "Cotton Club Murder Case." The case revolves around drug dealing and shady money transactions allegedly involved in the financing of Evans' film, *The Cotton Club*.

1991: Marlon Brando's thirty-two-year-old son Christian is sentenced to ten years in prison for killing his sister Cheyenne's fiancee. Four years later, she takes her own life at age twenty-five. . . . Actor Paul Reubens is arrested for indecent exposure in a porn theater, ending his career as impish Pee-Wee Herman and the popularity of his zany children's TV series, "Pee-Wee's Playhouse."

1992: Actress Mia Farrow discovers that her longtime companion, actor and film director Woody Allen, is having an affair with her adopted teenage daughter. Farrow later accuses Allen of abusing their youngest daughter, but Allen is cleared after an investigation.

1993: On Halloween night, rising film star River Phoenix, twenty-three, dies of a drug overdose outside the Viper Room, a Sunset Strip nightclub co-owned by another actor, Johnny Depp.

1994: Pop superstar Michael Jackson makes a payoff, reported between $15 to $50 million, to a boy who claims Jackson sexually molested him when he was thirteen. Jackson avoids a court trial and continues to be seen frequently in the company of children. . . . "Hollywood Madam" Heidi Fleiss is convicted of pandering after actor Charlie Sheen testifies that he paid to use her call girls at least twenty-six times. Her alleged "black book," rumored to list many top Hollywood names among her clients, never surfaces. . . . Nicole Brown Simpson, ex-wife of former football star and entertainment personality O.J. Simpson, is brutally murdered, along with Ronald Goldman. In what is billed as the "Trial of the Century," Simpson is tried and acquitted of murder charges, but found responsible and financially liable for the two deaths in a subsequent civil trial.

1995: British actor Hugh Grant is arrested when he is caught having sex in his car with a Hollywood street hooker. He later apologizes on NBC's "Tonight Show with Jay Leno". . . . Hugh O'Connor, son of TV star Carroll O'Connor and an actor on his father's TV series, "In the Heat of the Night," commits suicide after years of battling drug addiction. Carroll O'Connor decries the "rampant" drug use on the show's set. . . . Custody of *Home Alone* child star

Macauley Culkin is awarded to his mother, amid allegations that his demanding father has mismanaged and nearly wrecked his career.

1996: Film-TV star Howard E. Rollins, Jr., another "In the Heat of the Night" cast member, dies of AIDS after drug addiction has ruined his once-promising career. . . . Mega-producer Don Simpson (*Top Gun, Batman*) dies of a drug overdose as police are investigating the mysterious circumstances surrounding the drug-related death of Simpson's personal doctor months earlier at Simpson's Malibu estate. . . . Rap star and budding film actor Tupac Shakur is gunned down gang-style in Las Vegas while riding in a car driven by Death Row Records founder Marion "Suge" Knight. . . . Fading film-TV star Jan-Michael Vincent, his golden boy looks gone, breaks his neck in a drunk driving accident, after a long history of arrests for drug and spousal abuse. . . . TV star Kathie Lee Gifford weeps on her morning talk show after public revelations that her profitable clothing line is produced with sweatshop child labor.

1997: Actor-comedian Eddie Murphy is stopped by police after picking up a transsexual prostitute in an L.A. neighborhood notorious for its cross-dressing street hustlers. The hooker is arrested but no charges are filed against Murphy, who was merely being "a good Samaritan" by offering the prostitute a ride, according to his publicist. . . . Prominent sportscaster and exfootball great, Frank Gifford, husband of the aforementioned Kathie Lee, is "caught on tape" in a hotel dalliance with another woman and exposed in a tabloid newspaper. . . . Popular comedian Bill Cosby admits making secret payments totalling $100,000 to a former mistress after her daughter attempts to extort $40 million from the TV star, claiming he is her father. This follows soon after the murder of Cosby's son Ennis in Los Angeles, which is unrelated to the extortion attempt. . . . Actor Christian Slater, already saddled with two drunk driving convictions, is sentenced to ninety days in jail for engaging in a drug-induced brawl. . . . Popular sportscaster Marv Albert pleads guilty to sexually assaulting a woman in a hotel room, in a plea bargain that negates more serious rape and sodomy charges. He is immediately fired by NBC, ending his thirty-year broadcasting career. . . . Actor Robert Downey, Jr. is sentenced to six months in jail for repeated drug violations. . . . Following the path of his idol, John Belushi, beefy comedian Chris Farley dies of a drug combination overdose.

August 30, 1997

Half a world away from Hollywood, the reputation of tabloid photographers (paparazzi) hits a new low when their high-speed pursuit of Princess Diana in Paris ends in a collision that claims her life and those of two others. Because of the media's culpability—and because drugs and alcohol were found in the blood of the chauffeur—the shocking death of the princess has special reverberations in Tinseltown, where fast living, fan obsession, publicity-seeking celebrities and a predatory press are so much a part of the mix. A musical tribute to the late princess by singer Elton John, himself an admitted former abuser of drugs and a once-closeted gay man, becomes the biggest-selling CD in history, with the proceeds going to Diana's favorite charities.

Glossary of Hollywood Terms

Like any industry or company town, Hollywood has its own lingo and special jargon consisting of terms and phrases that fall (for our purposes) into three general categories: professional, technical and slang.

The following three selected lists are divided along those lines, although, through common use over many years, the lines between the categories sometimes blur. "Wrap," for instance, is a slang term meaning to end shooting or finish a production, but is so common that it is used almost as a formal, professional term, as in, "That's a wrap!"

What's important is not the category in which I've placed these terms and phrases, but their meaning and the reader's understanding of them within the context of workaday Hollywood. (For a select list and definitions of unusual or technical job titles, such as *best boy*, *script girl*, and *gaffer*, see chapter four.)

Professional Hollywood Terms

ABOVE THE LINE Film costs before the cameras roll (see also *below the line*).

ABOVE THE TITLE Contractual placement ("above the title billing") of a star's name above a film's title in the credit sequence, advertising, posters and related promotional material (see also *billing*).

ACQUISITION The process of acquiring distribution rights to a film or program produced by another company, for syndication, foreign release, etc.

AUTEUR A director who imprints each film with his or her distinct personal vision and style, often by also writing and producing (for example, Woody Allen, John Sayles, Martin Scorsese).

AVAILABILITY The status of an actor, writer or director's availability to work on a project, free of scheduling conflicts.

BACK END   Final profits of a movie after all expenses are tallied and met.

BACKDOOR PILOT   A made-for-TV movie that is not designed as a pilot (see *pilot*) but is thought to have the potential to spawn a series because of a central situation or character.

BACKSTORY   A condensed history of a character's life and personality worked into a script before the character appears (unless told in flashback), i.e., where they are from, what their family life was like, what the key conflicts are that they face, and so on.

BELOW THE LINE   The actual production costs of the movie.

BILLING   The order in which actors' names appear in film credits, ads, etc.

BIT PLAYER   Actor with a very small part but who may speak some lines or do some specific action, as opposed to an extra, who is usually used just for background purposes.

BLAXPLOITATION   Term denoting genre of gritty, urban action thrillers with African-American story lines and stars; shot low-budget, exploitation style; popular in the early 1970s. *Shaft* (1972), starring Richard Roundtree, is the prototype.

BLIND COMMITMENT   The promise to a "talent" (actor, director and so on) of a future but unspecified assignment, such as the chance to produce another TV pilot if the current pilot is not picked up (see *picked up*).

BOUTIQUE AGENCY   A small but successful agency with a specialized client list.

BOX OFFICE   The gross ticket receipts taken in at movies theaters, which can be either *domestic* (in the U.S.) or *worldwide*.

BREAKDOWN   A term related to the analysis of a script that can refer to a list of characters, a concise but detailed description of each scene, or a reader's report (see *coverage*).

BREAKDOWN SERVICE   A company that distributes breakdowns of available roles in movie or TV projects to talent agencies around town.

CAMEO   Appearance by a prominent actor in only a single scene, sometimes unbilled.

CINEAST   A film buff or movie enthusiast.

CINEMA VERITÉ   Filmmaking style emphasizing realism, often containing un-edited sequences and lacking narration, such as the documentaries of Frederick Wiseman.

CLIP Short section excerpted from film footage for viewing or promotional screening, or the other way around—as an "insert" into a film or program. ("We need an action clip from *Speed* to get this documentary moving.")

COLORIZATION A technical process that adds color to old black-and-white films to increase their current commercial value; used widely in the 1980s, it generated controversy because many movies were colorized against the wishes of the films' original directors.

COMPILATION FILM A film comprised of clips from other films.

CONTINUITY Maintaining consistency of small filmic details, such as the clothes or hairdo an actor wears in a scene shot on different days, or of script elements, e.g., character names.

COVERAGE Synopsis of a script or treatment (see *treatment*), including a log-line (one-sentence summation) of the story line and a section of critical comments.

CROSSOVER To bridge disparate audience segments with broad appeal or talent (e.g., "Ray Charles started out in R&B but proved to be the ultimate crossover singer").

CROSS-PLUG Promotional announcement "plugging" another program on the same station or network (see also *synergy*).

DAILIES Footage shot the previous day, prepared overnight for viewing by the producers and production executives (a.k.a. "rushes"); on some productions, the entire cast, crew and production team is welcome to view the dailies.

DEAL MEMO A preliminary outline of a working agreement, often issued prior to a final, detailed contract, and considered binding.

DEFICIT The difference between the cost of producing a program and what a network pays the producer (the network license fee), as in "deficit financing" (see chapter three).

DEMOGRAPHICS Breakdown and analysis of audience characteristics, such as gender, age, race, level of spending income and so on.

DEVELOPMENT The process of converting source material—books, plays, treatments and so on—into screenplays, or putting optioned or purchased screenplays through revisions.

DIRECTOR'S CUT The version of a film edited to the director's satisfaction, which may or may not be the version released (see *final cut*).

DISASTER FILM Big-budget picture whose formula pits a diverse group of people in a battle against the awesome forces of nature; the prototype was producer Irwin Allen's 1972 hit, *The Poseidon Adventure*. Others: *Earthquake*, *Towering Inferno*, *Twister*, *Titanic*.

EPIC   A film of great or epic proportions in terms of themes, cast, sets and settings, budget, etc. (*The Ten Commandments, Ben-Hur, Lawrence of Arabia*).

EPISODIC TELEVISION   Series television as opposed to one-shot programming.

EXHIBITOR   Movie theater or its owner.

EXPOSITION   Vital background information an audience needs to follow the logic of a story, as in, "Give us more exposition about how they pulled off the heist, but don't overdo it."

FEED   Transmission of programming or audiovisual content from a remote site, for example, "We're getting the report on the Tel Aviv bombing via the 12 noon satellite feed."

FILM NOIR   A distinct genre of film characterized by a dark, downbeat mood and style, often featuring a gritty urban setting and a femme fatale; particularly associated with films of the 1940s (*Laura, Double Indemnity, The Postman Always Rings Twice*), but also seen in scattered modern-era films (*Chinatown, Body Heat, Pulp Fiction, L.A. Confidential*).

FINAL CUT   The version of a film actually released; "final cut" in a director's contract indicates his or her right to dictate or approve which cut the public will see, which is rarely granted.

FIRST LOOK   An agreement that gives a studio or production company first consideration of a producer's or writer's projects; a.k.a. "first look deal."

FORESHADOWING   Information that "sets up" a later scene, either spoken or visually (e.g., a gun glimpsed in a drawer that foreshadows later violence).

FREE OPTION   An option deal that allows the studio or producer rights to a script for an initial period at no cost.

FRONT END   Beginning of the production, as in, "I'll take my money at the front end." Signifying a "front end deal."

GRAPHICS   The visual material used in a TV program other than live or taped sections.

GROSS   The total amount of box-office revenue generated by a movie during its theatrical release; a.k.a. "box-office gross," "gross revenues." (Also, see sidebar on page 63.)

HIGH CONCEPT   (*adj.*) A screen story that can be summed up snappily in a line, and more easily promoted by the studio, often used to describe more obviously "commercial" films.

HOUSEKEEPING DEAL   Arrangement in which a studio or production company gives a producer or a producer hyphenate office space and services in exchange for a first look agreement (see *hyphenate* and *first look*).

HYPHENATE   Person with more than one role, as in a writer-producer-director.

IMAGE SYSTEM   Visual mood and pattern of specific symbols in a film or show that underscore the theme (such as the distorted or broken "vision" symbols in *Chinatown*: broken glasses, mirrors, windshields, eyes, etc.).

INDEPENDENT   A producer who makes movies without a studio deal, or a company that specializes in financing the projects of such "indie" producers.

INFOMERCIAL   TV commercials presented—some would say disguised—as information and entertainment programs, often thirty minutes or an hour long, mimicking the standard TV format.

INTERACTIVE   Two-way communication, particularly through computer programming that invites the active involvement of the participant in viewing, instruction, entertainment and so on.

INTERNET   The vast universe of information that one can access by going on-line with the proper computer equipment, software programming and know-how; a.k.a. "cyberspace."

LICENSE FEE   A network's payment to a producer that guarantees the network exclusive rights to a specific number of broadcasts on a particular program.

LOCATION   Setting for a scene to be shot, usually existing and natural rather than set-designed (e.g., "We'll be shooting the drug smuggling scene on location at the Santa Monica Pier").

LOGLINE   One-sentence description of a story line, used in script coverage, pitch meetings, TV program listing guides, etc.

LONG FORM TELEVISION   TV movies and miniseries, which run longer than the standard hour and half-hour "episodic" television.

MADE-FOR-VIDEO   A feature-length film deliberately made for the video market, circumventing theatrical release; a.k.a. "direct-to-video."

MAGAZINE FORMAT   TV program format featuring several segments that may not be related in theme or content; "20/20," "60 Minutes" and "Dateline" are all magazine shows.

MAILROOM   A studio or agency department that handles mail, photocopying and other inside deliveries, and a traditional entry-level assignment for young aspiring executives.

MAJORS The major film studios (see chapter two for a complete list).

MERCHANDISING Toys, clothing, posters and other products based on characters or other concepts from a movie or television show.

MULTIMEDIA Term that describes a person or company who works with or produces projects in several media simultaneously (e.g., "DreamWorks/SKG is a new multimedia company that produces feature films, animation, music and television and Internet programming").

NARROWCASTING Specialized TV programming aimed at a niche audience, particularly prevalent on cable, with such "niche programming" as history, children's shows and sports.

NEGATIVE COSTS The money spent to produce a completed film (or TV project), for example, a "negative" from which prints can be struck, including added sound, music and special effects.

NEGATIVE PICKUP A film acquired ("picked up") by a studio that has been completely financed, produced and edited independently of the studio, which then handles distribution.

NET POINTS A negotiated percentage of the net profits of a film (see *net profits*). Also, see sidebar on page 63.

NET PROFITS The profits from a film after the deduction of all expenses.

NOTES A report or memo identifying problems in a script with suggestions for changes; also refers to a meeting in which such notes are discussed, as in, "It's time for notes."

NOVELIZATION A novel adapted from or based on a screenplay.

OPEN POINT An unresolved point in contract negotiations.

OPTION A deal by which a producer or studio pays a percentage of a property's total purchase price for the rights to that property for a limited period, customarily used to develop a script.

OPTION RENEWAL Payment made for a second or subsequent time period to extend the contract on the property.

PACKAGE A deal in which one agency supplies the major elements for a single film (stars, writer, director), taking a "packaging fee" for its services.

PACKAGING AGENT Agent who specializes in package deals.

PASS When agents or producers reject or "pass on" a submitted script.

PASS LETTER Rejection letter that accompanies a script being returned.

PAY OR PLAY Contractual agreement by which a creative talent is guaranteed a certain payment whether the movie actually goes into production or not; a.k.a. "pay or play deal." Most commonly involves top actors.

PICKED UP Renewed or given the go-ahead (a pilot is picked up when it is ordered as a series, a series is picked up for a second season and so on).

PILOT A prototype episode of a projected TV series shot with full production values and budget, used to test audience appeal.

PIRACY The illegal act of duplicating and selling films, tapes and other copyrighted material.

PITCH The act of verbally presenting a film concept and basic story line to a producer in a way that makes him or her want to buy the idea and/or the script.

POLISH A final, fine-tune rewrite that addresses minor problems in a script.

POSTPRODUCTION Editing, sound recording and mixing and other production activities that follow the completion of principal photography; a.k.a. "post" (see *preproduction* and *principal photography*).

PREINTERVIEW Conversation with an interview subject prior to the interview to establish the general line of questions (and possibly the general nature of the answers); also, from the interviewer's side, to "test" the appropriateness, articulateness and other qualities of the subject, or lack thereof.

PREMISE Idea or assumption that opens the presentation of a story, around which the rest of the action pivots, or on which its credibility hangs.

PREPRODUCTION The planning stage of a production when selections are made regarding casting, budgeting, scheduling, design and locations.

PRESS KIT A folder, provided by a studio or network publicity department, with plot synopsis, cast biographies, production notes, photos and other material of use to the media.

PRINCIPAL PHOTOGRAPHY The actual shooting of the major scenes of a film.

PRINT Copy made from the film's negative to be used in theatrical exhibition; a.k.a. "release print."

PRODUCTION BONUS Additional payment due upon the start of principal photography, often as part of a writer's contract.

PRODUCTION REWRITE Script changes made after a film is underway.

PRODUCTION VALUES The overall visual quality and "look" of a film.

PRODUCT PLACEMENT The promotional placement in movies of brand name products, from hamburgers to automobiles, often in exchange for cash or other compensation, for example, Paul Newman, who drives for the Budweiser racing team, drinking a can of Bud in obvious fashion in *Absence of Malice*.

REALITY Non-news shows that are nonetheless fact-based and designed to show "real life" in a documentary vein, though some may use "dramatic reenactments" to tell their true stories. Examples: "Cops," "Rescue 911," "America's Most Wanted."

RESIDUALS   Payments due actors or other talent upon rebroadcast of a TV program or rerelease of a film; a.k.a. "resids."

ROLODEX   Registered trademark for a specialized address and phone card file system.

ROUGH CUT   The first version of a film considered viewable by the editor.

RUNNER   Production company driver assigned to make deliveries, often scripts and tapes. Slang: gofer.

RUSHES   See *dailies*.

SEQUENCE   Succession of scenes that comprise a section of the film's story, with beginning and end points, such as a chase sequence made up of numerous cuts from various moments that build the action.

SET   Background setting designed and constructed within a studio for shooting a particular scene or scenes; sometimes outdoors (see *hot set* under slang).

SEXPLOITATION   A movie, usually of shoddy or marginal production values, which blatantly exploits the more titillating aspects of the story (*Valley of the Dolls, Night Call Nurses*).

SHOOT   The filming of a movie, as in, "All things considered, the shoot went very well."

SHOOTING SCRIPT   Final version of a script to be used during shooting, not necessarily with all revisions complete but with all existing scenes arranged in their proper order.

SHOP AROUND   Attempt by a producer to make a deal on a property without having the rights to it, such as "shopping around" a novel to the studios to see if there's interest in it.

SHOT   The single unedited piece of film that is the basic building block used to build the film's narrative, shot by shot, with close-ups, cutaways, dissolves and other techniques used to enhance the storytelling and call attention to the film's *content*, rather than the film itself.

SHOWRUNNER   Someone capable of writing-producing ("running") a TV show.

SIDES   Script pages given to actors to read during auditions.

SOUND STAGE   Special building, usually cavernous and featuring a high, arched roof, that can accommodate the construction of sets, grids for lighting, catwalks and so on.

SPEC SCRIPT   Screenplay written purely on speculation, without a contract or deal.

SPOT   TV or radio commercial (e.g., "Let's spend our money on thirty-second TV spots").

STEP OUTLINE   An incremental plot outline (one sentence to describe each scene of a script, one paragraph to summarize each chapter of a novel).

STOCK FOOTAGE   Film or video footage previously shot for another production (often unused) that is purchased from a "stock house" or "stock agency," or taken from one's own library (for instance, to be used in longshot war scenes or storm sequences).

STORYBOARD   Drawings laid out in comic strip fashion that illustrate key shots or scenes as they will be filmed or taped, and will eventually comprise the completed show.

STRIP   A television show that runs five weekdays in succession, usually in syndication.

SYNDICATION   Originally, the licensing of television programs for reruns after the completion of their original network licensing run; later, shows produced for first-run syndication.

SYNERGY   The cross-promotion of product within company-owned venues by entertainment conglomerates (Disney, for example, plugging one of its films on one of its TV shows).

TABLOID   Quasi-investigative news shows with a sensational bent. Examples: "HardCopy," "Inside Edition," "American Journal."

TAKE   Filming a shot with a particular camera setup (e.g., "We needed fourteen takes before we got the shot we wanted," or, "Nice work, that's a take!").

TALENT   Agent's actor client, or another creative element, such as a writer or director.

TELEFILM   A movie made for television.

TELEPLAY   Script for a TV program as opposed to a *screenplay* for a feature film.

TEST SCREENING   The presentation of an unreleased film in a theater by a studio's marketing department, often followed by audience surveys.

TRAILER   Fast-paced compilation of highlight clips used to promote an upcoming movie ("coming attractions" reel).

TREATMENT   The description of a proposed movie, preceding the screenplay, written in prose style that includes characters, settings, turning points and other key story elements.

TURNAROUND A property is "in turnaround" when a studio decides against going forward with it and puts it on the open market, hoping to recoup development costs.

TvQ Periodic research surveys conducted to evaluate the qualitative appeal of TV programs exclusive of their ratings performance, and also to determine, for casting purposes, the public appeal of individual performers. (For more, see *Les Brown's Encyclopedia of Television*.)

URBAN Hollywood code word for black or African-American (e.g., "The Keenan Ivory Wayans show plays well to the urban audience").

VOICE Literary term referring to the writer's attitude or tone that is inherent and consistent in a particular piece of writing, sometimes referred to as the "writer's voice" or "narrative voice."

WRAP Complete shooting, as in, "That's a wrap!" or "We've wrapped."

WRITER LIST List of writers available (or approved) for an assignment, with pertinent information, such as credits and agent.

WRITING SAMPLE A screenplay, not necessarily produced, presented to an agent or producer by a writer as an example of his or her best work.

Technical Production Terms

(Film, Video, Broadcasting)

ANSWER PRINT The first print assembled by the laboratory combining picture and sound that is submitted to the client for approval.

ASPECT RATIO The width-to-height ratio of a movie frame to a movie screen; the standard aspect ratio is 1.33 to 1, while CinemaScope uses a 2.35 to 1 ratio.

AVID A brand name for computerized non-linear editing systems that replaced the older, much more cumbersome linear method.

BACKLIGHTING Placing the main source of light behind the subject to be filmed and toward the camera, to create a silhouette effect.

BACKTIMING Adjusting the lengths of segments within a script or show to properly meet time requirements, often accomplished with alternative script endings, shorter or longer.

BITE A.k.a. "sound bite," a recorded quote, relatively brief, used in news and documentaries.

BLOCKING THE SCENE Establishing the positions and movements of the actors and camera.

BRIDGING SHOT A shot or sequence of shots used to cut away from the main action and convey the passage of time, such as calendar pages flipping, seasonal changes.

BUMP To suddenly increase the intensity, as in, "Bump the audio so we can hear what she's saying"; also, nontechnically, to remove or "bump" a guest from a program lineup.

BUMPER Material added to the beginning or ending of a program (or commercial break) to "pad" that section if it comes up short on timing.

CHEAT A SHOT To make the viewer think he or she is seeing something in a scene that really isn't there, such as cutting to a generic shot of any city to "cover" narration or dialogue about a specific city with a similar look.

CHIRON Cut letters into an image electronically, particularly used to identify an interview subject by name and title at the bottom of the picture, or a place, date and so on.

CHROMA KEY Electronic effect that can remove a specific color from an image and replace it with another visual; often used in news by placing a newscaster in front of a blue background screen, keying out the color blue, and projecting another graphic on the screen.

COMPOSITE PRINT Strip of motion picture film that combines both sound and picture.

CONTROL BOARD Panel of instruments that regulate audio output and can mix sounds from two or more sources.

COVERAGE Shots ordered by a director that include reverse angles, close-ups and other takes of scenes and settings to supplement the master shot (see *master shot*). For example: "Are you sure you got sufficient coverage of the crowd scene to allow for cutaways?" (Also, see *coverage* on page 254.)

CRANE SHOT Shot accomplished with a camera mounted on a movable, overhead boom.

CRAWL Movement of titles on screen, as at the end of a TV show (see *scroll*).

CROSS-CUTTING Cutting back and forth between different scenes to suggest parallel or simultaneous story action.

CUTAWAY A brief shot that interrupts the ongoing action of a film to cut in related story material at a given point, or simply for editing purposes, because a shot is going on too long, goes bad, etc. and the editor needs to "cut away" before "cutting back" to the main action; frequently used during documentary or news interviews to cover edits and jumps in the conversation.

CUTTING   The hands-on editing of a video or film reel, which includes the selection and technical assembly of scenes and sequences.

DAY FOR NIGHT   A shot filmed during the day, using film and lighting techniques that make it appear as a night shot in the finished film.

DEEP FOCUS   Camera technique that allows objects both close and faraway to be in focus in the same shot.

DIFFUSION   The use of a screen, glass filter or smoke to reduce the glare or intensity of light.

DIGITIZE   Conversion of standard videotape into digital format for digital editing.

DISSOLVE   The gradual merging of one scene (or sound) into another to avoid an abrupt or jarring cut, accomplished by overlapping a fade-out with a fade-in; a.k.a. "cross-fade." (An editor does a "slow dissolve" when he or she wants an especially gentle, smooth transition).

DOLLY SHOT   Moving shot captured by a camera mounted on a wheeled platform or "dolly" (see *dolly puller* under jobs, chapter four).

DUB   To record new dialogue in a special studio after filming is completed, or to record dialogue in foreign translation to replace original dialogue (see also *looping*).

DUPE   A duplicate negative made from a master or an original negative.

EDGE NUMBERS   Numbers calibrating film footage that are printed along one edge of the reel outside the perforations (also known as *key numbers*).

EFFECTS TRACK   Soundtrack on which sound effects are laid down before the final mix.

END TITLE   Title that comes at the end of the film.

ESTABLISHING SHOT   A shot that usually opens or comes near the beginning of a scene that establishes important information, such as time and place; a typical establishing shot at the beginning of a movie would be a slow pan of the city or building where the main character lives.

FADE   An optical effect that gradually replaces an image with a uniformly light or regular exposure ("fade-in") or a uniformly dark exposure ("fade-out").

FLASHBACK   A scene or sequence from the past inserted into the present time of a film story.

FLASHFORWARD   The insertion of scenes or sequences from future time.

FLAT   A section of a studio set, such as a room or rooftop, constructed on a wooden frame for ease in transporting or tearing down.

FLOOD A lamp that bathes or "floods" the entire set with general, diffuse light, eliminating shadows and dim or dark areas.

FLOP Reverse an image from right to left in editing, either for visual appeal or to use an image a second time while creating the appearance of a different shot; a.k.a. "flop-over."

FOLLOW SHOT Shooting a moving subject by moving a camera alongside on a carriage.

FORMAT The size or aspect ratio of a motion picture frame (see *aspect ratio*).

FRAME A single, rectangular unit of movie film; for example, 35mm film is comprised of sixteen individual frames per foot; the standard American film speed is twenty-four frames per second; and so on.

FREEZE-FRAME The illusion of a still photograph in a film, created by printing an identical frame of the same shot over and over (sometimes seen at the end of a film prior to a fade-out).

HARD Harsh or glaring light on a film set (also, high contrast chemical film developer.)

INSERT A "detail shot" cut into the film for the purpose of providing specific information at a key point in the story, such as a map, road sign, newspaper headline or letter.

INTRO A formulized bit of material that regularly opens a show; a.k.a. "stock opening."

JUMP CUT An abrupt, awkward cut that interrupts the continuity of a scene and calls attention to itself (e.g., "You've got a jump cut in the middle of the chase scene—find a better place to cutaway, or lose the cut altogether"); sometimes done deliberately to shorten a scene.

KEY Optical effect that cuts a foreground into a background image, combining two or more video sources (see also *Chroma key*).

KEY LIGHT The primary light directed at the subject being filmed, usually angled at 45 degrees.

KLIEG LIGHT Enormous lights (carbon-arc lamps) often seen sending their powerful beams into the night sky at film premieres and other promotional events; also used in filmmaking.

LETTERBOX Technique used to preserve the original aspect ratio of widescreen movies—such as those processed in CinemaScope—when they are shown on television by filling in the "empty" top and bottom areas of the TV screen with black rectangular bars.

LIP FLAP   Visual flaw created when subject remains on camera with lips moving but no words coming out, frequently caused when a producer cuts off a sound bite in mid-sentence or without sufficient pause for a clean visual edit.

LOOPING   The rerecording of an actor's dialogue, either by the original actor or a substitute, to both match and improve the audio quality or the reading of the line or lines; achieved by reading the lines in a special studio while watching a piece of the scene and attempting to stay "in sync" with the original reading.

MASTER SHOT   A long take of an entire scene, usually from a distance, to help with the editing when cutaways are needed for close-ups and other details.

MATTE SHOT   A complicated process utilizing a frame or piece of film that has a blank or opaque section, which can be printed with a normal shot to mask unwanted content in that frame; a "reverse matte" allows the printing of another scene in the blank or masked-off area.

MIX   A sound mix of separate recording tracks; visually, a dissolve.

MODEL SHOT   A shot using small models executed to create the illusion that they are full-size, for example, the destruction of bridges in *Earthquake*, skyscrapers in *Godzilla* and so on.

MONTAGE   Several brief scenes edited together in a quickly paced sequence, compressing the passage of time ("time-lapse").

MOTION CONTROL   The process of transferring still images, such as photos or news clippings, to videotape, animated by simple techniques such as pans and zooms.

OFF-LINE   A rough-cut video edit, completed prior to the final, high-tech "on-line" edit, which produces a broadcast quality tape.

ON-LINE   See *off-line*.

OPTICAL EFFECTS   Catchall term referring to special editing or "trick" effects such as dissolves, fades, wipes and freeze-frames.

OUTTAKE   Shot or scene not used for printing or assembling the final film.

OVERCRANK   To speed up the camera, shooting faster than the normal twenty-four frames per second, to create the illusion of slow motion.

OVERLAP SOUND   Allowing the sound to run on after the cut in a shot, overlapping into the next shot or scene.

PAN   Moving camera shot from side to side (horizontally) from a fixed point.

POINT OF VIEW SHOT   A shot in which the camera views the scene as if from the character's eyes; a.k.a. POV.

POST-SYNCHRONIZATION   Recording the sound after filming is completed.

PRACTICAL   Object or device on the set, such as an adjustable lamp or movable prop, that can be operated while the scene is in action.

PROCESS SHOT   A shot involving "process projection," a technique that films live action being performed in front of a screen on which the background is projected via another film, for example, an actor running toward the camera while a locomotive speeds toward him from behind.

PULL-BACK SHOT   A tracking shot or "reverse zoom" that pulls away from the subject to reveal his or her background or surroundings in wider context.

REACTION SHOT   A cutaway shot that abruptly leaves the main action, scene or speaking actor to reveal the reaction on another character's face (e.g., "We need a reaction shot just after she sees the dead body").

RELEASE PRINT   A final, polished print combining all the elements of the film, from opening shots and credits to the end title, for distribution to exhibitors.

RIGGING   Positioning studio lights according to the lighting director's plan.

ROLL CAMERA   Direction to set the cameras in movement for imminent action and filming.

RUNDOWN SHEET   Detailed outline of the planned segments and scripting of a program, for use in budgeting, gathering visual elements, scheduling, setting up interviews and so on.

SCROLL   Prior to state-of-the-art equipment, credits were shot on a rolling screen or scroll; now the term is more commonly used to refer to moving a computer screen up or down.

SETUP   The arrangement and positioning of cameras and lights.

SKIP FRAME   Optical effect during the printing stage that eliminates selected frames from a scene to speed up the action while allowing it to still appear natural.

SLATE   The clapboard that is held in front of the camera just before the take to identify both the shot and the take by number, to assist later shot selection during the editing phase.

SOFT   Diffuse lighting on a set that "flattens" the look or contrast between highlights and shadows (also, low contrast photographic developer); opposite of "hard" (see *hard*).

SOFT FOCUS   The creation of a soft or romantic effect through the use of special camera lenses, filters and even petroleum jelly; sometimes requested by actresses wishing to hide age lines or other blemishes, or automatically accorded them by amenable directors.

SOUND MIX   Creation of a film's final soundtrack by integrating music, sound effects, rerecorded dialogue and other audio elements in a high-tech studio.

SPLICE   As a verb, to join two pieces of film; as a noun, the resulting splice.

SPLIT SCREEN   The projection of two or more separate images within the same frame that do not overlap.

SPOT LAMP   Generic term for common studio lamps similar in design; they come in different sizes, referred to as baby, junior, senior and so on.

STEADICAM   Apparatus that is balanced hydraulically and harnessed to a camera operator's body, allowing a smooth "tracking shot" on foot.

STRIP   As in "film strip," a length of film with a width suitable for motion picture use cut from a wider roll of manufactured film.

SYNC, SYNCHRONIZATION   The correct relative placement of picture and sound; when the timing or spacial relationship is off, it is considered "out of sync," such as an actor's lips moving "out of sync" with recorded dialogue.

TAG   Brief section at the end of a segment that sums up or makes a concluding point to complete the segment, often seen in news, documentary and reality shows, often on-camera.

TEASE   Brief section just before a commercial break that promotes an upcoming segment, designed to "tease" or encourage the viewer to stay tuned (e.g., "When we return, O.J. Simpson reveals the truth about that awful night").

TILT   Moving camera shot vertically, from top to bottom, or vice versa.

TIME-LAPSE PHOTOGRAPHY   Photography speeded up to extreme degrees to compress hours into minutes.

TRACKING SHOT   A shot captured by a camera moving sideways in or out, in one plane, usually on a fixed track and dolly (see *dolly puller* under jobs in chapter four).

UNDERCRANK   To slow down a camera to create the illusion of fast motion (see *overcrank*).

VIDEO ASSIST   The use of a videotape camera and monitor by a film director on the set that offers an "instant replay" of a scene just completed.

VIEWFINDER   Device on a camera that frames and shows exactly what will be filmed, for use in placing the camera and preparing for the shot.

VOICEOVER   Narration delivered by an unseen narrator or lines delivered by an off-camera actor, laid over the footage seen on screen.

WALK-THROUGH Initial rehearsal on the set, sometimes using stand-ins instead of the stars, for the purpose of positioning and adjusting the cameras, lights, microphones.

WIDESCREEN Refers to film presentation in which the screened picture has an aspect ratio greater than 1.33:1 (see *aspect ratio*).

WILD Shooting without synchronized sound recording, particularly in fast action scenes or other scenes where dialogue is not precisely heard and sound effects will later be mixed in.

WILD RECORDING Recording sound off-camera, usually to create "natural" sound effects; e.g., an actor knocking over a chair and groaning or pounding on a wall.

WIPE Optical effect, gimmicky and seen frequently in the 1930s but now rather dated, in which an image or scene appears to be wiped off the screen by a newly appearing image.

WORK PRINT A print put together from unedited dailies that passes through various editing stages, becoming a rough cut and then a fine cut, prior to final mixing.

ZOOM Adjusting the variable focal length of a lens while the shot is in progress to bring the viewer close to or farther away from the subject (e.g., "Let's zoom in on the girl's eyes just before she shoots the winning basket").

Common Hollywood Slang

A-LIST The very best, as in, "I want nothing but A-list talent for this picture!"

ANGEL Private investor willing to provide seed money for an independent film project.

ANKLE To depart a talent agency, usually to join a competitor.

B- To signify second-rate, as in B-movie or B-material.

BANKABLE A star with enough clout or popularity to guarantee a project's financing.

BIMBO Female performer better known for her face and body than her acting skills (see *hunk*).

BLOCKBUSTER Huge hit movie; also applied to other entertainment forms.

B.O. Abbreviation for box office; movie ticket sales.

BOFFO To be successful at the box office.

THE BUSINESS The television business (as opposed to *The Industry*, signifying movies), though sometimes used to refer to the combined film and TV business.

BUZZ Entertainment industry word-of-mouth, often hyped by publicists or the media.

CHOPSOCKY A martial arts film, with Bruce Lee and Jackie Chan the two major stars of the genre, which peaked in the 1970s and originally came by way of Hong Kong.

COLD OPEN The opening material at the very top of a TV show preceding the first segment.

CRASH TV A sexy/violent sports show such as "American Gladiators."

CREATIVE DIFFERENCES Euphemism often used to explain the departure of a top talent from a film project after a battle of egos (e.g., "He left the project because of creative differences").

CYBERSPACE see *Internet* in Professional Terms.

D-GIRL Term for development assistant or executive, a job often filled by a young woman. Considered sexist, used less often in recent years.

DEVELOPMENT HELL The frustrating span of time in which a purchased or optioned script is put through revisions or awaiting a green light for production.

"DIAL IT UP!" Directive to a writer or editor to increase the excitement level (often the pacing) of a script or show (see *"Punch it up!"*).

DISEASE-OF-THE-WEEK Reference to made-for-TV movies about sick or dying characters, especially prevalent in the 1970s and 1980s (e.g., "Not another disease-of-the week movie!").

DONE DEAL Promised agreement on a film or TV project, as in, "It's a done deal!"—though often spoken insincerely.

EAR CANDY Light, easy listening music; a.k.a. "elevator music."

EXEX Executives.

FANZINE Shorthand for fan magazine.

FAVE Favorite.

FLACK Unflattering term for a publicist.

FLASH AND TRASH Derisive term for local news specials that feature sensational topics to boost ratings, particularly during ratings sweep weeks.

FLOP SWEAT Extreme performance anxiety, often associated with comics who are bombing (and sweating) before a live audience.

F/X Shorthand for special effects.

GOFER A low-level employee, usually at a production company, whose job is to handle any small errand or menial task required (i.e., to "go for" something).

GREEN LIGHT To OK a film project, as in, "Give it the green light!"

HANDSHAKE DEAL When two parties agree to work together on trust without a formal contract.

HEAT Strong word-of-mouth about a talented new performer or property.

HEAVY Villain or bad guy in a film or television show.

HELMER Agent's director client (who "helms" movies).

HONEY WAGON The string of trailers, comprised of "cast rooms" (individual trailers) and portable toilets, set up on location for the comfort of cast and crew.

HOT CONCEPT A particularly appealing or promotable story idea or premise.

HOT PROPERTY Script that's getting a lot of "heat" as a potential big film (see *heat*).

HOT READ A piece of material that must be read quickly, often because of competitive interest.

HOT SCRIPT A screenplay thought to have unusually high box-office potential or written by a "hot" screenwriter, to be read and considered quickly.

HOT SET A set that's set up for shooting and not to be disturbed.

HUNK Male performer better known for his face and body than his acting ability; male bimbo.

HYPE As a verb, to promote extravagantly (e.g., "to hype a movie"); as a noun, the resulting publicity and exposure created by hype (e.g., "The hype on this movie is incredible!").

IDIOT CARD Cue card for performer reading his or her lines.

IN THE CAN A film that has finished shooting but is not yet ready for release.

THE INDUSTRY The motion picture industry, though sometimes the entire TV-film industry.

INDY Independent producer (also "indie").

INDY PROD Independent production (also "indie prod").

INFOTAINMENT Sacrificing substance and informational content to make news more entertaining and attractive to viewers.

INK To sign a contract or new agency client.

INK SESSION Contract signing session.

IOWA Strictly amateur.

KIDVID TV or video programming for children.

LEGS Showing longevity at the box office, as in, "That film's got legs!"

LENS Used as a verb, meaning to shoot a film.

"LET'S DO LUNCH!" Invitation to meet for a business lunch (often insincere).

MAJORS The major studios.

MISTER BOYS Mail room (m.r./Mr./mister) employees working their way up in an agency.

NETS The major TV networks.

NONPRO Person from outside the entertainment business.

NUMBERS Box-office figures, ticket sales ("*Batman* racked up huge numbers").

OATER A Western, referring to the oats fed to horses.

ON THE NOSE Trite, overly pointed or direct writing, lacking in subtext or subtlety, telling too much straight out, as in, "I like the plot, but your dialogue is much too on the nose."

ORPHAN PROJECT Project that has lost its support within the studio.

PASADENA To reject ("pass on") a script.

PHONE IT IN To make a halfhearted effort, especially an uninspired performance.

PIMP FEE Agent's commission, usually 10 percent.

PLAYER Someone who wields significant clout or influence in The Industry.

P.O.W. Agency lingo for "perpetually overwritten" script.

POWER LUNCH Business meeting of Hollywood players (also "power break-fast" and so on).

PUFF PIECE An article written in a lightweight, fawning manner, often a celebrity profile.

"PUNCH IT UP!" Directive to a writer to improve a script, often specifically the dialogue, in terms of making it crisper, funnier and so on.

SCHMOOZEFEST A party or gathering where "schmoozing" takes place.

SCI-FI Shorthand for science fiction.

SCRIPT DOCTOR Rewrite specialist.

SITCOM Situation comedy.

SIX-FIGURE DEAL Contract paying a sum in the hundreds of thousands (compared to "in the five figures").

SKED Schedule, as in, "My show is finally on the network sked!"

SLAM DUNK Exclamation signifying completed deal or big success (e.g., "Slam dunk, baby!").

SLASHER MOVIE Horror movie in which many victims are slashed and bloodied (similar to "splatter movie").

SOAP Soap opera; daytime TV serial drama.

SPIN To put a positive or favorable slant on a potentially negative story; a savvy publicist or public relations person is a "spin master" who engages in "spin control."

STRETCH   Actor attempting a more challenging or unusual role.

SUIT   A noncreative executive, especially one who meddles in the creative process.

TAKE A MEETING   Conduct or get together for a business meeting.

TINSELTOWN   Campy term for Hollywood.

TOPLINE   To receive top billing.

TOPPER   A top executive.

THE TRADES   The three Hollywood trade papers: *Variety*, *Weekly Variety* and the *Hollywood Reporter* (or, more generally, all entertainment industry trade publications).

TRASH TV   Derogatory term for talk shows known for their sleazy or sensational topics and guests; a.k.a. "sleaze TV," "sluts-and-nuts."

TURKEY   poorly made movie that bombs (e.g., "It's a real box-office turkey!").

WANNABE   Someone, usually younger, who is trying to get into the business.

WEB   TV network.

WHODUNIT   A murder mystery in which the villain is not revealed until the end as opposed to a *thriller* in which the villain is usually known early on, at least to the audience.

WILLIS   Action-adventure script (after actor Bruce Willis of *Die Hard* fame).

WORD-OF-MOUTH   What people are saying, particularly about a new film (see *buzz*).

YAWNER   Boring show or movie.

30/10   To read or skim only the first thirty and last ten pages of a screenplay.

While most of the terms and phrases presented above are in common usage, some were compiled from various sources, including: *The World of Film and Filmmakers*, edited by Don Allen; *Scriptwriting for High-Impact Videos*, by John Morley; *Writing for Television and Radio*, by Robert L. Hilliard; *The 1997 A&E Entertainment Information Please Almanac*, edited by Robert Moses, Alicia Potter and Beth Rowen, and the Kodak website http://www.kodak.com/mptvi Home/tradition/glossary.shtml.

Other sources include: *Hollywood and the Best of Los Angeles*, by Gil Reavill; *How to Make It in Hollywood*, by Linda Buzzell; *Slang!*, by Paul Dickson; the *Los Angeles Times Magazine* "L.A. Speak" section; and the trade paper *Variety*, whose writers and editors over the years have been responsible for originating countless Hollywood slang terms.

Hollywood Organizations, Research Resources and Other Specialty Lists

This chapter is devoted to a wide assortment of select lists—organizations, publications, resources, specialty libraries and bookstores, web sites, refer-ddence books, film festivals, award shows and so on.

Please be aware that addresses, phone numbers and other details are subject to change, and that some entities may change names, merge with other groups or even cease to exist.

To stay current, consult the directories list for compendia that are up-dated on a quarterly basis, such as the *Hollywood Creative Directory* books, listed further on.

Professional Organizations & Associations

Academy of Motion Picture Arts and Sciences (AMPAS) (8949 Wilshire Blvd., Beverly Hills, CA 90211; 310/247-3000)

Academy of Television Arts and Sciences (ATAS) (5220 Lankershim Blvd., North Hollywood, CA 91601; 818/754-2800)

Action for Children's Television (ACT) (20 University Rd., Cambridge, MA 02138; 617/876-6620)

Actors Advisory Board (9000 Sunset Blvd., Suite #905, Los Angeles, CA 90069; 310/550-7104)

Alliance of Motion Picture and Television Producers (AMPTP) (14144 Ventura Blvd., Sherman Oaks, CA 91423; 818/995-3600; fax: 818/789-7431)

American Academy of Independent Film Producers (2067 S. Atlantic Ave., Los Angeles, CA 90040; 213/264-1422)

American Cinematheque (Hollywood Roosevelt Hotel, 7000 Hollywood Blvd., Hollywood, CA 90028; 213/461-9623)

American Film Institute (2021 N. Western Ave., Los Angeles, CA 90027; 213/856-7600; fax: 213/467-4578)

American Film Marketing Association (10000 Washington Blvd., Suite S-226, Culver City, CA 90232-2728; 310/558-1170; fax: 310/558-0560)

American Humane Association (15503 Ventura Blvd., Encino, CA 91436; 818/501-0123)

American Society of Cinematographers (ASC) (P.O. Box 2230, Hollywood, CA 90078; 213/969-4333; fax: 213/882-6391)

American Society of Composers, Authors and Publishers (7920 Sunset Blvd., Suite #30, Los Angeles, CA 90046; 213/883-1000)

American Women in Radio and Television (Southern California Chapter) (P.O. Box 3615, Hollywood, CA 90028; 213/964-2740)

Art Directors Club of Los Angeles, The (7080 Hollywood Blvd., Suite #410, Los Angeles, CA 90028; 213/465-1787)

ASIFA Hollywood International Animated Film Society (5301 Laurel Canyon Blvd., Suite #250, North Hollywood, CA 91607; 818/508-5224)

Association of Independent Commercial Producers (2121 Avenue of the Stars, Suite #2700, Los Angeles, CA 90067-5010; 310/557-2900)

Association of Talent Agents (9255 Sunset Blvd., Suite #318, Los Angeles, CA 90069; 310/274-0628)

Behind the Lens (Association of Professional Camerawomen) (P.O. Box 868, Santa Monica, CA 90406)

Broadcast Promotion and Marketing Executives (6255 Sunset Blvd., Suite #624, Los Angeles, CA 90028; 213/465-3777; fax: 213/469-9559)

Casting Society of America (6565 Sunset Blvd., Suite #306, Los Angeles, CA 90028; 213/463-1925)

Cinewomen (9903 Santa Monica Blvd., Suite #461, Beverly Hills, CA 90212; 310/855-8720)

Conference of Personal Managers/West Coast (10707 Camarillo St., Suite #308, North Hollywood, CA 91601; 818/762-6276)

Film Advisory Board/Ratings System (7000 Hollywood Blvd., Suite #322, Hollywood, CA 90028; 213/461-6541)

Friars Club of California, Inc. (9900 Santa Monica Blvd., Beverly Hills, CA 90212; 213/879-3375)

Greater Los Angeles Press Club (7000 Hollywood Blvd., Los Angeles, CA 90028; 213/469-8180)

Hollywood Arts Council (1502 Crossroads of the World, P.O. Box 931056, Hollywood, CA 90093; 213/462-2355; fax: 213/465-9240)

Hollywood Chamber of Commerce (7000 Hollywood Blvd., Suite #1, Los Angeles, CA 90028; 213/469-8311)

Hollywood Foreign Press Association (292 S. La Cienega Blvd., Suite #316, Beverly Hills, CA 90211; 310/657-1731)

Hollywood Heritage (historic preservation foundation located in the historic Wattles Mansion and Gardens) (1824 N. Curson Ave., Hollywood, CA 90046; 213/874-4005)

Hollywood Press and Entertainment Industry Club (P.O. Box 3381, Hollywood, CA 90028; 213/466-1212)

Hollywood Radio and TV Society (HRTS) (5315 Laurel Canyon Blvd., Suite #202, North Hollywood, CA 91607-2772; 818-789-1182)

Hollywood Screen Parents Association (P.O. Box 1612, Burbank, CA 91507-1612; 818/955-6510)

Hollywood Women's Press Club (342½ N. Sierra Bonita Ave., Los Angeles, CA 90036; 213/960-5725)

Independent Feature Project/West (1625 W. Olympic Blvd., Santa Monica, CA 90404; 310/392-8832)

International Documentary Association (1551 S. Robertson Blvd., Suite #201, Los Angeles, CA 90035; 310/284-8422)

International Television Association (6311 N. O'Connor Rd., Suite #230, Irving, TX 75039; 214/869-1112)

Motion Picture Association of America (MPAA) (15503 Ventura Blvd., Encino, CA 91436; 818/995-3600)

Motion Picture Health and Welfare (11365 Ventura Blvd., Studio City, CA 91604; 818/769-0007)

Motion Picture Industry Pension Plan (P.O. Box 1999, Studio City, CA 91604; 818/769-0007)

Motion Picture and Television Credit Association (1653 Beverly Blvd., Los Angeles, CA 90026; 213/250-8278

Motion Picture and Television Fund (23388 Mulholland Dr., Woodland Hills, CA 91364; 818/876-1888)

National Academy of Recording Arts and Science (NARAS) (3402 Pico Blvd., Santa Monica, CA 90405; 310/392-3777)

National Association of Television Program Executives (NATPE) (10100 Santa Monica Blvd., Suite #300, Los Angeles, CA 90067; 310/282-8802; fax: 310/282-0760)

Permanent Charities Committee (11132 Ventura Blvd., Suite #401, Studio City, CA 91604)

Production Assistants Association (8644 Wilshire Blvd., Suite #202, Beverly Hills, CA 90211; 310/659-7416; fax: 310/659-5838)

Screen Composers of America (2451 Nichols Canyon, Los Angeles, CA 90046; 213/876-6040)

Scriptwriters Network, The (11684 Ventura Blvd., Suite #508, Studio City, CA 91604; 213/848-9477)

Set Decorators Society of America (11333 Moorpark St., Suite #504, Toluca Lake, CA 91602; 818/848-2849)

Stuntmen's Association of Motion Pictures, Inc. (4810 Whitsett Ave. 2nd Fl., North Hollywood, CA 91607; 818/766-4334)

Stuntwomen's Association of Motion Pictures, Inc. (12457 Ventura Blvd., Suite #208, Studio City, CA 91604; 818/762-0907; fax: 818/762-9534; Web Site: www.stuntwomen.com)

Women in Film (WIF) (6464 Sunset Blvd., Suite #530, Los Angeles, CA 90028; 213/463-6040)

Youth in Film/Television International (5632 Colfax Ave., North Hollywood, CA 91601; 818/761-4007)

For a select list of minority/advocacy organizations and support groups, see chapter eight. In general, when researching organizations and associations, you might consult the *Encyclopedia of Associations*.

Labor Unions

Actors' Equity Association (AEA) (6430 Sunset Blvd., Suite #1002, Hollywood, CA 90028; 213/462-2334)

Affiliated Property Craftspersons (IATSE Local 44) (11500 Burbank Blvd., North Hollywood, CA 91601; 818/769-2500)

American Federation of Guards, Local 1 (4147 West Fifth St., Suite #220, Los Angeles, CA 90020; 213/387-3127)

American Federation of Musicians (AFM) (1777 N. Vine St., Suite #401, Hollywood, CA 90028; 213/461-3441; fax: 213/432-8340)

American Federation of Television and Radio Artists (AFTRA) (6922 Hollywood Blvd., Hollywood, CA 90028-6128; 213/461-8111; fax: 213/432-9041)

American Guild of Musical Artists (AGMA) (15060 Ventura Blvd., Suite #490, Sherman Oaks, CA 91403; 818/907-8986)

American Guild of Variety Artists (AGVA) (4741 Laurel Canyon Blvd., Suite #208, North Hollywood, CA 91607; 818/508-9984)

Association of Film Craftsmen (NABET Local 531) (1800 N. Argyle St., Suite #501, Los Angeles, CA 90028; 213/462-7484; fax: 213/462-3854)

Broadcast TV Recording Engineers and Communications Technicians (IBEW Local 45) (6255 Sunset Blvd., Suite #721, Los Angeles, CA 90028; 213/851-5515)

Choreographers Guild (256 S. Robertson Blvd., Suite #1775, Beverly Hills, CA 90211; 310/275-2533)

Costume Designers Guild (IATSE Local 892) (14724 Ventura Blvd., Penthouse C, Sherman Oaks, CA 91403; 818/905-1557)

Directors Guild of America (DGA) (7950 Sunset Blvd., Los Angeles, CA 90046; 213/289-2000; fax: 213/289-2024)

Dramatists Guild (2265 Westwood Blvd., Suite #462, Los Angeles, CA 90064)

IATSE and MPMO (AFL-CIO) (13949 Ventura Blvd., Suite #300, Sherman Oaks, CA 91432; 818/905-8999; fax: 818/905-6297)

Illustrators and Matte Artists (IATSE Local 790) (14724 Ventura Blvd., Penthouse B, Sherman Oaks, CA 91403; 818/784-6555)

International Brotherhood of Electrical Workers Local 40 (5643 Vineland Ave., North Hollywood, CA 91601; 213/877-1171 or 818/762-4239)

International Photographers (Cameramen) (IATSE Local 659) (7715 Sunset Blvd., Suite #300, Los Angeles, CA 90046; 213/876-0160)

International Sound Technicians, Cinetechnicians, Studio Projectionists and Video Projection Technicians (IATSE Local 695) (11331 Ventura Blvd., Suite #201, Studio City, CA 91604; 818/985-9204)

Laboratory Film-Video Technicians (IATSE Local 683) (2600 W. Victory Blvd., P.O. Box 7429, Burbank, CA 91505; 818/955-9720; fax: 818/955-5834)

Makeup Artists and Hairstylists (IATSE Local 706) (11519 Chandler Blvd., North Hollywood, CA 91601; 818/984-1700)

Motion Picture Costumers (IATSE Local 705) (1427 N. La Brea Ave., Los Angeles, CA 90028; 213/851-0220)

Motion Picture Craft Service (IATSE Local 727) (14629 Nordhoff St., Panorama City, CA 91402-1816; 818/891-0717)

Motion Picture First Aid Employees (IATSE Local 767) (8303 Gustav Ln., Canoga Park, CA 91324; 818/884-8894)

Motion Picture Screen Cartoonists (IATSE Local 839) (4729 Lankershim Blvd., North Hollywood, CA 91602; 818/766-7151)

Motion Picture Set Painters and Sign Writers (IATSE Local 729) (11365 Ventura Blvd., Suite 202, Studio City, CA 91604; 818/984-3000)

Motion Picture Sound Editors (MPSE) (P.O. Box 8306, Universal City, CA 91606; 818/762-2816)

Motion Picture Studio Grips (IATSE Local 80) (6926 Melrose Ave., Los Angeles, CA 90038; 213/931-1419)

Motion Picture and Television Editors Guild (Film Editors) (IATSE Local 776) (7715 Sunset Blvd., Suite #220, Hollywood, CA 90046; 213/876-4770)

Motion Picture and Video Projectionists (IATSE Local 150) (2600 Victory Blvd., Burbank, CA 91505; 818/842-8900)

National Association of Broadcast Employees and Technicians (NABET Local 53) (1918 W. Burbank Blvd., Burbank, CA 91506; 818/846-0490; fax: 818/842-7154)

Producers Guild of America (PGA) (400 S. Beverly Dr., Suite #211, Beverly Hills, CA 90212; 310/557-0807)

Production Office Coordinators and Accountants Guild (IATSE Local 717) (14724 Ventura Blvd., Penthouse Suite, Sherman Oaks, CA 91403; 818/906-9986)

Publicists Guild (IATSE Local 818) (14724 Ventura Blvd., Penthouse, Sherman Oaks, CA 91403; 818/905-1541)

Scenic and Title Artists (IATSE Local 816) (14724 Ventura Blvd., Penthouse 5, Sherman Oaks, CA 91403; 818/906-7822)

Screen Actors Guild (SAG) (7065 Hollywood Blvd., Hollywood, CA 90028-6065; 213/465-4600; fax: 213/856-6671)

Screen Story Analysts (IATSE Local 854) (14724 Ventura Blvd., Penthouse B, Sherman Oaks, CA 91402; 818/784-6555)

Script Supervisors (IATSE Local 871) (7061-B Havenhurst Ave., Van Nuys, CA 91408, 818/782-7063)

Set Designers and Model Makers (IATSE Local 847) (14724 Ventura Blvd., Penthouse B, Sherman Oaks, CA 91402; 818/784-6555)

Society of Motion Picture and Television Art Directors (IATSE Local 876) (14724 Ventura Blvd., Penthouse Suite, Sherman Oaks, CA 91403; 818/905-0599)

Studio Electrical Lighting Technicians (IATSE Local 728) (14629 Nordhoff Blvd., Panorama City, CA 91402; 213/851-3300)

Studio Teachers (IATSE Local 884) (14724 Ventura Blvd., Penthouse, Sherman Oaks, CA 91403; 818/905-1175)

Studio Transportation Drivers (Teamsters Local 399) (4747 Vineland Ave., Suite E, North Hollywood, CA 91602; 818/985-7374; fax: 818/985-8305)

Studio Utility Employees Local 724 (6700 Melrose Ave., Hollywood, CA 90038; 213/938-6277)

Writers Guild of America (WGA) (7000 W. Third St., Los Angeles, CA 90048; 213/951-4000)

Conventions

American Film Market (AFM) (10850 Wilshire Blvd., 9th Fl., Los Angeles, CA 90024; 310/446-1000)

Digital Hollywood, American Expositions, Inc. (110 Greene St., Suite #703, New York, NY 10012; 212/226-4983 or 212/226-4141)

Interactive Media Festival (448 Bryant St., San Francisco, CA 94107; 415/357-0100 or 800/573-1212)

NATPE International Programming Conference (National Association of Television Program Executives (NATPE), 2425 W. Olympic Blvd., Suite #550E, Santa Monica, CA 90404; 310/453-4440)

Showbiz Expo (Advanstar, 201 E. Sandpointe Ave., Suite #600, Santa Ana, CA 92707)

Directories

The main publishers of directories are Hollywood Creative Directory, 3000 W. Olympic Blvd., Suite 2525, Santa Monica, CA 90404; 310/315-4815; fax: 310/315-4816 and Lone Eagle Publishing, 2337 Roscomare Rd., Suite #9, Los Angeles, CA 90077-1815; 310/471-8066.

Actors
Academy Players Directory (Academy of Motion Picture Arts and Sciences, 8949 Wilshire Blvd., Beverly Hills, CA 90211; 310/247-3000)
Film Actors Guide, Steven A. Lukanic (Lone Eagle Publishing)

Agents
Film Producers, Studios, Agents and Casting Directors Guide, David M. Kipen and Jack Lechner (Lone Eagle Publishing)
Hollywood Agents Directory (Hollywood Creative Directory)

Below-the-Line Talent and Information
Cinematographers, Production Designers, Costume Designers and Film Editors Guide, Susan Avallone (Lone Eagle Publishing)
Hollywood Creative Directory: The Film and Television Industry Bible (Hollywood Creative Directory)
Hollywood Reporter Blu-Book, The (The Hollywood Reporter, 5055 Wilshire Blvd., Los Angeles, CA 90036; 213/525-2000)
International Documentary Association Membership Directory and Survival Guide (International Documentary Association, 1551 S. Robertson Blvd., Suite #201, Los Angeles, CA 90035; 310/284-8422)
Motion Picture, TV and Theater Directory (Motion Picture Enterprises Publications, Inc., P.O. Box 276, Tarrytown, NY 10591; 212/245-0969; fax: 212/245-0809)
Special Effects and Stunts Guide, Tassilo Baur and Bruce Scivally (Lone Eagle Publishing)
Studio Directory (Pacific Coast Studio Directory, P.O. Box V, Pine Mountain, CA 93222; 805/242-2722)
U.S. Directory of Entertainment Employers (Monumental Communications, P.O. Box 8297, Van Nuys, CA 91409; 800/640-4836)

Composers
Film Composers Guide, Vincent J. Francillon (Lone Eagle Publishing)

Directors
Directors Guild Directory (Directors Guild of America, 7920 Sunset Blvd., Los Angeles, CA 90046; 310/289-2000)

Feature Directors 1980-92, Their Credits and Their Agents (Hollywood Creative
  Directory)
Film Directors: A Complete Guide, Michael Singer (Lone Eagle Publishing)
Television Directors Guide, Lynne Naylor (Lone Eagle Publishing)

Distributors
Hollywood Distributors Directory (Hollywood Creative Directory)

Interactive and Multimedia
Hollywood Interactive Entertainment Directory (Hollywood Creative Directory)
Multimedia Directory, The (The Carronade Group, P.O. Box 36157, Los Angeles,
  CA 90036; 213/935-7600 or 800/529-3501; fax: 213/939-6705; E-mail:
  samsel@infomedia.com)

Producers
Film Producers, Studios, Agents and Casting Directors Guide (Lone Eagle Publishing)
Producer's Masterguide, The (330 West 42nd St., 16th Fl., New York, NY 10036-
  6994; 212/465-8889; fax: 212/465-8880)

Production Companies, Studios, Networks
Film Producers, Studios, Agents and Casting Directors Guide (Lone Eagle Publishing)
Hollywood Creative Directory: The Film and Television Industry Bible (Hollywood
  Creative Directory)

Writers
Feature Writers 1980-92, Their Credits and Their Agents (Hollywood Creative
  Directory)
Film Writers Guide, Susan Avallone (Lone Eagle Publishing)
Television Writers Guide, Lynne Naylor (Lone Eagle Publishing)
Writers Guild of America Directory (Writers Guild of America, west, 7000 W. Third
  St., Los Angeles, CA 90048; 213/951-4000)

Encyclopedias, Compilations, and Dictionaries
Biographical Dictionary of Film, A, David Thomson (Morrow)
Book of Video Lists, Tom Weiner (Andrews and McMeel)
*Box Office Hits: A Year-by-Year, Behind-the-Camera Look at Hollywood's Most
  Successful Movies*, Susan Sacket (Billboard)
Complete Directory of Prime Time Network TV Shows, 1946–Present (Ballatine
  Books)
Dictionary of Film Makers (University of California Press)
Dictionary of Films (University of California Press)

Entertainment Weekly Guide to the Greatest Movies Ever Made, The (Warner Books)
Facts on File Dictionary of Film and Broadcast Terms, The (Facts on File)
Film Encyclopedia (HarperCollins)
Filmmaker's Dictionary (Lone Eagle Publishing)
Halliwell's Filmgoer's Companion and Video Viewer's Companion (HarperCollins)
Halliwell's Film Guide (HarperCollins)
Les Brown's Encyclopedia of Television, Les Brown (Gale Publishing)
Leonard Maltin's Movie and Video Guide (Signet Books)
Motion Picture, TV and Theater Directory (Motion Picture Enterprises)
Movies Made for Television (New York/ZOETROPE)
Program Book (Daily Variety; see trade publications)
Variety Movie Guide (Prentice Hall/Simon and Schuster)
Variety Who's Who in Show Business (R.R. Bowker)
Who's Who in Television and Cable (Facts on File)

To find any titles listed in this chapter, you may want to consult the libraries and bookstores listed below, although some titles may be out of print.

Specialty Museums, Libraries and Archives

In Southern California:

Academy of Motion Picture Arts and Sciences, Margaret Herrick Library (333 S. La Cienega, Beverly Hills, CA 90211; 310/247-3020) (Motion pictures)

American Cinematheque (Hollywood Roosevelt Hotel, 7000 Hollywood Blvd., 3rd Fl., Hollywood, CA 90028; 213/466-3456)

American Film Institute, Louis B. Mayer Library (2021 N. Western Ave., Los Angeles, CA 90027; 213/856-7655) (Motion pictures and television, with extensive script collection)

Bruce Torrence Hollywood Historical Collection (Private; contact Bruce Torrence, 714/760-2652) (Hollywood, motion picture studios)

Gene Autry Western Heritage Museum Research and Publications (4700 Zoo Dr., Los Angeles, CA 90027-1462; 213/667-2000, ext. 323) (Westerns, wild west shows, western music)

The Getty Center (310/440-7300)

Institute of the American Musical, Inc. (121 N. Detroit St., Los Angeles, CA 90036; 213/934-1221) (Musical theater and film)

Museum of Television and Radio (465 N. Beverly Dr., Beverly Hills, CA 90210; 310/786-1000) (Television and radio programming; limited personnel and services)

National Archives, Pacific Southwest Region (24000 Avila Rd., P.O. Box 6719, Laguna Niguel, CA 92607-6719; 714/643-4241) (Covers Southern California, Arizona, and Clark County, Nevada)

Pacific Pioneer Broadcasters (P.O. Box 4866, North Hollywood, CA 91617; 818/346-6363) (Radio broadcasting)

UCLA Film and Television Archive (46 Powell Library, 405 Hilgard Ave., Los Angeles, CA 90095-1517; 310/206-5388; E-mail: arsc@ucla.edu) (Maintains large video library of old TV programs; open to the public at no charge)

UCLA University Research Library (U.R.L.), The Arts Library (450 Hilgard Ave., Los Angeles, CA 90095; 310/825-3817) (Includes extensive collection of entertainment industry periodicals and publications. Access limited to UCLA students and Sustaining Members of the Friends of the UCLA Library; contact the library regarding membership.)

USC Cinema-Television Library (213/740-7610) (Contains over three hundred donor collections, the complete Warner Bros. archives, and half a dozen partial collections from other studios covering both film and TV.)

Walt Disney Archives (500 S. Buena Vista St.; Burbank, CA 91521; 818/560-5424) (The official Walt Disney Co. archives)

Warner Bros. Studio Research Library (5200 Lankershim Blvd., Suite #100, North Hollywood, CA 91601; 818/506-8693) (Wide-ranging visual and historical research materials)

Writer's Guild of America, west, James R. Webb Memorial Library (7000 W. Third St., Los Angeles, CA 90048; 213/782-4544) (Film and TV writing and related fields).

The following public libraries are considered among the best in Los Angeles County for entertainment industry research:

Beverly Hills Public Library (444 N. Rexford Dr., Beverly Hills, CA 90210; 310/288-2200)

Burbank Public Library, Warner Research Collection (110 N. Glenoaks Blvd., Burbank, CA 91502; 818/953-9737)

Frances Goldwyn Regional Branch Library (formerly the Hollywood Public Library, 1623 N. Ivar, Hollywood, CA 90028; 213/467-1821)

Los Angeles Public Library (630 W. Fifth St., Los Angeles, CA 90071; 213/612-3200)

In addition, the *Los Angeles Times* library offers a research service, *Times on Demand*, which offers quick searches (specific *Times* articles since 1985), topic searches (list of stories published since 1985) or in-depth research for varying fees (800/788-8804, 8 A.M.–5 P.M., Monday–Friday). The free *Los Angeles Times* web site (http://www.latimes.com) also offers various features, including movie reviews, entertainment calendars and the Times Archives, back to 1990. For new technology data, access latimes.com/metahollywood.

Outside Southern California:

American Museum of the Moving Image (3601 35th Ave., Astoria, NY 11106; 718/784-4520)

American Film Institute/National Center for Film and Video Preservation (John F. Kennedy for the Performing Arts, Washington D.C. 20566; 202/828-4000)

George Eastman House (900 East Ave., Rochester, NY 14607; 716/271-3361)

Harvard Film Archive (Carpenter Center for the Visual Arts, Harvard University, 24 Quincy St., Cambridge, MA 02138; 617/495-4700)

Library of Congress, Motion Picture, Broadcasting and Recorded Sound Division (Washington D.C. 20540-4690; 202/707-5840).

Museum of Modern Art, Department of Film and Video (11 W. 53rd St., New York, NY 10019; 212/708-9602)

National Museum of Natural History/Human Studies Film Archives, Smithsonian Institute (Room E307, MRC 123, Washington, D.C. 20560; 202/357-3349 or 202/357-3356).

Wisconsin Center for Film and Theater Research, Film and Photo Archive (816 State St., Madison, WI 53706; 608/264-6466)

Specialty Bookstores (Los Angeles Area)

Book City (6627 Hollywood Blvd., Hollywood, CA 90028; 213/466-2525)

Bookie Joint, The (7246 Reseda Blvd., Reseda, CA 91335; 818/343-1055)

Book Soup (8818 Sunset Blvd., West Hollywood, CA 90069; 310/659-3110)

Collectors Book Store (1708 N. Vine St., Hollywood, CA 90028; 213/467-3296)

Eddie Brandt Saturday Matinee (6310 Colfax Ave., North Hollywood, CA 91606; 818/506-4242)

Larry Edmund's Cinema Bookstore (6644 Hollywood Blvd., Hollywood, CA 90028; 213/463-3273)

Samuel French Theatre and Film Bookshop (7623 Sunset Blvd., Los Angeles, CA 90046; 213/876-0570; fax: 213/876-6822; In the valley: 11963 Ventura Blvd., Studio City, CA 91604; 818/762-0535) (Samuel French provides free catalogs of its books upon request, broken down by category, such as writing, producing, acting and so on. Call or write for a catalog, specifying area of interest.)

Schools and Study Programs

Academy of Entertainment and Technology (Santa Monica Community College, 1900 Pico Blvd., Santa Monica, CA 90405-1628; 310/452-9277)

American Film Institute (AFI) (2021 N. Western Ave., Los Angeles, CA 90027; 213/856-7600)

American Film Institute Directing Workshop for Women (see AFI)

California Institute of the Arts ("Cal Arts," 24700 McBean Parkway, Valencia, CA 91355-2397; 805/255-1050)

Discovery Program (directing) (% Chanticleer Films, 1680 Vine St., Suite 1212, Hollywood, CA 90028; 213/462-4705)

Hollywood Film Institute (P.O. Box 481252, Los Angeles, CA 90048; 800/366-3456; fax: 800/933-1464; Online: HollywoodU.com/HFI)

Sundance Institute (screenwriting/filmmaking) (225 Santa Monica Blvd., 8th Fl., Santa Monica, CA 90401; 310/394-4662 or P.O. Box 16450, Salt Lake City, UT 84116; 801/328-3456)

UCLA Extension (Department of Entertainment Studies and Performing Arts, or The Writers' Program) (10995 Le Conte Ave., Los Angeles, CA 90024-2883; 310/206-1542 or 800/554-8252)

UCLA School of Theater, Film and Television (P.O. Box 951622, Los Angeles, CA 90095-1622; 310/825-5761)

USC School of Cinema/Television (University Park, Los Angeles, CA 90089-2211; 213/740-8358)

Visual Effects Society (818/789-7083)

Writer's Boot Camp (1525 S. Sepulveda Blvd., Los Angeles, CA 90025; 310/268-2288)

Writer's Connection (P.O. Box 24770, San Jose, CA 95154-4770; 408/445-3600)

Databases

Baseline (213/659-3830 or 800/242-7546 outside Los Angeles). Comprehensive database of entertainment industry credits and information; includes current box-office information and headline news from *The Hollywood Reporter*. Cost: $2 to $3.50 per minute. Also does for-fee research. Also, information on week-end box-office figures, industry headlines and upcoming films is available by calling Baseline's 900 service: 900/230-FILM (900/230-3456). Cost: 95 cents per minute.

Celebrity Service International (8833 Sunset Blvd., Suite #401, Los Angeles, CA 90069; 310/652-9910)

Entertainment Data, Inc. (EDI) (8350 Wilshire Blvd., Suite #210, Beverly Hills, CA 90211; 213/658-8300)

Hollywood/Entertainment Web Sites

(*Please note*: All web sites are preceded by *http://www.* unless otherwise noted.)

Academy of Motion Picture Arts and Sciences—oscars.org

Academy of Television Arts and Sciences—emmys.org

Ain't-It-Cool-News—aint-it-cool-news.com

American Broadcasting Company (ABC)—abctelevision.com

American Cybercast—amcy.com

American Film Institute—http://afionline.org

Cinema Sites—webcom.com/~davidaug/Movie_Sites.html

Columbia Broadcasting System (CBS)—cbs.com

CyberStudios—cyberstudios.com
Directors Guild of America—dga.org/dga/index.html
Discovery Channel—discovery.com
Drive-in Theater (history, locations, etc.)—driveintheater.com
E! Entertainment Television—eonline.com
Electronic Frontiers Foundation—eff.org/
Film Festivals—film.com
Film Music—filmmusic.com
Film Scouts—filmscouts.com/index.html
Find a Grave (celebrity burial locations)—orci.com/personal/jim
Fox Broadcasting Network (FOX)—foxnetwork.com
Gay & Lesbian Alliance Against Defamation (GLAAD)—glaad.org
Hollywood Film Institute—HollywoodU.com/HFI
Hollywood Network—HollywoodNetwork.com
Hollywood Online—Hollywood.com
Hollywood Stock Exchange—hsx.com
Integrated Media System Center (USC)—imsc.usc.edu
International Association of Technical Stage Employees—iatse.com/
Internet Movie Database—http://imdb.com
Internet Screenwriters Network—http://screenwriters.com
Los Angeles Times—latimes.com (add /metahollywood for new technology
    updates)
Magid Institute (entertainment industry web sites)—magidweb.com/
    entmedia.htm
MCA/Universal Studios—mca.com
MGM/United Artists—mgmua.com
Microsoft Multimedia Productions—http://m3p.msn.com
A Minor Consideration—minorcon.org
Motion Picture Association of America—mpaa.org
Movie Critics—moviecritic.com
Movielink—movielink.com
MovieWeb—movieweb.com
Mr. Showbiz—web3.starwave.com/showbiz/
National Association of Television Program Executives—natpe.org
National Broadcasting Company (NBC)—nbc.com
National Endowment for the Arts—arts.endow.gov
OnVideo—cyberprod.com/cyberprod/onvideo.htm
Paramount Studios—paramount.com
Screen Actors Guild—sag.com
Screenwriters Network—screenwriters.com/screenet.html
Screenwriters and Playwrights Home Page—teleport.com/cdeemer/scrwriter.html
ShowBizWomen: Opening the Doors to Hollywood—showbizwomen.com
Sony Pictures Entertainment—spe.sony.com/pictures/index.html

Sound Bytes: The WWW TV Themes Home Page—parkherre.com/tvbytes/
StarComp—leonardo.net/starcomp/
Sundance Channel, The—sundancefilm.com
Twentieth Century Fox Studios—fox.com
UCLA Extension Writers' Program (Screenwriting)—unex.ucla.edu/writers
Ultimate Hip-Hop Directory—http://ubmail.ubalt.edu/~rmills/hiphop.html/
The Ultimate TV List—www.tvnet.com
United Paramount Network (UPN)—upn.com
Usenet (newsgroup devoted to TV talk)—rec.arts.tv
Vibe Online (talk show/entertainment news)—vibe.com
Virtual L.A. (free photo service via e-mail)—geocities.com/Broadway/144/
    virtuala.html
Walt Disney Studios—disney.com
Warner Bros. Studios—warnerbros.com
World Wide Arts Resources—http://war.com
Writers Guild of America (WGA)—wga.org

Note: A number of resourcebooks list web sites. One of the most comprehensive is *What's On the Internet* (current edition), edited by Eric Gagnon and Edwinna von Baeyer (Peachpit Press).

Nonfiction/Reference Books

A&E Entertainment (Information Please) Almanac, Robert Moses, Alicia Potter and
    Beth Rowen
Adventures in the Screen Trade, William Goldman
All You Need to Know About the Movie and TV Business, Gail Resnik and Scott Trost
American Entertainment: A Unique History of Popular Show Business, Joseph Csida
    and June Bundy Csida
Backstory: Interviews With Screenwriters of Hollywood's Golden Age, Pat McGilligan
Beginning Filmmaker's Business Guide, The, Renee Harmon
Best American Screenplays (Volumes I, II, III), Sam Thomas
Black Film, White Money, Jesse Rhines
Black Hollywood: The Black Performer in Motion Pictures, Gary Null
Career Opportunities in Television, Cable and Video, Second Edition, Maxine K. Reed
    and Robert M. Reed
Celluloid Closet: Homosexuality in the Movies, The, Vito Russo
Censored Hollywood: Sex, Sin and Violence on Screen, Frank Miller
City of Nets: Hollywood in the 1940s, Otto Friedrich
City of Quartz, Mike Davis
CNN: The Inside Story, Hank Whitmore
David O. Selznick's Hollywood, Ronald Haver
Devil's Candy: "Bonfire of the Vanities" Goes to Hollywood, The, Julie Salamon
Dictionary of Film Makers, Georges Sadoul
Dictionary of Films, Georges Sadoul

Disney That Never Was, The, Charles Solomon
Due to Circumstances Beyond Our Control, Fred W. Friendly
Empire of Their Own: How the Jews Invented Hollywood, An, Neal Gabler
Enchanted Drawings: The History of Animation, Charles Solomon
Film Before Griffith, edited by John L. Fell
From Sambo to Superspade: The Black Experience in Motion Pictures, Daniel J. Leab
From Script to Screen: The Collaborative Art of Filmmaking, Linda Seger and Edward
    Jay Whetmore
Genius of the System: Hollywood Filmmaking in the Studio Era, The, Thomas Schatz
Grammar of the Film, A Raymond Spottiswoode
Great Movie Stars: The Golden Years, The, David Shipman
Hello, He Lied: And Other Truths From the Hollywood Trenches, Linda Obst
Hollywood vs. America, Michael Medved
Hollywood Anecdotes, Paul Boller
Hollywood and the Best of Los Angeles, Gil Reavill
Hollywood Be Thy Name: The Warner Brothers Story, Cass Warner-Sperline and
    Cork Millner with Jack Warner, Jr.
Hollywood on the Couch, Stephen Farber and Marc Green
Hollywood Days, Hollywood Nights, Ben Stein
Hollywood: The Dream Factory, Hortense Powdermaker
Hollywood: The First Hundred Years, Bruce T. Torrence
Hollywood Job-Hunter's Survival Guide, The, Hugh Taylor
*Hollywood: Stars and Starlets, Tycoons and Flesh-Peddlers, Moviemakers and
    Moneymakers, Frauds and Geniuses, Hopefuls and Has-Beens, Great Lovers and Sex
    Symbols*, Garson Kanin
Hollywood Walk of Fame, The, Marianne Morino
How to Make It in Hollywood, Linda Buzzell
Inside Oscar: The Unofficial History of the Academy Awards, Mason Wiley and
    Damien Bona
*Inside Warner Bros. (1935-1951): The Battles, the Brainstorms, and the Bickering—
    From the Files of Hollywood's Greatest Studio.* Rudy Behlmer
Indecent Exposure: A True Story of Hollywood and Wall Street, David McClintick
Independent Filmmaking, Lenny Lipton
International Film Encyclopedia, The, Ephraim Katz
Kenneth Anger's Hollywood Babylon I, Hollywood Babylon II, Kenneth Anger
Killer Instinct, Jane Hamsher
Lights, Camera, Action!: A History of the Movies in the Twentieth Century, Steve
    Hanson and Patricia King Hanson
Los Angeles A to Z: An Encyclopedia of the City and County, Leonard Pitt and Dale Pitt
Making of Citizen Kane, The, Robert Carringer
Making Movies, Sidney Lumet
MGM: When the Lion Roars, Peter Hay
Monster, John Gregory Dunne

Movie Business Book, The, Jason E. Squire

Movies, The, Richard Griffith and Arthur Mayer

Naming Names, Victor S. Navasky

Novels Into Film, George Bluestone

Oscar Dearest: Six Decades of Scandal, Politics and Greed Behind Hollywood's Academy Awards 1927-1986, Peter H. Brown and Jim Pinkston

Outrageous Conduct: Art, Ego, and the Twilight Zone Case, Stephen Farber and Marc Green

Out of Thin Air, Reuven Frank

Parade's Gone By, The, Kevin Brownlow

Pound of Flesh: Producing Movies in Hollywood—Perilous Tales From the Trenches, A, Art Linson

Power and the Glitter, The, Ronald Brownstein

Raising Kane: The Citizen Kane Book, Pauline Kael

Real Oscar: The Story Behind the Academy Awards, The, Peter H. Brown

Reel Power: The Struggle for Influence and Success in the New Hollywood, Mark Litvak

RKO Story, The, Richard Jewell and Vernon Harbin

Special Effects: Disaster at "Twilight Zone," the Tragedy and the Trial, Ron La Brecque

Story of Cinema, The, David Shipman

Studio, The, John Gregory Dunne

TV and Movie Business: An Encyclopedia of Careers, Technologies, and Practices, The, Alexandra Brouwer and Thomas Lee Wright

Technological History of Motion Pictures and Television, A, edited by Raymond Fielding

They Can Kill You But They Can't Eat You, Dawn Steel

This Business of Television: A Practical Guide to the TV/Video Industries, Howard J. Blumenthal and Oliver R. Goodenough

Translating L.A.: A Tour of the Rainbow City, Paul Theroux

Ultimate Hollywood Tour Book, The, William A. Gordon

Wannabe: A Would-Be Player's Misadventures in Hollywood, Everett Weinberger

What a Producer Does, Buck Houghton

When Women Call the Shots: The Developing Power and Influence of Women in Television and Film, Dr. Linda Seger

Who Killed CBS? Peter J. Boyer

Without Lying Down: Frances Marion and the Powerful Women of Hollywood, Cari Beauchamp

Woman's View: How Hollywood Spoke to Women, 1930-1960, A, Jeanine Basinger

Working in Hollywood: 64 Film Professionals Talk About Moviemaking, Alexandra Brouwer and Thomas Lee Wright

You'll Never Eat Lunch in This Town Again, Julia Phillips

Film Festivals

American Film Institute (AFI) Los Angeles International Film Festival

American Film Market (Los Angeles)

Asian American International FilmFestival (New York)

Aspen Filmfest

Berlin International Film Festival

Black Filmworks Festival of Film and Video (Oakland)

Boston Film Festival

Boston International Festival of Women's Cinema

Cannes Film Festival

Cape Town International Film Festival

Chicago International Children's Film Festival

Chicago International Film Festival

Chicago Latino Film Festival

Cleveland International Film Festival

Copenhagen Film Festival

Denver International Film Festival

European Film Market

Festival of Latin Film (Gramado, Brazil)

FilmFest DC (Washington, DC)

Florida Film Festival (Maitland, Florida)

Hawaii International Film Festival (Honolulu)

Hollywood Film Festival

Hong Kong Film Festival

Independent Feature Film Market (New York)

Inside/OUT Lesbian and Gay Film and Video Festival of Toronto

International Festival of Latin American Cinema

International Film Festival of Brussels

International Film Festival of India

Israel Film Festival (Los Angeles)

Jerusalem Film Festival

Latin American Film Festival (London)

London Film Festival

London Lesbian and Gay Film Festival

Los Angeles Asian Pacific American Film and Video Festival

Los Angeles Independent Film Festival

Los Angeles International Latino Film Festival

Melbourne International Film Festival

Miami Film Festival

MIDEM (film market, Paris)

MIFED (film market, Milan)

Minneapolis/St. Paul International Film Festival

Montevideo International Film Festival

Montreal International Festival of New Cinema

New Directors/New Films (New York)

New York Film Festival

Nordic Film Festival

Nortel Palm Springs International
Film Festival

Outfest: The Gay and Lesbian Film
Festival (Los Angeles)

Palm Beach International Film
Festival

Palm Springs International Film
Festival

PanAfrican Film Festival (Los
Angeles)

Philadelphia Festival of World
Cinema

Pordenone Silent Film Festival

Prix Italia

San Francisco International Asian
American Film Festival

San Francisco International Film
Festival

San Francisco International Gay
and Lesbian Film Festival

Santa Barbara Film Festival

Sao Paulo International Short Film
FestivalSarasota French Film
Festival

Showbiz Expo West (Los Angeles)

Sundance Film Festival

Sydney Film Festival

Telluride Film Festival

Toronto International Film Festival

USA Film Festival (Dallas)

Vancouver International Film
Festival

Venice International Film Festival

Washington International Film
Festival (Filmfest DC)

Women in Cinema Film Festival

Worldfest—Charleston
International Film Festival

These are among more than 250 film festivals scheduled annually around the world. For further
information on international film festivals, check the web site http://www.film.com.

Entertainment Awards Shows and Events

Academy Awards (Oscars)—Academy of Motion Picture Arts and Sciences

Adolph Caesar Awards—Negro Ensemble Company (NEC)

AFI Lifetime Achievement Award—American Film Institute (AFI)

AGLA Media Awards—Alliance of Gay and Lesbian Artists

American Latino Media Arts Awards—National Council of La Raza

Antoinette Perry Awards (Tony Awards)—American Theater Wing

Blockbuster Entertainment Awards—Blockbuster Entertainment

CMA Awards—Country Music Association (CMA)

Comedy Hall of Fame Awards—Comedy Hall of Fame

Daytime Emmy Awards—Academy of Television Arts and Sciences (ATAS)

Emmy Awards—Academy of Television Arts and Sciences (ATAS)

Frank Capra Achievement Award—Directors Guild of America (DGA)

GLAAD Media Awards—Gay and Lesbian Alliance Against Defamation (GLAAD)

Golden Globe Awards—Hollywood Foreign Press Association

Golden Laurel Awards—Producers Guild of America (PGA)

Golden Raspberry Awards (The Razzies)—Golden Raspberry Foundation

Grammy Awards—National Academy of Recording Arts and Sciences (NARAS)

Independent Spirit Awards—Independent Feature Project/West

Jimmie Awards—Association of Asian Pacific American Artists (AAPAA)

Kennedy Center Honors—Kennedy Center

MTV Movie Awards—Music Television (MTV)

NAACP Image Awards—National Association for the Advancement of Colored People (NAACP)

Nosotros Golden Eagle Awards—Nosotros, Inc.

Paddy Chayefsky Laurel Award—Directors Guild of America (DGA)

Peoples' Choice Awards

Platinum Circle Award—American Film Institute Associates

SAG Awards—Screen Actors Guild (SAG)

Soap Opera Digest Awards—*Soap Opera Digest*